"In working with college students, I believe the most important thing for them to understand is that everyone can be a leader. This book communicates that and helps students learn about themselves in a way that will assist them as they understand their own leadership. They'll be able to see how their college experience helps them become better leaders and then consider how to use that beyond their campus into their professional lives"—**Shelly Morris Mumma**, Director of Leadership, Student Engagement & First Year Experience and Campus Center, St. Norbert College

"This is not your typical leadership development book for college students. *College Student Leadership Development* so wonderfully addresses 'how' students should learn leadership by drawing on Sessa's vast experience and research. The book successfully accomplishes what every leadership educator and student hopes for: an insightful and rich model to give emerging leaders a process to learn about leadership."—**Matthew Sowcik**, Assistant Professor of Leadership Education, University of Florida

# COLLEGE STUDENT LEADERSHIP DEVELOPMENT

*College Student Leadership Development* introduces the idea that we all play a part in producing leadership and that learning how to participate in the process of leadership is something that all college students need to learn as part of their college academic experience. Rather than approaching leadership from the traditional model emphasizing specific skill sets, this book acquaints students with how to learn leadership using the ReAChS model of leadership development (Reflection, Assessment, Challenge, Support). It then encourages students to directly engage their own experiences to hone their leader identity and understanding of leadership as well as improve their leadership knowledge and skills. Step-by-step exercises lead students in reflecting on their experiences, assessing themselves, choosing challenges, creating support networks, and finally capturing and communicating to others what they have learned. Throughout, examples of student leaders' experiences provide readers with powerful examples of others' successes and struggles in leadership alongside the latest psychological research on learning and development.

**Valerie I. Sessa** is a Professor and Graduate Program Coordinator in the Department of Psychology at Montclair State University. Prior to MSU, she worked as a research scientist and director at the Center for Creative Leadership.

# Leadership: Research and Practice Series
A James MacGregor Burns Academy of Leadership Collaboration

## Series Editors

**Georgia Sorenson, PhD**, Møller Leadership Scholar and Møller By-Fellow, Churchill College, University of Cambridge, Founder of the James MacGregor Academy of Leadership at the University of Maryland, and co-founder of the International Leadership Association.

**Ronald E. Riggio, PhD**, Henry R. Kravis Professor of Leadership and Organizational Psychology and former Director of the Kravis Leadership Institute at Claremont McKenna College.

**George R. Goethals**
*Presidential Leadership and African Americans: "An American Dilemma" from Slavery to the White House*

**Michael Genovese**
*The Future of Leadership: Leveraging Leadership in an Age of Hyper-Change*

**Al Bolea and Leanne Atwater**
*Applied Leadership Development*

**Barbara C. Crosby**
*Teaching Leadership: An Integrative Approach*

**Dinesh Sharma (Ed.)**
*The Global Hillary: Women's Political Leadership in Cultural Contexts*

**Valerie I. Sessa**
*College Student Leadership Development*

# COLLEGE STUDENT LEADERSHIP DEVELOPMENT

*Valerie I. Sessa*

Routledge
Taylor & Francis Group

NEW YORK AND LONDON

First published 2017
by Routledge
711 Third Avenue, New York, NY 10017

and by Routledge
2 Park Square, Milton Park, Abingdon, Oxon, OX14 4RN

*Routledge is an imprint of the Taylor & Francis Group, an informa business*

*Library of Congress Cataloging in Publication Data*
A catalogue record for this book has been requested

ISBN: 978-1-138-94047-5 (hbk)
ISBN: 978-1-138-94048-2 (pbk)
ISBN: 978-1-315-67432-2 (ebk)

Typeset in Bembo
by Swales & Willis Ltd, Exeter, Devon, UK

# CONTENTS

# ILLUSTRATIONS

## Figures

## Tables

# SERIES EDITORS' FOREWORD

As both teachers and scholars of leadership, we are very pleased to add this book, *College Student Leadership Development*, by Valerie Sessa, to our series, because it exemplifies what the book series, "Leadership: Research and Practice," is all about. Valerie Sessa has written a guide to student leadership development that is solidly grounded in research, but draws on her experience of years of teaching and working closely with students.

Many guides to leadership development focus on the Leader, as Dr. Sessa tells us, "with a capital 'L'"—learning what it takes to be *the* leader. This book is about learning how to participate in the process of leadership, and how we all play a part in producing leadership. Sessa draws on her own research, and a wealth of research by other leadership scholars, on what truly works in student leadership development. We learn about student leadership development both through data and from firsthand accounts from Sessa's students who participated in her research. What this all leads to is a practical and sensible guide for any student who seeks to learn about leadership while developing his or her own capacity to lead. Indeed, this book will prove so valuable to a student's personal growth and development that completing a college degree without learning the lessons contained within is to fall short of a full college academic experience.

*Georgia Sorenson*
*Ronald E. Riggio*

# PREFACE

Why yet another book on leadership development for college students? Many colleges and universities across the nation provide their students with leadership courses, curricular programs, and co-curricular programs that are designed to develop students' formal knowledge about leadership as well as opportunities and experiences to develop students as leaders and actually practice leadership (Dugan & Komives, 2007). Additionally, student leader development theory and research is alive and well (Dugan & Komives, 2007). However, how to best approach the task of developing student leaders remains a gray area with college professors and administrators often left to their "best guess" regarding how to proceed (Allen & Hartman, 2009).

Most current leadership development books available to students use a skills-based approach to leader development. The books focus on a handful of skills students *should* develop to become leaders, and give students exercises they can do to develop those particular skills. Science, in particular social science, does not lend itself to absolutes—and our understanding of what leadership is and how to develop that leadership continuously evolves. Thus, while the currently available books provide behaviors and skills based on theories that students can strive to attain, they do not cover the full spectrum of what is needed to be a successful leader in today's or tomorrow's world.

This book concentrates less on the "what" to learn and more on the "how to" learn. Instead of targeting a set of skills to learn, students are introduced to the idea that they can use experiences to learn and develop the skills that they need. By looking systematically at stories of successful student leaders and checking them against what research has shown about learning and development in general, this book provides students with what it takes to take charge of their own leader development while in college. The book covers learning in general, learning leadership in particular, and how the entire university system (and beyond) can be utilized by students as a place where leadership development occurs. It presents a model of how learning through experience works (focusing both on the student as a learner and on the environment), then leads students step by step in how to gain experience and better learn through those experiences. Throughout the book, students read examples of other student leaders' experiences: what worked, what challenged them, and what hurt them, and what they learned as a result.

## Roots of the Book

This book is an integration of work I have accomplished in two major areas of my life. I worked as a research scientist at the Center for Creative Leadership (CCL), in Greensboro, NC from 1993 to 2001. Since then, I have been working as a faculty member in the psychology department at Montclair State University (MSU). While at MSU, I participated in the development of the Leadership Development through Civic Engagement minor, which I then directed from 2012 to 2016.

While at CCL, I became acquainted with classic leadership development research conducted by researchers Morgan McCall, Michael Lombardo, and Ann Morrison, and a number of other colleagues, which resulted in the book *Lessons of Experience* (1988). The original research focused mainly on white male senior executives and how they learned leadership through experience. CCL has since replicated and extended the findings from *Lessons* to many other populations in organizations . . . but never to college students. This research served as the impetus for my own research, conducted years later, as a faculty member. The research on college students that I refer to in this book (Sessa, Morgan, Kalenderli, & Hammond, 2014) replicates and extends the original CCL work into the college student population. And the original *Lessons* book also served as a model for the book presented here.

Also at CCL, I became acquainted with their ACS (Assessment, Challenge, Support) model of leadership development (see McCauley, VanVelsor, & Ruderman, 2010). Years later at MSU, I developed theory and conducted research with Manuel London on learning at the individual, group, and organizational levels (see London & Sessa, 2006 and Sessa & London, 2005). As I was writing this book, I realized that there were similarities between the original CCL model of leadership development and the theory London and I had developed on learning across individual, group, and organizational levels. As a result, I melded together CCL's ACS model with London and my model of learning into the ReAChS model of leadership development. ReAChS stands for Reflection, Assessment, Challenge, and Support.

Finally, I had the pleasure of many discussions with research scientists at CCL, which resulted in cutting edge ideas about leadership. In the 1990s, we were tasked by then President Walt Ulmer to define leadership. Many hotly debated conversations later, we realized that there were no agreed upon definitions of leadership among ourselves, and that as a result of these discussions, our own views on leadership were changing. Drath ultimately published a book, *The Deep Blue Sea* (2001), based on this realization. In that book, he suggested that an individual's understanding of leadership could be categorized into one of three principles and that, as we grow and mature, our understanding about leadership grows and matures as well. One extension of this realization is the DAC (Direction, Alignment, and Commitment) framework of leadership (Drath, McCauley, Palus, Van Velsor, O'Connor, & McGuire, 2008). Both understanding of leadership and the DAC framework serve as important elements in the book presented here.

## Audience

This book is written for college students. All college students: those who already see themselves as leaders, those who aspire to be leaders, and those who have no intention of ever being in a leader role. Based on CCL's DAC model, I define leadership in Chapter 1 as the accomplishment of three tasks: direction, alignment, and commitment. Defining leadership in this way does three things. First, we realize that while leadership is important and requires hard work, it is not something held by special people who are different from others. We all can and do participate in direction, alignment and commitment in some fashion, regardless of our role or title. Second, it takes the weight off individual leaders. They don't need to do leadership all by themselves. And third, everyone and anyone can learn how to do these tasks better, again, regardless of our role, title, or leadership development aspirations. This book can be used in a class, such as a freshman orientation course or a leadership development course. It can be used in a leadership development program open to all students. It can be used in training programs for particular on-campus positions, such as workshops for R.A.s or Student Government Association retreats. Finally, students who do not have these opportunities for a number of reasons, such as busy lifestyles in which school is only one part of a complex life, or attending school on-line, but who wish to develop themselves as leaders (or in terms of this book, "to participate in leadership") can read this as a stand-alone book and do the exercises on their own.

## Acknowledgments

Like I say about participating in leadership in this book, writing a book, even when you are the sole author, involves many, many other people. The people at CCL who have had some role in the development of my thinking about leadership are too numerous to count. Thank you to CCL as an organization. Professor

Jennifer Bragger took over as my leadership discussion and learning companion once at MSU, thank you to Jennifer. Professor Manuel London, Dean of the College of Business and Director of the Center for Human Resources at SUNY StonyBrook, Jillian Ploskonka, Assistant Director for the Center for Leadership at Montclair State University, and Professor Michael Reuter, Director of the Gerald P. Buccino '63 Center for Leadership Development at Seton Hall University, and the anonymous reviewers—thank you for patiently reading numerous drafts of my book prospectus and giving critiques, comments, suggestions, feedback, and encouragement. This book is entirely different, and much better as a result. Thank you to MSU I/O psychology program graduate students Gaynell Schettino and Nicole Alonso for reading, commenting on, and editing some of the early chapters that I wrote, which gave me confidence that I was on the right track. Thank you to MSU I/O psychology program alumnus and colleague Chris Pingor for reading the final draft of the book. Thank you to my husband, Joseph Fung, for reading outlines, discussing ideas, and sending me articles on chapter topics as I was writing them. Thank you to Christina Chronister, my editor at Taylor and Francis, and Julie Toich, her editorial assistant for helping me keep my book on track. Finally, who knew that writing is a debilitating endeavor? Thank you to Dr. Dominic Frio, DC, Dr. Ron Ben-Meir, DO, and Dr. Juan Nunez, DPT, for keeping my neck and shoulder in working order despite my poor posture while writing.

## References

Allen, S. J. & Hartman, N. S. (2009). Sources of learning in student leadership development programming. *Journal of Leadership Studies 3*(3), 6–16.

Drath, W. (2001). *The deep blue sea: Rethinking the source of leadership.* San Francisco, CA: Jossey-Bass.

Drath, W. H., McCauley, C. D. Palus, C. J., Van Velsor, E., O'Connor, P. M. G., & McGuire, J. B. (2008). Direction, alignment, commitment: Toward a more integrative ontology of leadership. *The Leadership Quarterly 19*, 635–653.

Dugan, J. P. & Komives, S. R. (2007). *Developing leadership capacity in college students: Findings from a national study.* College Park, MD: National Clearinghouse for Leadership Programs, Multi-Institutional Study of Leadership.

London, M. & Sessa, V. I. (2006). Continuous learning in organizations: A living systems analysis of individual, group, and organization learning. In Francis J. Yammarino & Fred Dansereau (Eds.), *Multi-level issues in social systems: Research in multi level issues, volume 5* (pp. 123–172). Emerald Group Publishing.

McCauley, C. D., VanVelsor, E., & Ruderman, M. N. (2010). Introduction: Our view of leadership development. In E. VanVelsor, C. D. McCauley, & M. N. Ruderman, *Handbook of Leadership Development* (pp. 1–26). San Francisco, CA: John Wiley & Sons.

Sessa, V. I. & London, M. (2005). *Continuous learning in organizations: Individual, group, and organizational perspectives.* Mahwah, NJ: Lawrence Erlbaum.

Sessa, V. I., Morgan, B. V., Kalenderli, S., & Hammond, F. (2014). Key events in student leaders' lives and lessons learned from them. *Journal of Leadership Education 13*, 1–28.

# 1

# INTRODUCTION: STARTING WITH YOU

LEADERSHIP. We all know what leadership is, right? When you see or hear this word, what do you think of? How do you know when someone is a leader or doing leadership? Stop reading right now (four sentences into this book), pick up a pen or pencil, and jot down words or images that come to mind.

Look at your words or your image. Do they include descriptions of a leader? Did you list personal characteristics? Appearance? Skills? Behavior? Do your words or images include followers (and perhaps words such as influence or power)? Do your words or images include something about a goal to be accomplished? When they think about leadership, most people, including students, think about leaders, followers, and goals, or some combination. Interestingly, even though most people consider one or all these pieces when they think about leadership, they each define leadership a little differently. I begin this book by carefully defining what I mean by leadership.

However, you note, the title of this book includes the words "leadership development". The purpose of this book is to help you take charge of your own leadership development. Part of your leadership development is to think more deeply about what leadership is. You have already started your leadership development journey in the first paragraph of this chapter. And like that first exercise, rather than telling you "what" to learn to participate in leadership, this book concentrates on helping you learn "how to" learn what you need.

## Leadership Definition

In this book, I am approaching leadership from a different angle. One that will probably seem strange to you right now. Instead of concentrating on the "who" of leadership (that is, the leader), I concentrate on the "what" of leadership; that is, the tasks of leadership. What exactly is happening that is making us think that leadership is occurring? Using work done at the Center for Creative Leadership (McCauley, 2014), I believe that leadership happens when three activities or tasks are being accomplished. The first task of leadership is *setting direction*, which is people coming to agreement on what they are trying to achieve. This deals with solving questions such as "Where are we going?", "What are we going to do?", and "How will we get there?". It is envisioning the future. The second task is *alignment*, which is dealing with helping the group, organization, or community effectively coordinate and integrate all the different aspects of the work so that it fits together and heads everyone and everything in the shared direction. The third task is *commitment*, which is people willingly making the success of that direction and alignment a personal priority to accomplish.

Defining leadership in this way does three things. First, we tend to think of Leaders and Leadership with a capital "L." We think Leaders are different from others: Leaders have special characteristics, special skills, special behaviors. Leaders are important. Leaders do big important jobs. Leaders work hard. We want our Leaders to take care of us, to solve our problems. We want to blame Leaders when something goes wrong. Some of us aspire to be Leaders while others do not want to ever be a Leader. Leadership defined as setting direction, alignment, and commitment is leadership with a little "l." It is important but not special; it is actually rather mundane and everyday work. And everyone bears responsibility for participating. If something goes wrong, it is not the Leader's fault; the responsibility lies with all.

Second, it takes the weight of leadership off individual leaders. They don't need to do leadership all by themselves. If you do a web search on what Leaders do, you will find they are expected to do all sorts of things and do them well. And there is little agreement among articles; what they need to do and be is endless. And they need to do this all by themselves. No wonder we think we need big "L" leaders. My definition opens options regarding how these leadership tasks get accomplished. Individuals can "participate" in leadership in different ways, from alone to in a group:

- They can be hired to set direction, align people and processes, and motivate people to be committed.
- They can be elected to do these tasks.
- They can step up or volunteer.

These three are the usual ways we think of participating in leadership. But here are more ways that individuals can participate in leadership:

- They can participate in leadership tasks (setting direction, aligning people and processes, motivating people to be committed) in a formal setting (an organization, club, etc.) or in an informal setting (with friends).

- They can participate in leadership alone (set their own direction, align their life towards that goal, and create their own commitment to succeed).
- They can participate in leadership as part of a group with someone else who has the title of "leader" or "manager." Here, "a follower" participates in leadership by either helping set direction, helping ensure that all are aligned, and helping all to be committed, or by actively supporting the direction that was set, and being willing to work in alignment, and being aligned and committed, as defined by the leader.
- They can participate in leadership as part of a group that has no official leader and everyone works together to set direction, to align people and processes, and to commit to accomplishing the direction.
- And here is a real stretch; they can write a manual that lays out the direction, demonstrates how to align people and processes, and give ideas on how to become committed to accomplishing the direction. The constitution of the United States of America is such a document. It has helped citizens of the USA determine how to govern themselves for over 200 years!

In these options, all are participating in leadership regardless of their role. You may have the title of "leader" or may see yourself as "follower" but in truth, if setting direction, aligning people and processes, and motivating people to be committed is happening, you are all participating in leadership together.

Third, it is time to let go of the "Are leaders born or made?" argument. It is a moot point. Everyone participates in leadership in some capacity on a regular basis. Stories about storks and cabbage patches notwithstanding, so far everyone that participates in leadership is born (we will have to revisit this in the near future as Artificial Intelligence evolves). And everyone can use preparation and practice in how to participate in leadership more effectively in a wide range of circumstances. Furthermore, in terms of who steps into a leadership role, research shows that approximately 30 percent of leadership role occupancy is due to genetics, and 70 percent is developed (Arvey, Zhang, Avolio, & Krueger, 2007; Hannah & Avolio, 2010). Even if you think, right now, that there is absolutely no way anyone is ever going to convince you to "take a leader role," you still need to know how to participate in the tasks of leadership to ensure that good leadership happens, regardless of what your title or role is.

Thus, I firmly believe that all students need to be prepared to participate in leadership in the capacities above. If you are not yet convinced, here are some more reasons:

- *We live in a democracy, which is a type of government that gives the power of governing to the people.* For a democracy to be successful, all members of the population must be ready, willing, and able to participate. In college, it is generally expected that you prepare to participate in a democratic and progressive society as an active citizen. This includes participating in setting local, state, and national direction, aligning people and processes to reach that direction, and committing and help others commit to this direction.

- *We are heading towards a "maker culture" and "maker movement."* We are becoming a society of inventors, designers, and tinkerers rather than passive users of someone else's products. Many of you may find yourself as entrepreneurs sometime in the future. You need at minimum to set your own direction, to align your life to meeting that direction, and motivate and commit yourself to that direction. You will probably do this in the company of others struggling with the same issues.

- *Many of the problems we will be facing in the future are complex and global— population growth; aging population; shortages of food, water, and jobs; increased energy needs.* In this context, one person, group, or country cannot be considered in charge or in a primary position of power. Nations and non-governmental agencies will need to work, in an equal partnership, to solve such problems in a way that is beneficial to all. Students today will be facing these challenges, and will need to set complex multi-faceted directions to solve those problems and align massive numbers of people and processes, and create commitment across nations and the world.

- *Many of you plan to have a family some day (or may already have children).* Parents set direction (and teach their children to set direction). Parents need to align people, time, processes, equipment—ask your mom and dad or guardian; I'm sure they have many stories about this going awry. And parents need to stay committed to the direction they are setting for themselves, and for their family.

- *And finally, you already participate in leadership; you just may not have realized it yet.* Although they were measuring leader behaviors rather than participating in leadership tasks, Kouzes and Posner (2016) asked over 2.5 million people across the world in the past 30 years to complete their Leadership Practices Inventory (LPI). The LPI contains 30 leader behaviors. No one who has taken the instrument gave themselves a response score of "almost never" to all 30 leader behaviors. Everyone participates in leadership in some capacity.

## Developing Yourself to Participate in Leadership

That is my definition of leadership. But this book is about leadership development. Although this book is geared towards helping you develop your capabilities in participating in leadership, I'm not going to tell you what you should learn. Despite the many lists that you will find on Google regarding what you must be and do to be a Leader, there really are no sets of skills or characteristics that will magically turn you into a Leader if you perfect them. I believe that you will learn what you need to learn when you need to learn it. Instead, I'm going to acquaint you with how to learn.

## The Layout of the Book

The remainder of the book is divided into three parts. Part I includes two chapters. Chapter 2 contains the fundamentals of learning in general. Chapter 3 helps you apply what you learned in the previous chapter to learning leadership in particular. This chapter lays out the ReAChS model of Leadership Development. ReAChS stands for (Re)flection, (A)ssessment, (Ch)allenge, (S)upport. The remainder of the book will go into each of these in much more detail including lots of exercises to help you develop your leadership. Part II includes the bulk of the book, addressing each portion of the ReAChS model. Chapter 4 is on (Re)flection. Chapter 5 is on (A)ssessment and includes a number of instruments that you can use to assess yourself. Chapters 6, 7, 8, 9, and 10 cover a number of ways you can (Ch)allenge yourself to develop your leadership. Chapter 6 details challenging experiences; Chapter 7 details challenging people; Chapter 8 details leadership courses and leadership development programs; and Chapter 9 details how to turn hardships into leadership development lessons. Chapter 10 takes the information from these chapters and turns them into how-to exercises for you to determine what you have already learned about leadership, how challenging your current situation is, and how to challenge yourself in the future. Finally, Chapter 11 covers (S)upport, because you cannot do leadership development alone. The final part of this book contains only one chapter. As you are developing yourself to participate in leadership, you need to learn to capture and tell your leadership development story. This how-to chapter is chock full of exercises designed to help you do this and create a leadership development portfolio to showcase your experiences.

## My Expectations of You

I am hoping that as you proceed through this book you do five things. First, take charge of your own development. Teachers, staff, administrators, friends, people in your community, and people in your family can suggest things for you to do and accomplish, encourage you, and support you. But only you can learn and develop. They cannot do this for you. Second, be open to changing and growing. You will be asked to do things differently, to think differently, to be differently. You can only learn and develop if you are open to this. Third, be prepared to engage in a variety of challenging experiences. You cannot grow and change if you do the same thing and hang out with the same people all the time. Fourth, and this one is odd to find in a college textbook, be prepared to fail. In fact, if you are not failing at least occasionally as you develop yourself in leadership, you are not challenging yourself! Sometimes, the key to success IS to fail and then to extract the lessons from that. And finally (and I bet you haven't seen this in college textbooks), be open to and prepared to have fun. How many college courses do you take where the subject matter is YOU!

## Summary

- When I define leadership, I concentrate on the "what" of leadership, the tasks that need to be accomplished. These are setting direction, alignment, and commitment.
- Defining leadership in this way does three things. First, we realize that leadership is important, but it is every day work, not something special for special people to do. Second, it takes the weight off individual leaders—they don't have to do it all, everyone involved participates. And third, everyone can use preparation and practice in participating in leadership so that they can participate in a wide range of circumstances.
- There are many reasons for preparing and practicing. These include serving as an engaged citizen in the USA government (assuming you are reading this in the US), the growth of the maker culture and maker movement, future complex problems, and being the head of a family.
- In this book, I will not tell you what you need to learn. There are no magic skills or characteristics that you need to master to turn into a leader. Instead, I will tell you how to learn, and if you engage in learning, you will learn what you need to learn about leadership as you need it.
- I introduce the ReAChS model of leadership development. ReAChS stands for (Re)flections, (A)ssement, (Ch)allenge, and (S)upport. Much of this book explains this model and helps you develop using this model.
- I lay out my expectations of you: (1) Take charge of your own leadership learning and development; (2) Be open to changing and growing; (3) Challenge yourself; (4) Be prepared to fail; and (5) Have fun.

## Questions for Reflection and Discussion

1. Compare your description of leadership that you wrote in the very beginning of the chapter to other peoples' descriptions. What are the similarities and differences? Now compare your definition of leadership to my definition of leadership. What are the similarities and differences?
2. Evaluate my definition of leadership. Do you like it? Dislike it? Do you think it is a useful way to define leadership? Why or why not? What do you agree with? What don't you agree with?
3. I really pushed the leadership definition boundary by suggesting that the constitution of the USA is an example of leadership. Do you think a person does leadership? Do you think that a group of people can participate in leadership together, with no one as the Leader? Do you think something other than a single person or a team of people can participate in leadership?
4. What do you think of a book that doesn't tell you what to learn and develop in your leadership but instead concentrates on helping you understand how to learn and develop your own leadership?
5. How are you feeling right now about developing yourself to participate in leadership?

# References

Arvey, R. D., Zhang, Z., Avolio, B. J., & Krueger, R. F. (2007). Developmental and genetic determinants of leadership role occupancy among women. *Journal of Applied Psychology 92*, 693–706.

Hannah, S. T. & Avolio, B. J. (2010). Ready or not: How do we accelerate the developmental readiness of leaders? *Journal of Organizational Behavior 31*, 1181–1187.

Kouzes, J. M. & Posner, B. Z. (2016). *Learning leadership: The five fundamentals of becoming an exemplary leader.* San Francisco, CA: Wiley.

McCauley, C. (2014). *Making leadership happen.* White paper. Greensboro, NC: Center for Creative Leadership.

# PART I
# Fundamentals

# 2

# ALL THE LEARNING THAT STUDENTS EXPERIENCE IN COLLEGE

If leaders are made, and if you can take charge of your own "making," how do you get started? The answer is, the same way that you have with everything else you know how to do: through learning. In this theoretical chapter, I'm going to summarize the thinking and research that I have done with my colleague Manny London on learning (London & Sessa, 2006; Sessa & London, 2005). We approach learning from a slightly different angle than what you may have read in a psychology class or an education class, so I recommend spending some time reading this chapter. It will give you ideas on learning leadership beyond what I can do in one book. It also may give you ideas on learning many other things. In the next chapter, I will apply these ideas directly to learning leadership.

## What Is Learning?

Before reading on, spend a moment envisioning yourself "learning." What do you see in your mind? Many of you might be picturing yourself sitting in a large lecture hall either trying to absorb the words that the professor is speaking by osmosis (that is, hoping to soak it in while you sit with your eyes half closed) or by diligently copying words off the overhead screens supplemented by what the professor is saying (to be put aside until there is a paper due or a test). What we mean by learning is much more than that.

I'm going to start with an odd statement: Although individuals do not exist to learn, they have learning mechanisms built into their very being. According to Elliott Jaques, in his book, *The Life and Behavior of Living Organisms* (2002), at your core, you are engaged in "intention-bound work." In just about everything you do, you are engaged in selecting goals, choosing how to achieve them, overcoming obstacles on the way, and evaluating the outcomes of your work. Individuals learn in the process of trying to achieve valued goals. They find themselves in situations in which they want something. For instance, individuals may want to try a new activity, seek to do work that they find interesting or fulfilling, or impress parents, professors, and peers. In order to do this, they may need to learn about something new or how to do something new. So they explore and experiment and practice, and, in the process, set more goals, try new behaviors, seek feedback, and find ways of interacting that work best for them. Thus, learning is a by-product of intention-bound work; it is not an end in itself and only happens when there is a need or an expected future need. Everyone is continuously engaged in this learning—in judging, choosing, deciding, in order to establish goals and in order to overcome obstacles or uncertainties encountered while engaging in intention-bound work.

In addition, you need to maintain yourself in a changing environment. You moved from high school to college (and perhaps from home to a dormitory or apartment); each semester your classes change; and, in one single day, every professor expects you to behave differently (plus in that single day, you need to change as you move from the classroom to classroom, to a co-curricular activity, to work, to hanging out with your friends, to eating dinner with your family). Because of constant fluxes in the environment, you adapt, change, develop, and evolve, as you select and achieve (or not achieve) goals and new goals, overcome obstacles, and evaluate outcomes of your work; you can never be "still." You do this by constantly re-creating yourself (in small, medium, and large ways). And you don't just respond to changes and adapt to your environment. You can also explore new forms and behaviors and change the setting that you are in.

From this point of view, you engage in learning on a regular, continuous basis as you proceed through your day and your life—from the time you were born through old age. And it occurs in all settings—the classroom, the clubroom, the dorm room, the ball field, the mountain path, the workplace, church, the grocery store aisle. Knowing this, you can begin to harness your own learning processes to better learn leadership (and many other things, for that matter!).

Learning is a neurobiological process (Keeling, Dickson, & Avery, 2011); as you maintain yourself in your environment and are engaged in intention-bound work, your brain is constantly changing its structure and the way it functions so that you can be successful. *You are continually deepening and broadening your capabilities in (re)structuring yourself to meet changing conditions, adding new skills and knowledge, and (re)creating yourself into a more sophisticated individual.* Learning outcomes are changes in the neuro-patterns of the brain (Ratey, 2001) and manifest themselves in changes in what you know, the way you think, how you behave, and how you feel. These changes come about as a result of learning processes.

## What Are Learning Processes?

There are three processes that individuals use to acquire the behaviors, skills, feelings, ways of thinking, and knowledge that they need as they go about their intention-bound work in a changing environment. These are *adaptation*, which emphasizes the often unconscious changes of individuals as they react to a stimulus in their environment; *generation*, which emphasizes purposefully seeking out and adding what is needed; and *transformation*, which brings about a fundamental shift in the way they think or act as individuals learn from others and experiment with new behaviors.

## *Adaptive Learning*

At the simplest level, an individual demonstrates a relatively permanent change in behavior in reaction to a stimulus in the external environment (this type of learning is exemplified in the behaviorist tradition of learning theorists such as Guthrie, 1952; Pavlov, 1927; Skinner, 1971; Thorndike, 1932; Tolman, 1932; and Watson, 1924). Students pick up information from their environment on how they should act and change their behavior accordingly—without necessarily being aware that they are doing so. Indeed, the resulting changes may be unnoticed or difficult to express. For example, when you walk into your first class of the semester, the professor is standing at the lectern looking over her notes, barely noticing the students as they walk in. The students are sitting quietly with all desks facing forward. At 9 am sharp, she closes the door and begins to take attendance. She glares at the students who come in late. You make a mental note not to be late to this class, EVER—maybe a few minutes early is a better policy. And you decide that asking for extensions on assignments is probably out as well. For your second class, the teacher is perched on the edge of the table chatting with students. She smiles at you as you walk in and says hello. You notice that the chairs are set in a circle. Hm, you think to yourself, I think I'm going to be expected to talk in this class, and you make a mental note to have all your readings done ahead of time. As another example, you decide to join a club. For the first meeting, you want to make a good impression, so you put on some of your trendier clothes and spend a little time in front of the mirror making sure your hair is perfect. When you walk into the meeting room, you see that everyone is casual, and some look like they just came from the gym. For the next meeting, you go as you are.

In all three examples, learning has occurred. This learning is automatic, unconscious, and powerful. It could occur for many different phenomena, including how to behave, how to dress, how to greet others (a hello, a handshake, or a hug), how to treat others (formally or informally), how to solve problems (including when and how to search for information, what sources to approach, and who to ask), how to work with others (type of meetings, frequency of meetings, which technology to use, what times are appropriate), and many other things. You can even unknowingly pick up knowledge about your major by watching and emulating the behavior of your professor or knowledge about how to run a meeting, by watching and emulating the vice-president of the Student Government Association during a legislative meeting.

## Generative Learning

Generative learning is purposefully adding and using new behaviors, feelings, knowledge, ways of thinking, and skills. There are several ways of thinking about learning generatively. The first way emphasizes that your mind is more than an unconscious adaptive learning system (as was discussed above). Rather, a thinking person interprets incoming information and gives meaning to that information through such things as insight, information processing, memory, and perception, and their (re) structuring. The role of a teacher, mentor, or coach is to provide you with information and help you process it in such a way that it makes sense and can be used in some way (learning theorists associated with this learning orientation include Ausubel, 1968; Bruner, 1960; Gagné, 1978; Koffka, 1924; and Kohler, 1947).

The second way focuses on the fact that people can purposefully learn by observing others. This is called *social learning*. The purpose of education is to demonstrate new roles and behavior and allow students to practice these. The role of a teacher, mentor, or coach is to model and guide new roles and behavior (social learning theorists include Bandura, 1986 and Rotter, 1966). Modeling is a great technique, especially when you are not sure how to behave or fit in. For example, freshmen and transfer students may purposefully watch students who have been around awhile and emulate them in terms of what they wear, how they behave, how much they study (or not), how engaged they are in their studies and in their extra-curricular activities, whether they attend college sporting events, etc., to determine how they should behave at their college. The difference between the examples here and the examples given in learning through adaptation is that adaptation is unconscious. You are not aware that you are doing it. In generative learning, you are purposefully watching others to learn from them.

The third way of generative learning is based on the belief that humans can control their own destiny and are free to choose and act—that is, you determine what you learn. This model emphasizes human nature, human potential, and human emotions. Behavior is the consequence of human choice. The purpose of your learning and education is to become a self-actualized and autonomous adult, with the role of the teacher or mentor or coach to facilitate this process (theorists representative of this humanist tradition include Maslow, 1970 and Rogers, 1969). A label for this type of generative learning is called *andragogy* which includes the following assumptions: (1) Your self-concept as you grow into adulthood is one of being increasingly responsible for your own decisions and lives. Adults generally do not like other people's wills imposed upon them. (2) You are life/task/problem-centered and want to learn things that will help with your life, a task you are working on, or a problem you are dealing with. (3) You become ready to learn those things you need to know and are able to do in order to cope effectively with your real life. (4) So, you need to know why you need to learn something before undertaking to learn it. (5) You already have a large volume and quality of experience. While you can provide rich experiences to other students and learn from other students, on the downside, you already have mental habits, biases, and presuppositions that guide, and sometimes limit, your learning. (6) Although you can respond to external motivation to learn something (e.g., getting a good grade), the most potent motivators of your learning are internal (Knowles, 1975).

In summary of the three ideas in the paragraphs above, generative learning is purposeful. When you have a goal or see the need, you think about and choose a path to do what you need to attain that goal or satisfy that need including attending college, choosing a major, selecting certain courses over others, earning degrees, participating in activities, and observing others to keep your behaviors, feelings, knowledge, and skills up to date with what is needed in your life and your next life stage (e.g., your life after college). You control what you learn, and you can and need to take charge of your own learning. This means that you need to: (1) Be aware and open when life presents you with a new challenge and recognize that you need to learn; (2) Be open to learning about new things—actually acquiring new behaviors, skills, feelings, and knowledge generatively and monitoring that learning; and (3) Be open to learning how to do new things—using, evaluating, and reaping the benefits of learning.

## *Transformative Learning*

College is often a transformative learning experience for students. The world and ways of viewing it change as students move into and through their college years. The previous equilibrium of the forces in students' (perhaps simpler, pre-college) lives becomes unbalanced and they experience discomfort. Truths get tested forcing new ways of thinking. Students transform by reframing these experiences into a broader and more complex understanding in the way they see themselves and the world in which they live (this constructivist tradition is based on theorists such as Dewey, 1933/1986; Lave (cf. Cole, Sharp, and Lave, 1976); Mezirow, 1994; Piaget, 1952; Rogoff, 1990, von Glaserfeld, 1996; and Vygotsky, 1978). The result is a powerful and lasting change in who you are as a person. You develop an increasingly complex way of understanding the world. It means becoming more mature—able to be critical of yourself and to see weaknesses that can be overcome and strengths that can be enhanced. You develop a new understanding of your relationships with others. And not only do you change the content of what you know, but you change your previous assumptions—typically becoming more inclusive (open to new ideas), discriminating (able to understand fine points), and integrative (able to see interactions and linkages). This transformation can happen in two different ways: through experiences and through others.

## Transformative Learning Through Experiences

Learning from experience, or learning by doing, is one of the most powerful ways for individuals to learn, especially when it involves experiencing new challenges. Think about how you learned to ride a bike, or tie your shoes, or cook. With these, rather than reading a book or watching a video, you climbed on your bike, or you sat down with someone and they walked you through step by step how to tie your shoe, or you cooked with someone in order to learn.

However, experience alone does not lead to learning. Here, I draw from David Kolb's (1984) work with his colleagues on experiential learning theory to explain. In his theory, in order to learn from an experience, you need to engage in a four-step process. First, you engage in a concrete experience. You do something. Then you observe what happened and reflect on it. What worked, what didn't, what went differently from what you expected. These observations and reflections are then assimilated into an idea or theory and new implications are drawn. These implications are actively tested and serve as a guide in creating a new experience. Here is an example. You are hanging out on the college green soaking up the warm spring sun with your friends when another friend rides up on his unicycle. You ask if you can give it a try and you spend a few minutes attempting to ride the unicycle (concrete experience). You fail miserably, but there was a brief 5-second moment when you balanced by rocking back and forth a bit and held your feet horizontal on the pedals. "Hm," you think to yourself (observe and reflect), "when I put my weight on the seat and not the pedals, and I sat up straight, and I got those pedals horizontal by rocking my feet, I was able to balance a bit." "I bet," you continue (assimilating your reflections into an idea and new implications), "if I asked two friends to hold me until I get situated into that position, I might do a little better." So you convince two friends to join you (testing). They stand on either side of you and you put your arms around their shoulders. They wait while you mount the unicycle, sit up straight and get your weight on the seat, not the pedals. You rock back and forth a bit by holding the pedals horizontally and gently pedaling a bit. They let go and this time you last 10 seconds (concrete experience). Which leads you to . . . observe and reflect . . . This cycle lasts a few more times until your friends get tired of holding you up and you get tired of being laughed at. But you are now balancing on the unicycle for about 30 seconds and a few turns of the pedals. You are on your way to learning how to ride a unicycle.

## Transformative Learning Through Interactions with Others

You can develop a new understanding of yourself through your conversations with others (Gergen, 2009). As you interact with others and receive messages from them, you begin to see yourself and understand yourself through their eyes! As humans, we rely heavily on language to make sense of ourselves, others, and the world. That is, who you are is constructed and agreed upon through your conversations with others. When you were younger, this was simpler. You relied on your parents, your teachers, and your peers to help you understand yourself. In college (and as you add more and more social networking tools to your life), you can encounter and exchange with an almost limitless variety of people from all over the world with wholly different beliefs and even language (words) about life and truth, from your own. This has the potential to cause a major transformation in your understanding of yourself and your life while you are in college. For example, you may find that the various people within your life see you differently and treat you differently. You may find that your parents still see you and treat you like a little kid, while your favorite professor sees you as a mature and responsible adult with the ability to articulate sound critical thinking. Your high-school friends see you as the same old fun-loving and spontaneous person ready to drop everything for a party, while college classmates see you as capable of being ready, willing, and able to work on that class project on Saturday morning. And while you had always assumed you were a pretty fair and open-minded individual, your roommate (who has a vastly different background from you in terms of race or social economic status, or religion, or sexual orientation, etc.) argues that you act like you are biased and privileged.

In summary, transformative learning processes through experiences and other people lead to a dramatic shift in the way we think, feel, and act that irreversibly alters our very way of being in the world. We discover that we need to experience disequilibrium, let go of old ways, and take on new ways in order to continue being successful in our "intention-bound work."

## Combining Adaptive, Generative, and Transformative Learning

Individuals learn adaptively, generatively, and transformatively as they go about their intention-bound work and maintain themselves in a changing environment. Individuals build on, expand, and transform their behaviors, knowledge, feelings, ways of thinking, and skills. Often learning may be adaptive—student leaders may receive recognition for delegating and empowering their team members, and delegate and empower more as a result. Sometimes, learning is generative such as when a student leader purposefully seeks information by reading or watching others on how to delegate better and tries different methods to see what works. Also, learning may be transformative as the student leader is stretched and finds that the only way to get the job done is through delegation and empowerment of team members.

Individuals learn to apply their learning to an increasing variety of contexts, for example, moving learning from classroom to an internship, from student organization to organization, from non-work experiences to work experiences, etc. And again, the learning can be adaptive (using the same behavior in a new situation and discovering it works), generative (purposefully trying a technique learned in a psychology class with a friend who is struggling with a relationship problem), and transformative (realizing why a certain behavior, knowledge, or skill works across situations and deliberatively using that realization in a variety of novel ways).

## How Do Learning Processes Get Started?

In order to engage in one of the three ways of learning (adaptive, generative, and transformative), you need to be stimulated or triggered to learn and you need to be ready to learn.

### Triggers for Learning

Learning processes are triggered by pressures, demands, challenges, and opportunities that affect individuals such that they cannot continue what they are doing in the same way and be successful. When you are unfamiliar with a task or situation, or if you are exposed to a circumstance that is either extremely intense or highly meaningful, your activation level increases. This heightened arousal has been positively linked to the activation of the learning processes discussed above (DeRue & Wellman, 2009).

Although we tend to think of learning as something that happens in the college classroom, in reality, triggers for learning happen across the entire college campus as you go about your intention-bound work and maintain yourself in a changing environment. In "Learning Reconsidered: A Campus-Wide Focus on the Student Experience," the authors suggest that learning triggers can and do occur in the academic context (the classroom, a meeting with a professor, a lab, the library), the institutional context (in athletics, clubs, fraternities and sororities, committees, work-study positions, Residence Hall Assistants, Student Government, etc.), and even in the social context (hanging out with your friends) (Keeling, 2004).

And recent evidence demonstrates support for this idea. Learning is triggered when students are involved in activities that challenge and opportunities that move students out of their usual practices:

Researcher George Kuh (2008) found the following college experiences to be associated with student learning. He called these "high impact educational practices": first-year seminars and experiences, common intellectual experiences, learning communities, collaborative assignments and projects, research, diversity/global learning, service learning or community-based learning, internships, writing intensive courses, and capstone courses and projects. What is particularly interesting about these experiences is that while some of these occur solely in the academic context (for example, writing intensive projects and capstone courses and projects), others are designed to cross contexts. For example, first-year seminars and programs can occur in the classroom, but not necessarily; some of you reading this book may be in a first-year leadership development program that is offered outside of the classroom. Common intellectual experiences may ask students to participate in both classes and in co-curricular activities on the same topics at the same time. For example, student leaders at Montclair State University in New Jersey are encouraged to pursue a minor in leadership development (where they learn "about" leadership) at the same time as being engaged in their leadership roles within the school (where they learn "how to do" leadership). Some learning communities have a floor dedicated to them in a dormitory making them "living-learning communities" so that students have a chance to learn together both in the classroom and socially. In both service-learning/community based learning courses and internships, students are expected learn in the classroom, apply what they learn outside the classroom, and reflect back in the classroom (using David Kolb's experiential learning model discussed earlier).

Using data from the Wabash National Study of Liberal Arts Education, two researchers, James Barber and Patricia King (2014), found that exposure to new ideas, situations, and people from diverse backgrounds as well as experiencing discomfort all lead to the triggering of learning processes. What is key here is that students in this study mentioned that these triggers for learning happened all over the university, not just in the classroom. For example, while one student was exposed to new ideas about religion through his encounter with people from different religions in his honors roundtable discussions (academic context), another student was exposed to new ideas about religion by making a new friend who happened to be an atheist (social context). Both of them noted that this was a significant learning experience for them. And in both cases, students indicated that they expanded their ideas about religion, others, and themselves.

The Gallup Organization partnered with Purdue University to determine what matters most in college (Gallup-Purdue Index report, 2014). That is, they compared experiences that students had in college to how engaged they were in work and to their well-being after college. They found that the following experiences mattered most: (1) being involved in co-curricular activities and organizations; (2) working on projects that took a semester or longer to complete; (3) an internship or job where they were able to apply what they were learning in the classroom; and (4) a professor or mentor who cared about them as a person, who made them excited about learning, and who encouraged them to pursue their dreams. Similar to the findings from the high-impact educational practices and the Wabash National Study, in this study, people still recall important learning triggers happening both inside and outside the classroom long after they have left the university!

## Readiness to Learn

While triggers are needed to begin your learning process, they are not enough. You live in a complex environment that bombards you with continuous information.

You need to pick and choose what you will notice. That means your college or university, your teachers, mentors, and coaches can impose learning triggers and encourage you to begin the learning process, but they can't make you learn, predict what you will learn (if anything), or even make you use what you learn. When and how a student notices triggers for learning and responds by learning depends on their readiness to learn. Readiness to learn is how individuals recognize when triggers for learning are occurring and that they need to change accordingly: they must learn something in order to accomplish their task and then actually make a decision to take some sort of action.

In short: You choose the triggers that get your attention in the process of engaging in your intention-bound work.

Readiness to learn has stages. You don't go from not ready to ready in one step. James Prochaska and his colleagues have been working on understanding how people change for many years. Their theoretical model is called the Transtheoretical Model of Change and demonstrates that people move through stages of readiness to learn and change, including the following:

1.  *Pre-contemplation*: At this stage, there is an unawareness or under awareness that a trigger for learning and change is occurring. An individual doesn't recognize yet that there is a gap between what they are trying to accomplish and their current knowledge, skills, behaviors, or emotions, so they don't plan on taking any sort of action to close the gap.
2.  *Contemplation*: In this stage, there is a beginning awareness of a learning trigger, but the individual is not yet ready to make a commitment to change.
3.  *Preparation*: In this stage, an individual is aware of the trigger and is making plans to change or even starting to make small changes with the intention to make larger changes soon.
4.  *Action*: In this stage, individuals make specific, overt changes to their knowledge, ways of thinking, skills, behaviors, or emotions.
5.  *Maintenance*: Once a change happens, it needs to be maintained. In this stage, individuals work to practice and maintain the changes that they made in the action stage.

(Prochaska, Prochaska, & Levesque, 2001;
Prochaska, DiClemente, & Norcross, 1992)

Here is a behavioral change example. You have been noticing that your jeans are too tight when you put them on in the morning. At first, you blame the dormitory dryers: they are so hot, and all your clothes are shrinking. Here you are in the pre-contemplation stage, you haven't noticed yet that you are gaining weight. But, as you look in the mirror in the morning during the past few weeks, you begin noticing that the "Freshman 15" that you had sworn would not happen to you is becoming a reality. At this point, you might be thinking that maybe you should cut back on those late night snack fests with your roommates. But it's so much fun. And you have been needing new clothes anyway. Here you are in the contemplation stage. Then one day, you actually bust your zipper. In class. You pull your shirt down over your pants and after class you run back to your dorm and throw on some sweats. You decide you are going on a diet and will work out more. You dig out your old fitbit or turn on the fitness programming on your Apple Watch. You download a food diary application onto your smartphone and set your current weight and weight loss goals. You even do some Google searches on weight loss. But it is the weekend, and you decide to start the diet for real next week. Here, you have moved into the preparation stage, you are putting all your plans together. Finally, the day comes. You eat oatmeal for breakfast and head to the gym. You have calculated, at a pound a week, that you need to spend the spring semester diligently dieting and working out. Here you are in the action phase and actively modifying your eating habits and your fitness habits. Finally, you have reached your goal. But you vow not to go back to your first semester eating habits and to keep working out at the gym. You are in the maintenance stage. You also know more about nutrition, dieting, and your body. I have presented all these stages as happening quickly. They can happen quickly, but they can also happen much more slowly, perhaps even taking years. Or not at all (for example, some students might just go out and buy new clothes and complain that they need to diet as they eat that late night hot fudge sundae with extra fudge).

Research comparing learning readiness stage distributions across a range of behaviors and populations found that about 40 percent of "pre-action" individuals are in the pre-contemplation stage, 40 percent are in the contemplation stage, and only 20 percent are in the preparation stage (Laforge, Velicer, Richmond, & Owen, 1999). People in pre-contemplation and contemplation who are required to participate in some sort of learning situation are likely to see calls for change as imposed on them and be resistant to learning. But those who are ready to learn are more easily triggered, either by a current or expected trigger present in the environment, something that catches their interest, or even something unexpected.

Moving beyond the "pre-action" stages depends on three ways of thinking. First, you need to believe that you can learn and change. Second, you need to be motivated to learn. And third, you need to persist in your learning.

## Openness to Learning

You may notice a trigger in the environment that requires you to learn and change to be successful, but you don't believe that you can learn what is needed to deal with it. Have you ever been in a classroom at the beginning of the semester and the instructor asks "What do you want to get out of this course?" What did (or would) you say? Some students say they want to achieve an A or good grade in the class. Others indicate that they were curious about the topic or want (or need) to know more.

Carol Dweck and her colleagues, through their research, have discovered that people tend to fall in one of two categories regarding their beliefs about intelligence and ability, and corresponding two mindsets or "views you adopt for yourself" (Dweck et al., 2012: 6). Some people believe that intelligence and ability are fixed personal attributes. They are mainly concerned with demonstrating how smart they are and they prefer tasks they can already do well and avoid ones in which they may make mistakes and not look smart. They focus on demonstrating their competence and receiving favorable reactions from others, or on avoiding failure and negative reactions from others. This is called a fixed mindset, and individuals in this category tend not to believe that they can learn and change (but they can hone what they are already good at). Other people believe that intelligence and abilities are something they can change and develop through experience and effort. Individuals with this belief view effort as a way to develop the ability they need for mastering the task, and they are likely to exert effort to learn especially if they think they currently lack the ability needed to perform the task. This is called a growth mindset, and individuals in this category believe they can learn and change in anything they put their mind to.

Everyone learns (because they have to in order to pursue their intention-bound work and survive in a changing environment), however if an individual is more learning or mastery goal oriented, they are more open to learning and will more easily recognize triggers and move along the readiness to learn stages more quickly and with less support than individuals who are more performance goal oriented.

## Learning Motivation

Another factor that influences your readiness to learn is your motivation to learn. Motivation is an internal drive or desire that causes us to act (whether it is grabbing a glass of water because you are thirsty, reading your homework to gain knowledge in a class, or practicing an ice skating maneuver over and over). When we are motivated, we want something and we intentionally make things happen by our own energy and actions. That is, we set a goal, we put in place a plan of action to reach the goal, we put the plan into action and monitor ourselves (sometimes modifying the goal, the plan, or our actions along the way), and then we reflect on how well we accomplished the goal through the plan and our actions (Bandura, 2001).

When a person is motivated to learn something such as how to lead, it works the same way as motivation to do anything else. The person wants something and intentionally makes things happen by their own energy and actions. They set a goal. Goals can vary wildly and here are some examples: (1) I want to be a leader; (2) I want to be a good leader; (3) I want to be a leader in my field; (4) I want to be prepared to lead in case the situation calls for it; (5) I want to be the president of the SGA (or a club or team); (6) I am not sure I want to be a leader myself, but I'm curious about leadership; or even (7) I'm not sure I want to be a leader myself, but maybe there is something I can do to help a leader do a better job. With the goal in mind, the person puts in place a plan of action (if I want to succeed at my goal, I should take some workshops or courses or this certificate/minor, I should join the SGA or a club, watch how the eboard operates, and run for a position). Then the person puts that plan into action and monitors the plan and their behaviors and actions. Finally, they evaluate the plan, their behaviors and actions, and their own capabilities in doing so.

## Persistence in Learning (Grit)

A third factor that influences your readiness to learn is your perseverance and passion for long-term goals, or grit. Here, I draw on the research by Angela Duckworth and her colleagues (Duckworth, Peterson, Mathews, & Kelly, 2007; see also this TED talk: www.ted.com/talks/angela_lee_duckworth_the_key_to_success_grit?language=en). You may notice a trigger in the environment that requires you to learn and change to be successful; you may be motivated to learn it, but do not have the long-term stamina to follow through. Grit entails working strenuously toward challenges, maintaining effort and interest over years despite failure, adversity, and plateaus in progress.

Grit is different from intelligence or talent and is more important. Most of us are familiar with Aesop's fable on the race between the tortoise and the hare. At the starting line, it is the hare, without a doubt much quicker than the tortoise, who is expected to finish first. As expected, the hare quickly outpaces the tortoise, getting so far ahead that he lies down to take a nap mid-race. When the hare awakens, the tortoise, who all the while has been laboring toward his destination, is too close to the finish line to beat. Similarly, in their research, Duckworth and her colleagues found that "grittier" college students, like the tortoise, had higher GPAs and higher levels of educational attainment than students with less grit (and this was not related to SAT scores).

Life is hard. Every day, there are obstacles to what we want to do. Students with grit realize that they are supposed to suffer when working hard on a challenge that exceeds their capabilities. They are supposed to feel confused. When they are frustrated and overwhelmed, they know they need to persist and stay the course. Those with less grit may believe that suffering, confusion, frustration, and being overwhelmed are signs that they should not pursue a path or that the path is not worth pursuing. They are less likely to persist in their learning.

## Summarizing Triggers for Learning and Readiness to Learn

In this section, I discussed that learning processes are stimulated by triggers to learn and readiness to learn. As you live your life and go about your intention-bound work in an ever-changing environment, you encounter instances when you realize that you cannot continue what you are doing in the same way and be successful. You can encounter these learning triggers anywhere. We mostly think of learning happening in the classroom or the library, but learning can also be triggered in other college activities such as co-curricular activities, athletics, and fraternities and sororities, and non-college activities such as a job. You even learn when you are hanging out with your friends and family. While triggers are needed to get your attention, they are not enough to begin the learning process. You pick and choose the triggers that get your attention as you go about your intention-bound work. Whether you notice a trigger and whether you choose to do something about it is based on your readiness to learn. Students vary in their readiness to learn or in their recognition of triggers and the need to change. Although everyone learns, those who are open to learning, who are motivated to learn, and who are persistent are more ready to learn and will engage in the learning processes more readily than those who are less open to learning, do not find learning particularly motivating and engaging, and are not as persistent in their efforts.

When there is no trigger for learning and individuals have a low readiness to learn, little learning of any sort will occur: individuals can continue their intention-bound work with no change. When there is a trigger for learning, individuals who have low readiness to learn will respond by adapting. When there is a high readiness to learn, individuals will be easily triggered, either by a known or expected trigger present in the environment, something that catches their interest, or even something unexpected. High readiness to learn can lead to generative learning. In cases where there is both a trigger for learning and a high readiness to learn, individuals may respond with generative or transformative learning. See Table 2.1.

## Capitalizing on Your Learning Through Reflection

As I stated above in the transformative learning section, reflection is thinking about how or why we have perceived, thought, felt, or acted the way we did. As a result of the learning processes, you've made a change. But without reflection, you can't determine the extent to which you are moving toward your goals in your intention-bound work or whether you need to change in some other way to achieve those goals (or change the goals themselves). Reflection brings to light

**TABLE 2.1** Triggers to Learn and Readiness to Learn on Learning Processes

|  | Low readiness to learn | High readiness to learn |
|---|---|---|
| Low or no learning triggers | No learning | Generative learning |
| High learning triggers | Adaptive learning | Generative and/or Transformative learning |

to your experiences and gives meaning to your changes. Thus, without reflection, you can change, but you don't really "learn."

Reflection is a tool for transforming your experiences into information you can use. The meanings that you make can shape your future. For example, students can use their reflections to influence their triggers for learning and change their readiness to learn. You can deliberately put yourself in challenging situations to trigger your learning (or decide to go an easier route). You may be more likely to notice a gap between where you are and where you would like to be, and thus move into the ready to take action phase more quickly. In addition, reflection about a trigger, the learning processes, and the outcome can help students become more open to learning (I learned! I can do it again!), more likely to engage in learning (humans tend to repeat things they are successful at), and more willing to persist at least a little bit longer next time.

## Summary

- You do not exist to learn. But learning mechanisms are built into the core of your being and are necessary for you to be successful in your life.
- You need to maintain yourself in an ever-changing environment and in your intention-bound work. You learn in the process of living. You engage in learning on a regular, continuous basis as you proceed through your day and your life, in every activity that you engage in. That is, you are continually deepening and broadening your capabilities in (re) structuring yourself to meet changing conditions, adding new skills and knowledge, and (re) creating yourself into a more sophisticated individual.
- When you learn, your brain changes in structure and the way it functions. You may notice that you have changed what you know, the way you think, how you behave, and how you feel.
- There are three learning processes that you use to acquire the behaviors, skills, feelings, ways of thinking, and knowledge that you need. These are adaptive learning or a change in behavior as the result of a stimulus in the environment, generative learning or purposefully adding and using new behaviors, knowledge, ways of thinking, feeling, and skills, and transformative learning or reframing what you know into a broader and more complex understanding in the way you see yourself and the world.
- These learning processes are triggered by pressures, demands, challenges, and opportunities that affect you in such a way that you cannot continue what you are doing in the same way and be successful. That is, you don't learn unless you see a need to learn.
- But your world is complex and there are many potential triggers. When and how you notice a trigger for learning depends on your readiness to learn. People vary in their readiness to learn depending on their openness to learning, whether they find learning motivating and engaging, and their level of grit or persistence.

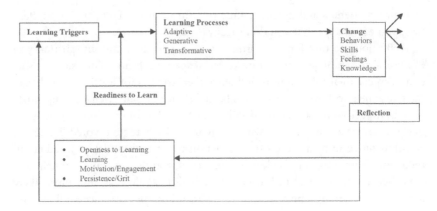

**FIGURE 2.1** How Learning Works.

Modified from London, M & Sessa, V.I. (2006), Continuous learning in organizations: a living systems analysis of individual, group, and organization learning, in Francis J. Yammarino, Fred Dansereau (ed.) Multi-Level Issues in Social Systems (Research in Multi Level Issues, Volume 5) Emerald Group Publishing Limited, pp.123–172.

- Changing your behaviors, skills, feelings, and knowledge is great, but not enough. You need to reflect on the changes to determine if the changes "worked." This in turn will allow you to deliberately choose triggers to challenge yourself (or deliberately choose an easier route) as well as strengthen your readiness to learn.
- Look at Figure 2.1 to see how learning works.

## Questions for Reflection and Discussion

1. How would you have described learning before you read this chapter? Did this chapter change the way you think about learning? How did your way of thinking about learning change? Discuss learning now, as you see it, in your own words.
2. What did you agree with in this chapter? What did you disagree with in this chapter? What surprised you in this chapter?
3. Think about your experiences in college so far. Consider the academic context, the institutional context, and your social context. What triggers for learning have occurred in each context? Are you satisfied with the amount of triggers that are occurring? Why or why not (and be specific)? What can you do to create a good balance (for some, you may need more triggers; for others, you may need fewer triggers)?
4. Have you engaged in any of the triggers listed above? Did you learn as a result (and what did you learn)? Now that you know that they are important to beginning your learning processes, are you interested in adding more of them to your own experiences? When and how might you do so? What other triggers would you explore and consider adding?

5. Generally, what is your readiness to learn? Be specific. Are there any gaps present that you need to close? Are you open to learning, are you motivated to learn, do you persist in learning? If through your reflection or discussion, you realize your readiness to learn is too low, what might you do to increase it? Can readiness to learn be too high? (Why or why not and be specific).

6. Why are you at college? Why are you attending this particular university or college? How is this impacting your readiness to learn?

7. Do you and how do you reflect on what you have learned? Think broadly, not just classroom learning. For example, if you learn something new that you can visualize, do you play back your movements in your head to determine what worked and what didn't. How can you deliberately add reflection into your life?

## References

Ausubel, D. P. (1968). *Educational psychology: A cognitive view.* New York: Holt, Rinehart & Winston.

Bandura, A. (2001). Social cognitive theory: An agentic perspective. *Annual Review of Psychology 52,* 1–26.

Barber, J. P. & King, P. M. (2014). Pathways toward self-authorship: Student responses to the demands of developmentally effective experiences. *Journal of College Student Development 55,* 433–450.

Bruner, J. S. (1960). *The process of education.* New York: Vintage.

Cole, M., Sharp, D., & Lave, C. (1976). The cognitive consequences of education: Some empirical evidence and theoretical misgivings. *Urban Review 9,* 218–233.

DeRue, D. S. & Wellman, N. (2009). Developing leaders via experience: The role of developmental challenge, learning orientation, and feedback availability. *Journal of Applied Psychology 94,* 859–875.

Dewey, J. (1933/1986). *How we think: A restatement of the relation of reflective thinking to the educative process.* Boston, MA: D. C. Heath & Company.

Duckworth, A. L., Peterson, C., Mathews, M. D., & Kelly, D. R. (2007). Grit: Perseverance and passion for long-term goals. *Journal of Personality and Social Psychology 92,* 1087–1101.

Dweck, C. (2012). *Mindset: How you can fulfill your potential.* New York: Random House.

Gagné, N. L. (1978). *The scientific basis of the art of teaching.* New York: Teachers College Press.

Gallup-Purdue Index report (2014). *Great Jobs, great lives: A study of more than 30,000 college graduates across the US.* www.luminafoundation.org/files/resources/galluppurdue index-report-2014.pdf.

Gergen, K. J. (2009). *An invitation to social construction* (2nd ed.). Los Angeles, CA: Sage.

Guthrie, E. R. (1952). *The psychology of learning* (Rev. ed.). New York: Harper & Brothers.

Jaques, E. (2002). *The life and behavior of living organisms: A general theory.* Westport, CT: Praeger.

Keeling, R. P. (2004). Learning reconsidered: A campus–wide focus on the student experience. American College Personnel Association. www.myacpa.org/pub/documents/ learningreconsidered.pdf.

Keeling, R. P., Dickson, J. S., & Avery, T. (2011). Biological bases for learning and development across the lifespan. In M. London (Ed.), *The Oxford Handbook of Lifelong Learning* (pp. 40–51). New York: Oxford University Press.

Knowles, M. S. (1975). *Self-directed learning.* River Grove, IL: Follett.

Koffka, K. (1924). *The growth of the mind* (R. M. Ogden, Trans.). London: Kegan Paul, Trench, Trubner.

Kohler, W. (1947). *Gestalt psychology: An introduction to new concepts in modern psychology.* New York: Liveright. (Reprinted 1959, New York: New American Library).

Kolb, D. A. (1984). *Experiential learning: Experience as the source of learning and development.* Englewood Cliffs, NJ: Prentice-Hall.

Kuh, G. (2008). *High-impact educational practices: What they are, who has access to them, and why they matter.* Washington, DC: Association of American Colleges and Universities.

Laforge, R. G., Velicer, W. F., Richmond, R. L., & Owen, N. (1999). Stage distributions for five health behaviors in the United States and Australia. *Preventive Medicine 28*, 61–74.

London, M. & Sessa, V. I. (2006). Continuous learning in organizations: A living systems analysis of individual, group, and organization learning. In Francis J. Yammarino & Fred Dansereau (Eds.), *Multi-level issues in social systems: Research in multi level issues, volume 5* (pp. 123–172). Emerald Group Publishing.

Maslow, A. H. (1970). *Motivation and personality* (2nd ed.). New York: Van Nostrand Reinhold.

Mezirow, J. (1994). Understanding transformation theory. *Adult Education Quarterly 44*(4), 222–232.

Pavlov, I. P. (1927). *Conditioned reflex* (G. V. Anrep, Trans.). London: Oxford University Press.

Piaget, J. (1952). *The origins of intelligence in children.* New York: International Universities Press.

Prochaska, J. M., Prochaska, J. O., & Levesque, D. A. (2001). A transtheoretical approach to changing organizations. *Administration and Policy in Mental Health 28*(4), 247–261.

Prochaska, J. O., DiClemente, C. C., & Norcross, J. C. (1992). In search of how people change: Applications to addictive behaviors. *American Psychologist 47*, 1102–1114.

Ratey, J. (2001). *A user's guide to the brain.* New York: Pantheon Books.

Rogers, C. R. (1969). *Freedom to learn.* Columbus, OH: Merrill.

Rogoff, B. (1990). *Apprenticeship in thinking: Cognitive development in the social context.* New York: Oxford University Press.

Rotter, J. B. (1966). Generalized expectancies for internal versus external control of reinforcement. *Psychological Monographs 80*(1, Whole No. 609), 1–28.

Sessa, V. I. & London, M. (2005). *Continuous learning in organizations: Individual, group, and organizational perspectives.* Mahwah, NJ: Lawrence Erlbaum Associates, Inc.

Skinner, B. F. (1971). *Beyond freedom and dignity.* New York: Knopf.

Thorndike, E. L. (1932). *The fundamentals of learning.* New York: Teachers College Press.

Tolman, E. C. (1932). *Purposive behavior in animals and men.* New York: Appleton-Century-Crofts.

von Glaserfeld, E. (1996). Introduction: Aspects of constructivism. In C. Twomey Fosnot (Ed.), *Constructivism: Theory, perspectives, and practice* (pp. 3–7). New York: Teachers College Press.

Vygotsky, L. (1978). *Mind in society: The development of higher psychological process.* Cambridge, MA: Harvard University Press.

Watson, J. B. (1924). *Behaviorism.* New York: Norton.

# 3

# LEARNING LEADERSHIP

The previous chapter was theoretical and went into depth on learning in general. I included that chapter to impact and broaden the way you think about learning and about your role as an active participant in the learning process. The purpose of this chapter is to apply that learning model to learning leadership specifically. You will see that learning leadership is similar to learning in general. Then the remainder of the chapters in this book will go into the topics from this chapter in more depth. In this chapter, I: (1) address leadership learning trajectories; (2) discuss the different leadership learning outcomes that you will encounter as you learn about leadership, learn how to do leadership, and experience leadership; and (3) introduce the ReAChS of leadership (based on triggers for learning, readiness to learn, and reflection from the last chapter) that will allow you to take charge of your own leadership learning, now and in the future.

## Leadership Learning Trajectory

When it comes to learning leadership, everyone starts from their own unique place, proceeds on their own unique path, and thus develops their own identity of leadership, their own understanding of leadership, and their own strengths and weaknesses. You will find that as you participate in leadership and reflect on your experiences, your leader identity will change and develop, your understanding of leadership will become more complex, and you are developing needed skills and competencies. Much of this learning will be adaptive—that is you will tweak or change the way you lead, discover it works better, and as a result continue on the new path without realizing it until you look back later. You will learn generatively. Reading this book about learning leadership and putting into place all or part of the recommendations, or attending a workshop on conflict resolution, are both examples of generative learning. And you will learn transformatively. The first time you step into a leadership position and discover that you were able to do it (and perhaps liked it) or being in a follower position and discovering that your leadership views, skills, and competencies could help you and your team in that position are both examples of transformative learning.

In this chapter, I will share information about leadership learning and development of adults and students. You may feel that you are starting from a similar place as the people that I describe. Or you may feel that they and their experiences are very different from your own. You may find yourself learning similar lessons to adults and students that I discuss. Or you may find that you are learning different leadership lessons. When you compare yourself to others at your school, you may find that the same experiences (for example, being a resident assistant (RA)) leads to different learning outcomes. In fact, you may even set out planning to learn one thing, and end up learning something else that is important. Some of you may feel like your trajectory is very steep, others may perceive theirs is quite flat. Your leadership learning trajectory is your own; it is neither right nor wrong, bad nor good. What matters is that you own and manage your leadership learning trajectory!

## Leadership Learning Outcomes

When you think about learning leadership, what outcomes enter your mind? What do you expect to learn? You probably realize right away that you need to learn leadership skills and competencies. And with a bit more thinking, you might realize that since you are in a school setting, you will be learning theories and other formal knowledge about leadership. But there are at least two additional outcomes you learn in your leadership development journey that are intertwined with the leadership skills and competencies, and the knowledge that you develop: You learn who you are as a leader, that is your leader identity, and you learn and develop your ways of thinking about leaders and leadership. These two actually impact your learning of leader skills, competencies, and knowledge, so I'm going to address them first.

### Who You Are as a Leader

A leader identity is an identity that a person holds regarding whether he or she thinks they are a leader, what sort of leader they are, and how they relate to others as a leader. Some of you reading this book may have a fairly sophisticated view of yourself as a leader. Others may still be wondering why you are even reading this book as you are not a leader, don't see yourself ever being a leader, and don't want to be a leader. "Leader" is not yet part of how you identify yourself. Before moving on to the next paragraph, take a moment and ask yourself the following three questions (even if you have not thought of yourself as a leader before): (1) Am I a leader? Or, from the first chapter, How have I participated in leadership?; (2) What sort of leader am I (or would like to be)?; and (3) As a leader, how do I relate towards other leaders? Towards followers? Towards peers?

Developing a leader identity is perhaps one of the most important leadership learning outcomes. As you develop your leader identity, or who you are as a leader, research suggests that you become more motivated to lead, you are more likely to engage in leadership, and you begin to seek out leadership responsibilities and opportunities to develop your leadership skills (DeRue & Ashford, 2010).

Identity can be described with regards to level, as well as type. Susan Komives and her colleagues (2005, 2006) have been researching the development of leader identities in students and young adults for many years. In their research, they found that people may proceed through up to six stages of leader identity (not all people proceed through all levels). In the first stage, children are aware that leaders exist out there somewhere—parents are leaders, the president of the United States is a leader, girl/boy scout leaders are leaders. At this point, leadership is external to the child and they don't identify as a leader. In the second stage, children begin joining groups and taking on responsibilities, but typically don't on take positional leadership roles. In addition, even if they are in a leader role (e.g., the president of the speech club), they still may not see themselves as a leader. In the leader-identified stage, individuals believe that leadership is a position, and therefore, the person in that position is the leader. The typical college student is at this stage. In the leadership differentiated stage, individuals still see leadership as what an individual does as a positional leader, but also perceives leadership being exhibited by non-positional group members. A group member could be "a leader without a title." At this stage, individuals become more aware that leadership is a process. In the generativity stage, individuals recognize the interdependence of people working together. They express a passion for their commitments and care for the welfare of others, including the sustainability of their own groups in which they are working. The final stage is integration and synthesis of leadership identity into a more encompassing identity. Individuals understand that they do not need to hold positional leader roles to engage in leadership. They now "engage in leadership" rather than "are a leader."

What are some things that successful college student leaders learn about themselves as leaders? Here, I will draw from my own research on successful student leaders in college (Sessa, Morgan, Kalenderli, & Hammond, 2014). These students said that they learned about themselves in general, and about themselves as leaders in particular.

Here are some lessons that successful student leaders in college said that they learned about themselves in general when they participated in leadership:

- It really does enrich you inside and it's not just about giving to people or being a leader; it's also self-enriching and it's finding out who you are and finding out what you can do for the world or for the community or just for yourself. So that's really what I learned, that it's not just giving to other people, or being a leader, or starting something or whatever, it is for yourself as well, which a lot of people miss.
- It was big for me in trusting myself. I tend to be my own worst critic and tend to blame myself when stuff goes wrong. With all I was doing I didn't have time for that. So I think it helped me stop doing that a little bit. It is not always my fault and even if it is, dwelling on it is not going to help.
- I was not very confident in myself, so that role really allowed me to develop confidence, public speaking skills, interacting with people on a weekly basis. That meant talking to administrators on a regular basis. That was something that really developed me because I was very shy and very timid, and didn't have the confidence to go up to someone and ask questions, but this role really allowed me to experience and try new things and really develop like I said, confidence.
- It is more fun than I thought it would be.
- I learned my passion in life. I learned that there is nothing more I want to do than become a doctor.
- I realized that I can make a legitimate difference, no matter how big or how little it is.
- I learned that I'm probably more of an orderly person than most people.

Here are some lessons the student leaders said they learned about who they are as leaders. As you can see from these examples, some of these students are in the leader- identified stage and some are in the leadership differentiated stage:

- I didn't really see myself as a leader. I never really thought that I could go ahead and take charge and have an impact like that until she (a professor) told me the kind of impact she could see I was having on others in that class. I remember thinking, wow, I'm going to be all right. If a tenured professor is telling me that I'm going to be good, then she is probably right. That definitely made an impact.
- I really liked having that leadership position. I liked the fact that, not to say I was superior to anyone else or above anyone else, but I liked overseeing and having all the little parts go together and then having not the final say, but reviewing the final product.
- Sometimes leadership is a sole position. You are alone. You have support and you have people that are higher than you but I think in single leadership positions there are a lot of being, not feeling alone, but you are kind of solo in being a leader.
- So I think what I really took away from that is that leadership isn't a title, you know, no one has cards that say "John Smith, Super Leader." You do

what you're expected to do. Because really, the membership aspect of it, as we progressed through the year became more and more apparent what was expected of me, and not just here at my college, what's expected of me later I think.

- Everybody plays their own role and you don't always have to be in a leadership position. There doesn't always have to be a leader. For example, we had a talent show portion of the training program. Every school was asked if they wanted to volunteer and put together a skit. One of the other leaders said we should do one. Everyone else was not interested, but I took his lead and we put together a great show.

There are two takeaways from this: (1) People hold leader identities and those identities differ from one another; and (2) Leader identities change and develop over time, from no identity, to fairly simple, to more complex.

## *Ways of Thinking about Leaders and Leadership*

Similar to your leader identity, the way that you think about leaders and leadership may change and develop over time. Leadership is not something that exists out in the real world, like a tree. The term "leadership" is a construct, not an object. A construct is something that is not directly observable in the visible world. We know beauty (another construct) when we see it, for example, but we can't describe it in inches or pounds in terms of how much there is, where it starts or ends, or even agree with others on what is beautiful and what is not. Leadership is like beauty in that regard. As you move through your life, not only does your understanding of yourself as a leader shift, but so does your understanding of what leadership "is" shift.

Wilfred Drath, in his book, *The Deep Blue Sea: Rethinking the Source of Leadership* (2001) proposes that there are three general ways of understanding leadership that he calls "principles of leadership." In Drath's first principle of leadership, "personal dominance," leadership is seen as coming directly from the formal leader. Leadership is what the leader does and is a personal characteristic of the leader. Most college students (and many adults) understand leadership from this principle. An individual in the formal role of leader who understands leadership from this perspective sees themselves as the "authority." Followers or observers who understand leadership from this perspective, think that if the leader's actions don't make sense, or if someone doubts or challenges the leader, then leadership is ineffective or is not happening. In Drath's second principle of leadership, "Interpersonal Influence," leadership is seen as an influence process and a leader emerges from a process of negotiation with the rest of the group where the individual(s) of greater influence emerge as the leader(s). The personal dominance principle, which sees leadership as being something inherent in the leader, differs from the emergence of a leader from a process of negotiation in that here, leadership is occupied by the most influential person and can change over time. An individual in the formal role of leader who understands leadership from this perspective would see their job as listening to and being influenced by followers but having greater influence on their followers through reason and negotiation and by virtue of their formal title as leader. In Drath's third principle of leadership, "relational dialogue," leadership is understood to happen when people participate in collaborative forms of thought and action to complete tasks and accomplish change. If there is a person who has the label of "leader," the role this person takes is only one aspect of participation in the larger process of leadership. An individual in the formal role of leader who understands leadership from this perspective might see their job as to "act with" the other members of the group and to use his/her talents and skill sets as needed to reach goals and effect change. For example, their contributions to leadership might involve facilitating the group in creating a direction together, and in submitting the actual report of progress or goals reached.

Similar to your leader identity, there are two takeaways from understanding leadership: (1) People hold ideas about what is and what is not leadership, and these vary by person; and (2) Understanding of leadership changes and develops over time, from fairly simple to more complex. As your leader identity and the way you understand leadership changes, this will impact the skills you deem important to learn and develop.

## Leader Skills and Competencies

The Society for Human Resources Management defines leader competencies as, "leadership skills and behaviors that contribute to superior (leader) performance" (www.shrm.org/resourcesandtools/hr-topics/behavioral-competencies/leadership-and-navigation/pages/leadershipcompetencies.aspx). In this section, I draw from a classic study conducted by the Center for Creative Leadership (CCL) (McCall, Lombardo, & Morrison 1988) as well as my own research (Sessa, et al., 2014). In both studies, successful leaders (executives and students in leadership positions who were seen as successful by others) were interviewed. In the original CCL study, the successful leaders were top-level executives. In my study, I focused on successful student leaders in college.

In both studies, we asked the following:

> When you think back over your career as a manager (on your collegiate leadership experiences), certain events or stories probably come to mind—things that led you to change or affirm the way you lead. Please identify at least three "key events" in your career (from your years in college), which helped shape you into the leader you are today. What happened and what did you learn from those experiences (the good and the bad)?

Here, I will summarize the lessons these successful leaders learned. I will start with what successful executives said they learned, then I will list what successful

**TABLE 3.1** Leadership Skills and Competencies Learned by Successful Executives

| | |
|---|---|
| Personal awareness | • The balance between work and personal life<br>• Knowing what excites you about work<br>• Personal limits and blind spots<br>• Taking charge of your career<br>• Recognizing and seizing opportunities |
| Executive temperament | • Being tough when necessary<br>• Self-confidence<br>• Coping with situations beyond your control<br>• Persevering through adversity<br>• Coping with ambiguous situations<br>• Use (and abuse) of power |
| Basic values | • You can't manage everything all alone<br>• Sensitivity to the human side of management<br>• Basic management values |
| Handling relationships | • What executives are like<br>• How to work with executives<br>• Dealing with people over whom you have no authority<br>• Handling political situations<br>• Getting people to implement solutions<br>• Strategies of negotiation<br>• Understanding other people's perspectives<br>• Dealing with conflict<br>• Directing and motivation subordinates<br>• Developing other people<br>• Confronting subordinate performance problems<br>• Managing former bosses and peers |
| Setting and implementing agendas, goals, and plans | • Technical/professional skills<br>• All about the business one is in<br>• Strategic thinking<br>• Shouldering full responsibility<br>• Building and using structure and control systems<br>• Innovative problem-solving methods |

*Source*: Lindsey, Homes, & McCall, 1987.

college student leaders learned. Finally, I will describe a resource for even more skills and competencies that students might draw from.

See Table 3.1, which lists lessons that the successful executives in the original CCL study said they learned (Lindsey, Homes, & McCall, 1987).

See Table 3.2, which lists lessons that successful student leaders from my study said they learned (Sessa, et al., 2014). As you can see, there are some similarities and some differences to what successful executives said they learned.

These are the skills and competencies that arose in my research and the research by CCL. But there are many more competencies that you may develop as you learn about and practice leadership while in college. Remember, that

**TABLE 3.2** Leadership Skills and Competencies Learned by Successful Student Leaders

| | |
|---|---|
| Personal or self-awareness | • Professionalism<br>• Balancing roles |
| Learning and reasoning | • Big picture perspective<br>• Decision-making<br>• Learning to teach/learn |
| Individual competencies | • Accountability and responsibility<br>• Adaptability and flexibility<br>• Resilience, persistence, and hard work<br>• Taking initiative |
| Support systems | • Developing and using support systems<br>• Being a support system |
| Working with others | • Communication<br>• Teamwork<br>• Dealing with conflict<br>• Dealing with diversity<br>• Delegation<br>• Inspiring and motivating others |
| Getting the job done | • Task skills<br>• Working in the school environment |

*Source*: Sessa et al. 2014.

in learning, you learn what you need to learn in order to continue with your intention-bound work in an ever-changing environment! The same is true for learning about leadership. Corey Seemiller, in her book, *The Student Leadership Competencies Guidebook: Designing Intentional Leadership Learning and Development* (2013), details 60 student leadership competencies (some of them related to those outlined above, some not) that cover learning and reasoning, self-awareness and development, interpersonal interactions, group dynamics, civic responsibility, communication, strategic planning, and personal behavior. Remember that the skills and competencies listed are examples of what you may learn.

In addition, you are never really finished learning leadership competencies. You continue to learn and hone them over your lifetime (and as your identity changes and your understanding of leadership changes, your manner of accomplishing competencies will also shift).

Stuart and Hubert Dreyfus (1986) developed a five-stage model of skill and competency acquisition that is widely used. Here you can see that skill and competency development doesn't happen all at once:

1. *Novices*: focus on accomplishing immediate tasks, they typically require clear rules that they follow closely.
2. *Advanced beginners*: use rules as guidelines, applying them in new situations, but not able to handle exceptions or unforeseen problems.

3. *Competent performers*: form conceptual models of what they are doing; can handle more complex situations based on their experience; typically rely on heuristics or surface features.
4. *Proficient performers*: have experienced a wide variety of situations and challenges; see the big picture, monitor their own performance, and interpret underlying principles to adjust their behaviors based on the context; can handle relatively novel or complex situations.
5. *Experts*: able to identify and solve problems intuitively, with little explicit analysis or planning; see underlying patterns effortlessly and adapt principles to generate and apply appropriate solutions, even to complex and unique situations, in such a way that they generate consistently superior performance. The "expert" level does not signify that development stops, as expert practitioners need to evaluate their practice and keep up-to-date with new evidence.

There are three takeaways from this section: (1) There are many skills and competencies you will be learning on your leadership journey; (2) You will continue to develop and hone these skills and competencies over your life-time; and (3) On your own unique leadership trajectory, you may find yourself learning similar skills and competencies as others. You may find that you are learning similar skills and competencies, but that you are at different levels of expertise. Or you may find that you are learning other skills and competencies.

## *Learning Formal Knowledge about Leadership*

A final outcome of what you may learn about leadership, especially in college, is formal knowledge, theory, and language about leadership. Many students reading this book may be in a course that discusses leadership theories. Being exposed to formal knowledge, theories, and language allows you to be able to express your identity, your understanding of leadership, and your skills and competencies in common leadership terms. Here are some examples from my research with students:

- I think it was really powerful working with a faculty advisor so I could see how she interacts with the students. It was interesting to see that dynamic and take things from the advisor and use them. For example, the way she interacted with the students. She was someone who really cared and she brought me towards really caring for the students as a *transformational leader*.
- We learned about the *servant-leader model*, the characteristics really stuck with me and I try to carry them out into my everyday life.
- And the last course I took, it was 5 hours on conflict management, which was pretty tedious but I did gain a lot of insight on how to deal with conflict. There's always conflict in any organization, especially our fraternity which has 100+ people. Whenever you get that many people together there is always going to be conflict. *And I learned, something that really stuck with me is that they defined conflict as merely the existence of two different ideas at the same place at the same time, and*

*I decided that's something that happens on a regular basis, and there are ways to deal with it and ways not to deal with it,* so I learned a lot there.

There is one main takeaway from learning formal knowledge about leadership. When you are aware of the formal knowledge, theory, and language about leadership, it gives you a better understanding of leadership, it helps you understand yourself as a leader, and it helps you understand how your skills and competencies relate to leadership. In addition, you can better discuss with others about leadership as you share a common language (for example, in a job interview, you can use common terms with the interviewer to discuss your skills and competencies and the levels of expertise that you have attained).

### Summary of Leadership Learning Outcomes

Each student reading this book is on their own unique leadership learning trajectory that will continue throughout their lifetime. As you engage in learning about and practicing leadership, you will learn adaptively, generatively, and transformatively. Along the way, your brain is changing its structure and the way it functions. This learning manifests itself in changes in how you think about yourself as a leader, how you understand leadership, how you participate in leadership in terms of your skills and competencies, and how you speak about leadership and yourself as a leader.

If you feel like you have a lot to learn with regard to leadership, you do. But keep in mind, you will learn what you need to learn as you need it. And you will continue to learn leadership over your lifetime. Like all learning processes, learning about leadership and how to do leadership is stimulated by pressures, demands, challenges, and opportunities, which affect individuals such that they cannot continue what they are doing in the same way and be successful. Learning about leadership and how to do leadership is also impacted by your readiness to learn. Finally, learning about leadership and how to do leadership is influenced by your critical reflections. In the next section, I introduce the ReAChS model of leadership learning, based on the learning model from the first chapter, that will allow you to take control of your own leadership learning and development while in college and beyond.

### ReAChS: Taking Control of your Leadership Learning

ReAChS stands for (Re)flection, (A)ssessment, (Ch)allenge, (S)upport during your leadership learning journey. This model is a combination of the learning model I presented in the last chapter with work by the Center for Creative Leadership (McCauley, VanVelsor, & Ruderman, 2010).

### Reflection

In the last chapter, I defined reflection as purposefully challenging ourselves to better understand how or why we have perceived, thought, felt, or acted the way we have. Reflection is vitally important in leadership learning as well. How you shape your learning experiences in your mind impacts both your leadership learning triggers and your readiness to learn leadership. As a result of reflection on the past, you can choose leadership learning triggers or challenges to propel you into the future. In addition, reflections about a trigger, the learning processes, and the outcome can help you become more open to learning more about leadership, more likely to engage in learning about leadership (humans tend to repeat things they are successful at), and more willing to persist at least a little bit longer in a difficult situation next time! In Chapter 4, I will go into much more depth on this topic as well as encourage you to begin a leadership learning journal. In all of the subsequent chapters, I will provide prompts and exercises for the learning journal.

## Assessment

As I stated in Chapter 2, you pick and choose what you notice regarding what is happening in the environment that is calling for you to change in some way, and that this noticing depends on your readiness to learn leadership. In this section, I will discuss how you can better recognize that learning and change is needed in yourself, in your leadership work, your openness to learning about or how to do leadership, your motivation to lead, and finally your persistence or grit in learning leadership. You can do this through self-assessments. Assessment is information that helps you understand who you are, where you are now, what your current strengths are, what development needs are important in your current situation, and what your current level of effectiveness is. In this book, I cover self-assessment, which is based on your own evaluations. In Chapter 5, I will go into much more depth as well as provide a number of self-assessments to help you get started. These self-assessments will help you learn more about yourself in terms of your personality and values, determine where you might want to learn and change next in your leadership journey, determine your learning goal orientation, better understand your motivation to learn leadership, and better understand your persistence or grit in learning about leadership.

## Challenges

Challenges are learning triggers; they are experiences that are new and that may call for skills and perspectives you have never used or developed; or experiences that create imbalance for you and provide an opportunity to question established ways of thinking and acting. In the previous chapter, I suggested that when you are unfamiliar with a task or situation, or if you are exposed to a circumstance that is either extremely intense or highly meaningful, your activation level increases. And that this activation level stimulates your learning processes. This is true for learning leadership as well. When you are engaged in, or are participating in leadership in some way, and you find yourself in a situation that you don't know how to proceed, your learning processes will be triggered. In this section, I will describe challenges that you may encounter in your learning, development, and practice of leadership that could trigger learning. I will draw from the same two studies that I drew from above in the discussion of leadership learning outcomes. However, in both of these studies, executives and students alike spoke of similar challenges! So I will combine my description of challenges over both studies.

In the original study, researchers collected 616 events. In my study, we collected 180 events. Both studies demonstrate that the main challenges for leadership learning are:

- challenging assignments including early (pre-leadership) experiences, short-term assignments, and major long-term roles;
- other people, including bosses, peers, and subordinates/followers—here it is not so much the event but the person or persons within the event that stimulate the learning process;
- coursework and leadership development programs;
- hardships—these events have three characteristics:

    1. During the worst of a difficult situation, individuals experienced a strong sense of aloneness or lack of control over events.
    2. The situation forced them to confront themselves.
    3. Individuals accepted appropriate personal responsibility for the mess they are in.

As you can see from this list, there are many ways to trigger leadership learning processes. Researchers estimate that 70 percent of all leadership learning is triggered through informal "on the job" experiences while formal leadership programs and other training programs contribute around 10 percent (McCall et al., 1988). While most of this research looked at leaders in the workplace, my study with student leaders showed very similar findings (Sessa, et al., 2014).

Additional research by the Center for Creative Leadership then asked the question: What was it about *these* challenging assignments, dealing with others, hardships, and courses/leadership development programs that caused leadership learning processes to be activated? Or what are the characteristics in the environment that are necessary to trigger leadership learning processes? (McCauley, C. D., Ruderman, Ohlott, & Morrow, 1994). They found five characteristics that are more likely to make experiences into leadership learning triggers. These are: dealing with unfamiliar responsibilities, higher levels of responsibility, creating change, working across boundaries, and managing diversity.

When you are in a situation with *unfamiliar responsibilities*, you may need to exhibit new knowledge, skills, behaviors, or feelings that you have not needed before. When you have *higher levels of responsibility* than you have encountered before, you may need to juggle more (and more important) initiatives than you have had to in the past. In addition, these initiatives may involve multiple parts (for example, when managing a large event, you need to oversee, coordinate, and manage other students who are involved in procuring the location, the technical set-up, the finances, the program, etc.). Sometimes, you may discover that some sort of *change is needed*. This includes fixing a problem that you discover, changes in the way your club is run, or changes in your own or others' behavior. Sometimes, you may need to *cross boundaries*, such as when you need to convince your school administration to support a proposal or work with another club or clubs to put on an event. And finally, you find that you are *leading a group of others who differ* in many different ways including culture, gender, race, ethnic, age, year in school, major, living arrangements (on or off campus), etc. In each of these cases, you may be called on to think critically about the situation, identify underlying causes and consequences of problems, and process new and ambiguous information. You may need to experiment with new ways of influencing people who are different from you. Finally, you may need to figure out how "things work around here," why they work that way, and if needed, how to change them.

Similar to learning triggers in general, leadership learning challenges can happen anywhere in the school environment: In the academic context (a classroom discussion, a team assignment, a study group, or even the class negotiating with the professor to change the syllabus); the institutional context (in athletics, clubs, fraternities and sororities, committees, work-study positions, Residence Hall Assistants, Student Government, etc.); and even in the social context (planning an event with your friends).

In Chapters 6, 7, 8, and 9, I will go into much more depth on the different kinds of challenges you might encounter that will trigger your leadership learning. In Chapter 10, I will provide a number of exercises to help you decide what challenges you would like to target in your leadership learning trajectory.

## Support

When you are facing tough assessments of yourself or difficult challenges, your support network can make the difference between turning these situations into learning experiences from ones that lead to frustration or failure. Your support network includes people with whom you can talk about your reflections, assessments, and experiences in a way that enhance your self-confidence and provide you with reassurance about your strengths, current skills, and established ways of thinking and acting. Support can come from parents, teachers, advisors, bosses, coaches, mentors, significant others, friends, peers, your direct reports, community volunteers, religious leaders, or anyone else. Some of your support network might:

- provide emotional support and encouragement and let you vent your feelings;
- express confidence in your current abilities and in your ability to learn and grow;
- keep you on track and reward you for your progress;

- be in a situation similar to yours and offer empathy;
- provide you with long-term support and guidance through experience and example;
- provide you with focused support geared toward acquiring a specific skill or overcoming a specific hurdle.

In Chapter 11, I will talk in more depth about support, give some guidance in building a support network, and also cover the fact that in your own leadership journey, you will need to be part of other people's support network as well.

## Summary of ReAChS

The purpose of this section was to introduce you to the ReAChS model of leadership development: (Re)flection, (A)ssessment, (Ch)allenge, (S)upport. This model gives you the information you need to take control of your own leadership learning trajectory. Now that you know about how you learn, reflection helps you reframe many experiences into learning experiences. In addition, through reflection you can choose leadership challenges to trigger your learning as well as assess yourself to stimulate your readiness to learn. Self-assessment can help you realize that there is a gap between where you are and where you want to be, and stimulate your readiness to learn. Once you realize that challenges stimulate the learning process you can learn to turn situations that you don't feel prepared for, or other demanding situations into challenges, to stimulate your learning. In addition, you can deliberately choose challenges to stimulate your own learning. Finally, this learning is difficult to do alone. It helps to have a support network that can provide you with emotional support, positive energy, empathy, and guidance, as well as help you analyze situations and keep you on track.

## Summary

- Learning leadership is similar to learning everything else you know or have learned already.
- Like learning everything else, you are on a leadership learning trajectory that is unique to you. You learn what you need to learn, when you need to learn it. In addition, you don't learn something all at once. You learn incrementally and will continue to learn in more depth or in a more complex fashion over your lifetime.
- When you learn leadership, you are learning about who you are as a leader (your leader identity), ways of thinking about leaders and leadership, leader skills and competencies, and formal knowledge about leadership.
- You can take control of your own leadership learning by ReAChS. (Re)flection helps you reframe past leadership experiences into learning experiences and prepares you to begin the next leadership learning experience.

(A)ssessment stimulates your readiness to learn. And (Ch)allenge, either those that happen to you or those you choose to engage in, trigger the learning processes. Finally, your (S)upport network is vital in your leadership learning process as it keeps you on track.

## Questions for Reflection and Discussion

1. As a result of reading this chapter, reflect on your own leadership learning trajectory to this point. How do you feel about embarking (or continuing) on your leadership learning journey at this point in time?

2. Susan Komives and her colleagues (2005) suggest reflecting on the following questions to begin to understand your own leader identity:

   a. Can you think of a time when you defined leadership differently than you do now? Describe it. How do you define leadership now and how is it different from your earlier view?

   b. When you have a position of authority in a group, what is your role with others?

   c. What is your role in a group when you do not have a position of authority?

   d. What strategies are you using to ensure that a group you are currently working in and its goals will continue after you are no longer a member?

3. As a class, do the following exercise. Individually, write/describe what you mean by leadership. Choose some sort of visual symbol (object, picture, etc.), song, or poem that represents that leadership to you (and make sure you explain this on your page). Bring your leadership description and visual symbol, song, or poem to class. Allow each person to present their definition of leadership and their symbol of leadership. Compare and contrast definitions and symbols with each other. What are some similar themes? What are some different themes? Any surprises? Compare your own leadership description to Drath's principles of leadership discussed above. Do you see any similarities?

4. Reflect on the same question I posed to the students in my research above: When you think back on your collegiate leadership experiences so far, certain events or stories probably come to mind—things that lead you to change or affirm the way you lead. Please identify at least three "key events" from your years in college, which helped shape you into the leader you are today. What happened and what did you learn from those experiences (the good and the bad)? How do your lessons compare and contrast to the lessons learned by executives? By students in my research? By students in your class or program?

5. If you have had courses or workshops on formal theories about leadership, which are your favorite theories and why? Have you tried to "use" any of the theories (or elements of the theory) in your own practice? How did that work?

6. Take one of the events from #4 and re-write it. This time, try to use formal terms from either this chapter or from the theories you are familiar with. Show it to someone in your support network for feedback. Practice telling the event like you would to a job interviewer or someone interested in your leadership experiences.

7. What is your reaction to the ReAChS model? How do you feel about it? Are there parts you like/don't like? Do you think it is useful? How might you use the model (either in its entirety or elements of it)? If you could talk with me (the author of this book), what don't you understand or what might you recommend I change or develop further?

   a. What is your initial reaction to the use of reflection in your leadership learning journey? How have you used reflection in the past? How do you see yourself using reflection from here on out?

   b. What is your initial reaction to assessment? Have you done any self-assessments before? If you have, I recommend including them as you move forward. What do you already know about yourself to be true?

   c. What are some leadership challenges that you have already encountered? How do these compare to the challenges listed above? What is your initial reaction to the idea that you can purposefully select challenges? How might you turn events that you didn't select into "challenges" now that you know about the idea of using situations as learning events?

   d. Who is part of your support network? Who might be good additions? What roles do they play? Whose support network are you a part of?

8. What is your next step in your leadership learning journey? What is your plan to get there? How will you capture your learning?

# References

DeRue, D. S. & Ashford, S. J. (2010). Who will lead and who will follow: A social process of leadership identity construction in organizations. *Academy of Management Review 35*, 627–647.

Drath, W. (2001). *The deep blue sea: Rethinking the source of leadership*. San Francisco, CA: Jossey-Bass.

Dreyfus, H. L. and Dreyfus, S. E. (1986) *Mind over machine: The power of human intuition and expertise in the age of the computer*. Oxford: Basil Blackwell.

Komives, S. R., Longerbeam, S. D., Owen, J. E., Mainella, F. C., & Osteen, L. (2006). A leadership identity development model: Applications from a grounded theory. *Journal of College Student Development 47*, 401–420.

Komives, S. R., Owen, J. E., Longerbeam, S. D., Mainella, F. C., & Osteen, L. (2005). Developing a leadership identity: A grounded theory. *Journal of College Student Development 46*, 593–611.

Lindsey, E., Homes, V., & McCall, M. W. (1987). *Key events in executives' lives*. Technical report no. 32. Greensboro, NC: Center for Creative Leadership.

McCall, M.W., Jr., Lombardo, M. M., & Morrison, A. M. (1988). *The lessons of experience: How successful executives develop on the job.* Lexington, MA: Lexington Books.

McCauley, C. D., Ruderman, M. N., Ohlott, P. J., & Morrow, J. E. (1994). Assessing the developmental components of managerial jobs. *Journal of Applied Psychology 79*, 544–560,

McCauley, C. D., VanVelsor, E., & Ruderman, M. N. (2010). Introduction: Our view of leadership development. In E. VanVelso, C. D. McCauley, & M. N. Ruderman, *Handbook of leadership development* (pp. 1–26). San Francisco, CA: Wiley.

Seemiller, C. (2013). *The student leadership competencies guidebook: Designing intentional leadership learning and development.* San Francisco, CA: Jossey-Bass.

Sessa, V. I., Morgan, B. V., Kalenderli, S., & Hammond, F. (2014). Key events in student leaders' lives and lessons learned from them. *Journal of Leadership Education 13*, 1–28.

# PART II
# ReAChS Model

# 4

# REFLECTION

*A life that is not reflected upon isn't worth living. It belongs to the essence of being human that we contemplate our life, think about it, discuss it, evaluate it, and form opinions about it. Half of living is reflecting on what is being lived. Is it worth it? Is it good? Is it bad? Is it old? Is it new? What is it all about? The greatest joy as well as the greatest pain of living come not only from what we live but even more from how we think and feel about what we are living.*

*(Henri J. M. Nouwen, 1996: 26)*

Leadership learning, like all learning, occurs in a cyclical fashion. As you learned in Chapter 2, an event triggers or activates your learning processes. Depending on the trigger and your readiness to learn, you adapt, you purposefully add or change your knowledge or skills, or you change the way you see and understand the world. This leads to some sort of change in what you know, the way you think, how you behave, or how you feel. Then, because you were in an out of the ordinary, perplexing, or unusual experience, where your environment changed or you were stuck and had to do something differently as a result, you tend to ponder the trigger, your experience, and your changes, and that reflection then impacts what triggers you notice and your readiness to learn, starting the cycle over again.

Therefore, it is not just the challenging experience, your learning processes, and your changes that are learning. Challenging experiences offer an opportunity for learning and development. While some learning may happen just by going through these steps, learning becomes more effective if deliberately coupled with the final step of reflecting on what you have been doing. You need to intentionally recall what you did after the fact, make meaning, and codify your experience and your reactions into your memory so that you can draw on the process and the changes you made, and integrate them into your responses again in the future. Your leadership learning and development will proceed more intentionally if you construct, reflect on, and make sense of your experience.

In the ReAChS model, I have chosen to address reflection first for two reasons. First, it is worth starting your leadership learning journey from here by deliberately reflecting on past experiences to determine where you are on your leadership trajectory, why you are where you are, and what your next step should be. Second, people are generally not good at reflection without practice. I will be introducing you to reflection exercises in this chapter and as you move through this book with the hope that these will help you get in the practice of reflecting. The purpose of this chapter is to familiarize you with what reflection is (and isn't), to describe why it is so important to your leadership learning and development, to describe how to reflect, and to get you started with some reflections.

## What Is Reflection?

Reflection is the process of stepping back from an experience to think about its meaning to yourself. You create meaning from your experiences and your reactions to those experiences, and these serve as a guide for future ways of thinking, ways of behaving, and ways of feeling. Reflection is actually a natural and familiar process that you do (although you may not have realized that's what you are doing). In our personal lives, we discuss troubling situations with friends, partners, spouses, counselors, or support groups. In school, we write papers, answer questions, engage in classroom discussions, and analyze cases, all as ways to develop new insights. In the business world, we analyze experiences and summarize our learning in reports, performance review sessions, and problem-solving processes. Reflection occurs in less formal ways as well—we may have experienced breakthroughs while jogging, showering, or mowing the lawn (Daudelin, 1996).

In this chapter, we are going to take regular everyday reflection up a notch to make it intentional and more powerful for your leadership learning and development. "Critical reflection" (Mezirow, 1997) is not just thinking about, but purposefully challenging ourselves to better understand how or why we have perceived, thought, felt, or acted the way we did during a challenging experience. In critical reflection, we discover our own biases and assumptions, and we look at our own behaviors, question them, and choose to modify or change them. Critical reflection can result in the following: (1) You can get a new perspective on the experience that you would not have gained had you not taken the time to think about it, discuss it with others, etc.; (2) You can become motivated to try out your insights from your reflection; (3) You can change your behavior, thoughts, attitudes, and feelings based on your reflection; and (4) You can become committed to action which will ultimately enhance your personal and leadership effectiveness (Rogers, 2001).

For example, to fulfill a general education requirement, you decided to take a class on Human Geography (because it fit your schedule). In the class, you are intrigued with the idea that variations in physical environments around the world interact with and drive the culture of the people who live in that environment— including their language, tools, religion, and even politics! You begin to reflect on how growing up in the US, in your small farm town in the Midwest, with plenty of clean air, food, water, and other resources is impacting YOUR ways of perceiving, feeling, thinking, and acting. As a result, you start to purposefully listen to college students from other environments to try to understand their assumptions and perspectives better. And you begin to question and modify your own ways as a result.

## What Reflection Is Not

Before getting too deep into this chapter, it is worth noting briefly what reflection is not. Reflection is NOT rumination. When a person is reflecting, they are both describing the event, what they have done, and what worked or didn't work (and why) AND prescribing what needs to be done next and how to get there. There is a sense of productivity, interest, and energy (even if what the person tried and is now reflecting on didn't work). Rumination, on the other hand, feels negative. Generally, a person is focusing on something that went wrong or caused distress and its causes and consequences. A person who is ruminating is dwelling on what went wrong (like a never-ending loop playing in your head), but never moves to problem solving.

As you work through the reflection exercises moving forward and you find yourself in a rumination loop (or anytime you find yourself in a rumination loop), try the following:

1. *Ask yourself whether rumination is solving your problem.* If not, try to identify a solution or solutions and commit to taking action. This will help move you from rumination to reflection.
2. *Set a time limit to your rumination.* If you've been thinking about the same issue for more than 10 minutes with no increase in insight or problem solving, it's not working. Time to do something else: take a walk, clean your room, make a (healthy) snack or cup of tea, have a conversation with someone about something else, do some sort of task that will take your mind off the rumination.
3. *Write it down.* Write the event, your experience, what you are thinking, feeling, doing as a result, and what worked and didn't work. Then add the next step of what you learned from this, what needs to be done next, and plans to get there.

4. *Talk to a trusted person (friend, parent, teacher, advisor, coach, etc.), but set some ground rules first.* You don't want to just ruminate to them, you want them to help you move from rumination to reflection. Ask them to let you talk (again go through the event, your experience, what you are thinking, feeling, doing as a result, and what worked and didn't work). Ask them for their perspective (perhaps they can help you see things a different way). Then ask them to help you determine what you learned from this, what needs to be done next, and plans to get there. End the conversation with a thank you and that you will take action on those plans.

5. If, as you are reading this, you realize that you ruminate on a regular basis, you might want to check in with your school's health facilities. They probably have workshops, support groups, and other tools to help you break the rumination habit.

## Struggles with Doing Reflection

Research has found that students can be reluctant to do reflection as part of their leadership development although they understand why reflection is important and useful (White, 2012). There are two reasons why people might be reluctant to reflect: (1) The current culture in the United States places a higher value on action than reflection; and (2) Leadership experiences can evoke an array of negative emotions (e.g., fear, anxiety) such that individuals find it uncomfortable to reflect and do not want to do it (DeRue, Nahrgang, Hollenbeck, & Workman, 2012).

Have you ever watched a hamster in a cage run on its hamster wheel, spinning away, not going anywhere, and fast? Look at people these days, and you may find a resemblance: we are like hamsters running on a wheel. In terms of the current United States culture, we are obsessed with productivity. We feel a constant pressure to perform. We are led to believe that to be successful, we need to do more, or life will fall apart. This leads us to tie our self-worth to achievement, doing, and productivity. If we slow down even for a moment, we'll get run down by all those behind us and everyone will move ahead of us. Therefore, we feel unworthy if we're not doing something. And ultimately, we become and stay busy. We rush to get the good things in life quicker, we chase money, we even rush so that we have more free time. There are many things we have to do, however, we also unnecessarily fill up our time with things we don't have to do because we want to feel productive and worthy. In the end, this becomes habitual and addictive. We learn to get our own "rush" from rushing.

Constantly doing and rushing from one thing to another also serves another purpose. When we are busy, we operate on automatic pilot. We don't have to think too deeply or feel too deeply, we just have to do. Experiences that evoke learning are challenging. We run into obstacles, our environment is changing, we are stuck and cannot move forward by thinking, feeling, or doing something the same way as we have in the past. By their very nature, these experiences can evoke negative emotions and discomfort. And most of us do not like to spend time going too deep. Our constant movement provides a distraction to these negative underlying feelings that cause us unease and discomfort.

Thankfully, research also shows that once busy leaders get in the habit of reflecting, they do so with greater ease over time. Morgan McCall, a researcher specializing on leadership learning in top-level executives, noted that when he first started interviewing executives, "it was a challenge for them even to remember what they had done in the previous two weeks, given the relentless pace and performance pressure of the executive job." But he found that after a few weeks of being exposed to his questions, "What, if anything have you learned?" managers began to attend to their experiences in a more purposeful manner; they were able to recall them more readily, and they were able to reflect on what they were learning (McCall, 2010).

In addition, people are starting to push back on this hamster-in-a-wheel lifestyle. A quick Google search on "mindfulness" (which involves intentionally bringing your attention to the present moment and being aware of your experiences as they are happening) turns up over 38,000,000 hits. On February 3, 2014, *Time Magazine* put "The Mindful Revolution" on its front cover. It is a billion-dollar industry (Seppala, 2015). Research is showing that meditation builds resilience, helps you regulate your emotions, enhances creativity, improves your relationships, and helps you focus. Apparently "doing nothing" has real results! (Seppala, 2015).

I am hoping that during the reading of this book, you will also get in the habit of attending to your experiences in a more purposeful and mindful manner, recalling your experiences more readily after the fact, and thus able to reflect on what you are learning from your experiences!

## Ways of Reflecting

There are two primary ways of reflecting. You can reflect with other people. And you can reflect on your own.

Reflecting with other people generally occurs in some sort of dialogue. These may occur in small groups reflecting together, or one-on-one with one person reflecting and the other person listening and commenting. See Table 4.1, which shows a list of group reflections.

**TABLE 4.1** Examples of Reflection with Others

- Informal discussions and conversations with friends and colleagues
- Conversations with mentors or coaches
- Individual or group therapy
- Performance appraisal discussions
- After event reviews
- After action reviews.

I am going to talk about an interpersonal reflection option and a group reflection option in depth, both developed by the United States Army. Both are used after a challenging event. The first, called an After Event Review (AER) is one that you would do with a coach, mentor, or other person who is familiar with AERs guiding you. AERs are reflection procedures that give individuals the opportunity to systematically analyze their behavior and to be able to evaluate the contribution of their behavior to their performance. The second, called an After Action Review (AAR) is similar, but a whole team reflects together. AARs are team structured reviews, debriefs, or reflections for analyzing what happened, why it happened, and how it can be done better by the team and those responsible for the event. These two are techniques that you may not be familiar with but you could try out and use as reflection tools with a little practice.

## After Event Review

AERs have been shown to have a positive effect on leadership development (DeRue, et al., 2012). According to the researchers who conducted a study, AERs have three parts: self-explanation, data verification, and feedback. Self-explanation involves individuals systematically analyzing their own behavior and developing specific explanations for how their behavior contributed to performance or outcome. Here you would describe your experience and explain in depth how you contributed to the performance or outcome observed in the experience. Once individuals develop a self-explanation, the data verification component asks them to imagine alternative interpretations of their experience and consider a range of alternative explanations for how their behavior contributed to performance. Here you would describe one or more different leadership approaches that could have been used in this experience and what might have happened if you had taken those approaches. Self-explanation and data verification help individuals more effectively reflect on experience by finding and clarifying the link between their own behavior and outcomes, and they promote more counterfactual thinking. Finally, the feedback component of AERs challenges individuals to develop specific recommendations for behavior change. In this step you would develop clear conclusions about what worked, what did not work, what you learned from the experience about your leadership capabilities, and, based on these lessons, how you will lead differently in the future. See Table 4.2 for a worksheet to help guide you through this exercise. Get in the habit of filling out these as a form after challenging events and saving them.

## After Action Review

AARs are a cyclical method for extracting lessons from any team event and applying them to other events (see Darling, Parry, & Moore, 2005). The full cycle actually starts before the event. Assuming there is one leader in charge, the

**TABLE 4.2** After Event Review

1. *Describe the experience*

   - What was the experience?
   - Who was involved in this experience?
   - What was your role in this experience? (For example, did you have to coordinate or did other people depend on you? Did you depend on other people?)
   - What exactly did you do prior to, during, and after this experience?

2. *Awareness*

   - How did you react to the experience?
   - How challenging was this experience? What about the experience made it challenging or not challenging?

3. *Critical analysis*

   - How did you contribute to the performance observed in this experience? (Was there an assessment of performance—what did it reveal?)
   - How effective were you as a leader in this experience?
   - Have you taken the same leadership approach to experiences before? How successful was it in previous situations? How effective was it in this situation? What was similar/different about these situations?
   - Do other people in your team or in other teams have similar approaches to leadership as you? How does it work for them?
   - What is a different leadership approach you could have taken in this experience? What might have happened if you had taken this approach?
   - Did you have the competencies (e.g., technical, thinking, and interpersonal skills) needed to be effective in this experience?

4. *New perspective*

   - What did you learn from this experience about your leadership capabilities?
   - Given what happened in this experience, how will you lead differently in the future?
   - In what ways could you develop your leadership skills in the future? What opportunities do you have to develop further as a leader?
   - In what ways do you need to change your attitudes, expectations, values, leadership approach to be a more effective leader?

5. *Action steps*

   - List at least two action steps you plan on taking, based on your learning from this experience.

*Source*: modified from DeRue et al. (2012).

leader drafts a "before action review" (BAR) or a plan of action that includes the task, the purpose of the task and its importance, the underlying intent (the why), the desired result, what was learned from similar situations, and what will ensure success this time. She shares the plan with the rest of the team and each member of the team describes the plan back to the leader to demonstrate that they fully understand the plan of action. Next, the team goes through a practice or rehearsal of the plan. During the practice session, discussions occur to determine if the plan is working or not (and fix it if it is not as smooth in practice as it is on paper), as well as discussions regarding what could go wrong in reality. Plans are built in to address what could go wrong. This BAR serves as the plan of action and also the discussion plan for the AARs. Brief AARs are held as each step in the plan of action happens with a lengthier AAR at the end of the event. Thus mini-cycles of short BARs, plans, and AARs occur throughout the event between the pre-liminary BAR and the AAR.

In the AARs, the members first go over the ground rules: (1) Participate; (2) Absolute candor is critical; (3) Take notes; (4) Focus on our issues, not the issues of others; (5) Focus on improving performance, not on placing blame; and (6) Acknowledge own mistakes (this is particularly important for the leaders). Then the members discuss the original plan (or that portion of the plan) and expected end state, along with a brief review of the events that actually occurred and the actual end state. Four questions are covered. What were our intended results? What were our actual results? What caused our results? And what will we sustain or improve? This final question covers the lessons learned and these are included in the next round of BARs. All along the way, notes are taken.

For anyone who has been in the armed forces or ROTC, plays music in an orchestra (or a marching band), who acts in plays, or who plays team sports, you are probably familiar with some version of this. But have you ever tried this when your club or association puts on an event?

## Examples of Solitary Reflection

You can also reflect on your own. There are two general ways of reflecting on your own: You can do it in your head or you can write it down. While we think of reflecting purposefully, now that you are more aware of reflection, you may find that you do it spontaneously while you are doing other activities. See Table 4.3 for a list of methods of doing reflection on your own.

In this book, I am going to give you a number of exercises to accomplish through journal writing. For the remainder of this book, I encourage you to keep a leadership learning journal. It can be any type of notebook. Pick one out that you like the look and feel of. Although you can keep either a paper journal or

**TABLE 4.3** Reflecting on Your Own

- Spontaneous thinking during rhythmic, repetitive, mindless physical exercise (jogging, swimming laps, mowing the lawn) or routine habits (driving an established route, showering, doing the dishes)
- Meditation
- Prayer
- Journal writing.

an electronic journal, I encourage you to write by hand. Each chapter (or set of chapters) will have reflection exercises for you to both discuss with others, then do on your own and capture your reflections and your learnings in the journal.

## Reflection Exercises to Get You Started

The rest of this chapter covers exercises encouraging you to begin reflecting with others or on your own.

1. *If there is a faculty member or staff person (or mentor or coach) who is willing to help you, try an AER.* Pick a recent experience that you were heavily engaged in. You do not need to have been in the role of the leader for this experience, but you should have been heavily engaged.
2. *Ask a team you are associated with if they would be willing to try out an AAR.* This could be any group or team (even a group project in a class). Read this article in preparation and pass it around to your team members for them to read as well: https://hbr.org/2005/07/learning-in-the-thick-of-it. If there is a faculty member or staff member associated with the team, ask them to help you facilitate this (give them the article too). Do a BAR, do a rehearsal, then do an AAR. Start simple. You are trying to learn a new reflection process at the same time you are using that process in your learning process.
3. *Meditate.* There are many many meditation techniques in existence. I'm going to mention two simple ones I am familiar with. If you meditate already and like it, do what you are familiar with. Try these two (or some variation). Or explore others.

   a. The first one, called 4-7-8 breathing by Dr. Andrew Weil (www.drweil. com/health-wellness/body-mind-spirit/stress-anxiety/breathing-three-exercises/) takes little time and can be done anywhere. Here is what you do: (1) Sit up in a comfortable position. Place the tip of your tongue on the ridge of your gums, just under your front teeth. Close your eyes. (2) Expand your diaphragm and slowly inhale through your nose for a count of four. (3) Hold your breath for another count of seven (4) Open your mouth slightly and exhale for eight counts, drawing your dia-phragm in. (5) Repeat this cycle four times in total. (6) Do this several times a day (for example, you can do this in the morning before you get out of bed, in your seat before each class begins, as a study break, and in the evening before you go to bed).
   b. The second meditation is called "mindfulness meditation" and I will give just a brief "how to" guide here: (1) Get into a comfortable posi-tion (this can be sitting or lying down). Your eyes can be closed, half closed, or even open. (2) Whether your eyes are open or not, focus them on one spot. (3) Sit quietly for a few moments. (4) Start to pay attention to your breathing. As you inhale and exhale, it helps to words

of some sort to yourself. For example, as you inhale, say "In." Exhale from your lungs and then your abdomen, saying, "Out." Do this each time you breathe. You can also use the words that have meaning to you. I learned to say upon inhale "ham" and upon exhale "sah" (which means "I am" in Sanskrit); (5) As you sit breathing, you will notice that thoughts arise. All kinds of thoughts. Notice the thoughts and say to yourself, "thinking has occurred." When you notice that you have gotten caught up in thoughts and that you are no longer thinking about your breath, gently bring yourself back to your inhale and exhale. This will occur any number of times during your meditation. Just bring yourself back to breathing.

c. Remember you can't do meditation wrong, nor can you do it poorly.

4. *Write in your leadership learning journal.* Here are two reflections, one to write before an event and one to write after an event:

a. In the first one, knowing that you will be participating in an event, you can reflect ahead of time to prepare yourself for learning while in the event. Just thinking this through and writing about it will help you keep your goals in mind. Ask yourself and write about: What do I intend to learn in this event? What skills related to leadership do I want to work on or develop? What do I already know now that will help me do this? What will make this a beneficial experience for me? How will I make sure this is a beneficial experience?

b. Choose a recent event that has already happened: an issue or incident that you think posed a problem or had a positive impact on your leadership learning or practice and take the following steps: (1) Write a detailed and clear, but concise, description of what happened. Include where and when it occurred, who was involved, what your role was, and a step-by-step description of what happened including your actions in the event. Use descriptive words here and not interpretive (for example, "the teacher smiled," not "the teacher was happy"). The key here is to be clear and descriptive so you can see the situation from different angles. (2) Write down the impact of what went on. Here are some questions that may help you do this: What were the consequences or results of my actions? What was exciting, puzzling, inspiring, frustrating, impressive, upsetting, or challenging about the event as it played out? How did it affect me? How did it affect others? How did I feel about the event at the time? What have I thought about and felt since the event? (3) Write about: Have I seen this before? Were the conditions the same or different? (4) If I were to do this again, what would I do the same? What might I do differently? What was omitted? What are the different options I could have tried? What might happen if I had [. . .]? How would [a peer of yours] have handled this? Did I have the skills and knowledge to deal with this? (5) What did I learn about myself during this event? How has this experience changed my thoughts, values, or opinions? Or, in what ways have my sense of self, values and self-confidence changed because of this experience? Or what skills and competencies did I improve on? And finally (6) What will I do differently next time based on what I've learned? How will I think, feel, act, or behave differently in the future because of this? What positive implications can I see this event having on my leadership for the future?

## Summary

- Reflection is the process of stepping back from an experience to think about its meaning. It is a natural process that you do but might not realize that you are doing it.
- The purpose of this chapter was to help you take your regular reflection up a notch to make it intentional and more powerful for your leadership learning and development.
- Critical reflection is purposefully challenging ourselves to better understand how or why we have perceived, thought, felt, or acted the way we did during a challenging experience. We discover our own biases and assumptions and we look at our own behaviors, question them, and choose to modify or change them.
- Reflection is not rumination. Rumination feels negative. When you are ruminating, you tend to dwell on what went wrong like a never-ending loop in your head. In reflection, while you describe the event and what went wrong, you are also prescribing what needs to be done next and how to get there.
- As a student, although you might understand and agree with this chapter, you might also find yourself reluctant to reflect. This is normal. In our culture, we place a higher value on action over reflection. And reflection can be uncomfortable. However, people are starting to push back on the push for constant action. They want the pace to slow down, be mindful, and reflect. And they are discovering that with a little practice, it becomes easier over time.
- There are two ways of reflecting. You can reflect with others, either one-on-one with someone, or as a group. Or you can reflect on your own, where the reflection either takes place in your head or you record it in some fashion. I recommend a leadership learning journal.

## References

Darling, M., Parry, C., & Moore, J. (2005). Learning in the thick of it. *Harvard Business Review* (July/August). https://hbr.org/2005/07/learning-in-the-thick-of-it.

Daudelin, M. W. (1996). Learning from experience through reflection. *Organizational Dynamics 24*(3), 36–48.

DeRue, D. S., Nahrgang, J. D., Hollenbeck, J. R., & Workman, K. (2012). A quasi-experimental study of after-event reviews and leadership development. *Journal of Applied Psychology 97*, 997–1015.

McCall, M. W. (2010). Recasting leadership development. *Industrial and Organizational Psychology 3*, 3–19.

Mezirow, J. (1997). Transformative learning: Theory to practice. *New Directions for Adult and Continuing Education 74*, 5–12.

Nouwen, H. J. M. (1996). *Can you drink the cup?* Notre Dame, IN: Ava Maria Press.

Rogers, R. R. (2001). Reflection in higher education: A conceptual analysis. *Innovative Higher Education 26*, 37–57.

Seppala, E. (2015). How meditation benefits CEOs. *Harvard Business Review*. https://hbr.org/2015/12/how-meditation-benefits-ceos.

White, J. V. (2012). Students' perception of the role of reflection in leadership learning. *Journal of Leadership Education 11*, 141–157.

# 5

# ASSESSMENT

## Prompting Your Readiness to Learn

*Know thyself*
*(Delphic Maxim)*

The second section of the ReAChS model of leadership development is "Assessment." As I have discussed previously, in the learning model, an event has the potential to trigger or activate your learning process. But you may not notice the trigger to learn or you may not act upon it if you are not ready to learn. If you do not recognize when a trigger for learning is occurring and that you need to change accordingly, then little or no learning will happen. In fact, you may even be resistant to learning. One way to understand your own readiness to learn and even help you to be ready to learn is through knowing about yourself: who you are, your current baseline of your readiness to learn in general and your readiness to learn leadership, and your strengths and developmental needs. The purpose of this chapter is to familiarize you with what assessment is, to describe why it is important to your leadership learning and development, to describe what can be assessed and how, and then give you the opportunity to assess yourself in a number of different ways.

### What Is Assessment and Why Is It Important for Leadership Development?

If you do not have a thorough understanding of who you are as you participate in leadership experiences, it is difficult to take charge of your own leadership development. Assessment is discovering information about yourself: who you are, what your current level of behavior or performance is, what your current strengths are, and what development needs are important in your current situation. Assessment provides a benchmark and an awareness of where you are right now—what is working, what is working well, and what is not working as well. The idea behind assessment is that the more we know about ourselves and how we are performing in the here and now (and what is working and what is not working), the readier we are to be triggered to learn. Assessment also pinpoints areas for learning and development so that you can make appropriate decisions on what to concentrate on.

Similar to reflection in the last chapter, assessment is continuous. As you move through the learning process and change as a result, you need to re-assess yourself: Now, after this experience, who am I as a result of the changes I made? Has my current behavior or performance changed? Did my changes hone my strengths? Did I improve on my developmental needs?

## What Can Be Assessed

You can learn many things about yourself including your personality and character, your values, your abilities, skills, and competencies, your behaviors, your performance, and the results of your behavior and performance. This gets pretty complicated, but here is a brief definition of each of these. *Personality* is a unique pattern of relatively permanent traits and characteristics that a person is born with that gives them both consistency and individuality to how they respond to situations and how they act. *Character* is similar to personality but refers to relatively permanent personal attributes that are developed early in life and become ingrained in people and are relevant to how we behave and how we see the world. *Values* are also similar to personality and character but are a set of life goals reflecting what is most important to a person. Although values are thought to be generally stable, as a person travels through life, their life goals may change accordingly. Similar to personality and character, values also govern our behavior and guide the way we look at the world.

*Abilities*, *skills*, and *competencies* are capabilities in carrying out tasks—what you are able to do. Abilities are believed to be something that you are born with, like a talent. While you can improve or hone an ability, skills and competencies are believed to be something you can learn and develop. *Behavior* is your actions or the way you conduct yourself in a particular situation. It is caused by a combination of the person: their personality, character, values, abilities, skills, competencies, and other things going on such as thoughts and feelings along with what is going on in the environment: other people, the situation. *Performance* is an evaluation of your behavior—did you do well or poorly. And *results* are what happens based on your behavior. As I am sure you are already aware (and even more so as a result of reading this paragraph), you are a complicated human being. Assessment helps you to begin unraveling and understanding all these different aspects of yourself. Being aware of and understanding these aspects of yourself helps you begin using these aspects purposefully. Or where possible (for example, your skills, competencies, and behavior) changing them.

## Ways of Assessing

Determining your personality, character, values, abilities, skills, competencies, behaviors, performance, and results, however, is not a simple task. In the natural world, you can weigh a rock on two different scales (assuming the scales are accurate) and be fairly certain of getting the same weight on both scales. Or two people can weigh the rock and get the same result. However, when you measure a person in terms of their personality, character, values, abilities, skills, competencies, behaviors, performance, and results, a person is rarely that consistent in different circumstances (e.g., at home, with friends, at school, in the community, etc.). In addition, scales differ—you can be one personality on one personality inventory and a different one on another. And you and other people will interpret all these variables differently. Therefore, it is helpful to use different methods to assess yourself and look for commonalities between and among the instruments.

When it comes to leadership assessment, there are a few common methods that range from fairly simple to very sophisticated. These are: self-assessment, feedback (informal, formal, and 360 degree), simulations, assessment centers, and individual psychological assessments.

## *Self-Assessment*

Self-assessment is the process of looking at yourself in order to assess your own personal attributes. This can be informal, such as through journaling. Or it can be formal through the use of reliable and valid self-assessment instruments. Reliability is the degree to which the self-assessment tool produces stable and consistent results. If you take an instrument and then take it again some time later, you should receive a similar score on it (unless you did something in between to impact your score such as learn how to do something new). Validity refers to how well a self-assessment instrument measures what it is supposed to measure. If you take an instrument measuring your character, you want to be certain that the results are accurate.

The emphasis of this chapter is on self-assessment—both formal and informal. There are opportunities for you to self-assess your personality, your character, your readiness to learn in general and your readiness to learn leadership in particular, and a few leadership competencies. With the exception of a few instruments that I have developed in my own research, the instruments in this chapter are all reliable and valid. At the end of the formal assessments, there is an informal reflective assessment where you will pull together all of the assessments you took and reflect on who you are as a leader.

Self-assessment does require honesty. When we self-assess, we have a tendency to inflate our strengths, minimize our weaknesses, and attribute failure or negative events to the situation (rather than to ourselves). Simply, people tend to empha-size their positive qualities, describing themselves in positive and optimistic terms (Greenwald, 1980; Taylor & Brown, 1988). So although I provide self-assessment instruments and opportunities in this book, it is important to supplement this with other assessments when you have the opportunity.

## Feedback

One way you can supplement these assessments is through the use of feedback. Feedback is information sent to an individual about his or her prior behavior so that the individual may continue with the same behavior or adjust his or her current and future behavior to achieve the desired result. Sometimes you can receive objective feedback: How many baskets did you make, how fast did you run, how many errors were on your test. But often, you get subjective feedback from other people. Another person holds up a mirror and says, "This is what I'm seeing about you from my angle" and gives you information about yourself from another point of view. You can receive *informal feedback* through ongoing conversations and in-the-moment advice. Students talk about having conversations (some impromptu, some planned) with their bosses, or senior students, or peers, or people that they are leading. Sometimes it is purposeful: a person is trying to tell them something about their behavior (either positive or constructive). Sometimes it is not purposeful; for example, after hearing a person speak about something that happened, you might realize that your own behavior was interpreted differently than you expected. You usually receive *formal feedback* via an annual performance review. You might receive an annual performance review at your job in which your boss assesses your accomplish-ments in the past year as well as discusses your developmental needs. *360-degree feedback* is a formal process in which a person receives confidential, anonymous feedback from the people who work "around" them and might include managers, peers, direct reports, and customers.

## Simulations

You might have the opportunity to participate in a simulation and receive infor-mation on how you performed in it. A simulation is an imitation of a real world process or system that you participate in as though it were real. Most of you, at this point, have been involved in computer simulation games and have built cit-ies, survived apocalypses, escaped zombies, raced cars, and flown airplanes. You can also use simulations to find out about your leadership. In this type of simula-tion, you might participate with classmates in a business simulation where you take on a specific role and have to solve a business problem in a certain amount of time. An observer might watch how you interact with others, how you communicate, how you handle pressure, and how you make decisions, to name a few. Or you might receive some sort of score based on objective measures. You would then receive a report rating your behavior with suggestions for what you do well and what you might want to work on.

## Assessment Centers

An assessment center is used to evaluate a number of individuals' behaviors across a variety of situations including job related simulations, leaderless group discussions, role plays, interviews, and psychological tests. Different observers look at your psychological assessments; interact with you in interviews; watch you during your leaderless group discussions, simulations, and role-plays; and then make judgments about your behavior. The observers then meet together and discuss their interpretations of what happened and evaluate your performance. You receive an individual feedback session and a written report outlining everything they measured, which could include: personality, character, values, abilities, skills, competencies, behaviors, performance, and results. What is rich about this experience is that trained observers have access to information about you from a number of different methods and techniques and have discussed their observations among themselves to develop a report.

## Individual Psychological Assessment

A final technique for assessment is an individual psychological assessment, which is similar to an assessment center except you go through it by yourself. You fill out professionally developed and validated measures of personality, leadership style, and cognitive abilities among other things. The process often includes individual simulations, role-plays, and an interview with the observer. The observer takes all the information and makes judgments about you from many different angles. This assessment method tends to be costly and time consuming.

In summary, assessment is an important component of your leadership learning and development. Assessment, or information about yourself, gives you an awareness of where you are right now: who you are, what your current level of behavior or performance is, what your current strengths are, and what development needs are important in your current situation. This information can help you be ready to learn when learning triggers occur and helps you focus on what to concentrate on in your learning and development. You can gather information on many things about yourself including your personality, character, values, abilities, skills, and competencies, your behaviors, your performance, and the results of your behavior and performance. And there are many ways of gathering information about yourself. You can self-assess, receive feedback, and when you have the opportunity, participate in simulations, assessment centers, and possibly even individual assessments. In this chapter, you will focus on self-assessment. The remainder of the chapter includes a personality inventory, a character strengths inventory, some instruments to determine your general readiness to learn (including your learning goal orientation and your grit), some instruments to determine your readiness to learn leadership (including your leader goals and your leadership self-efficacy), and finally a short instrument where you assess yourself on a number of common leadership competencies. At the end of this chapter, you will use these assessments to assess yourself on who you are as a leader. All the instruments in the remainder of the chapter are both reliable and valid with the exception of the leader goals and the leadership competency assessment, which I created for use in my own research.

## Assessment Instruments

### Who You Are: Personality

One of the ways a leader can undertake self-assessment is through personality inventories. These inventories do not predict who will be a leader, or who will be a good leader or poor leader. But once you understand your personality, you can use this knowledge to better understand yourself in situations calling for you to participate in leadership.

### Personality

Before reading about personality, take the BFI, Big Five Inventory (John, Donahue, & Kentle, 1991; John, Naumann, & Soto, 2008) using this link: www.outofservice.com/bigfive/. It is free, it takes about 10 minutes to complete, and you get a brief description of your results at the completion of the survey. If you can, print the results page. If not, note down your scores and the descriptions that the page gives you.

There are countless personality traits that exist in humans and distinguish us from each other. But research suggests that there are five broad dimensions of personality. That is what is measured in this test: the Big Five, which has been shown to be both reliable (that is, you can take it now and you can take it again in six months and score similarly) and valid (that is, assuming you are honest in your answers, you can be sure that the score you receive on each dimension is an accurate representation of who you are).

Your combination of the Big Five traits (with other traits not measured here) form how you uniquely express yourself in the world and gives you your distinctive "you-ness." It is the pattern of emotional qualities, behaviors, thoughts, feelings, attitudes and habits that make us who we are. These personality traits explain the underlying reasons why an individual leader behaves the way they do (in this section, I draw from Toegel, & Barsoux, 2012).

However, you should remember that these traits determine your preferences for behaving—sometimes the situation will suggest a different way to act, and you do so without thinking. In addition, you can choose to behave in a different manner than your preference suggests, if you decided to do so.

## Extroversion

Look at your extroversion score. Are you low, medium, or high? People who are high on extroversion are highly engaged in the external world. They like being with people and like excitement; they get their energy from engaging in the outside world. In groups, they like to talk, assert themselves, and draw attention to themselves. People who are low on extroversion are called introverts. Introverts tend to be quiet, low-key, and less engaged with the external world. This should not be interpreted as shyness; introverts simply need less stimulation than an extrovert and prefer to be alone or hang out with only a few people at a time. They get their energy from within as opposed to the external world. Are you extroverted, introverted, or in between? Do you agree or disagree with your score, and why? Think of some recent situations where this trait was in the forefront? Did it have a positive influence, negative influence, or mixed influence on the situation?

People who score high on extroversion are more likely to emerge as a leader and more likely to be perceived as leader-like than someone who is an introvert, but that doesn't necessarily mean they are better leaders! Yes, it can be an advantage in leadership situations to be energetic, outgoing, and assertive. But people that are high in extroversion can also be too energetic and tire people out, too outgoing and turn people off, and too assertive and talk too much and not listen enough. And introverts can be energetic, outgoing, and assertive when they want to, but they may just need to spend some alone time afterwards to get their energy back. In knowing that you are an extrovert, when you are in a leadership situation, you need to remember to practice listening skills, be patient with unhurried others, and temper your outgoing nature a bit. In knowing that you are an introvert, when you are in a leadership situation, you may need to encourage yourself to speak up and get heard, but you can capitalize on your listening skills and summarize points made. You can be energetic, outgoing, or assertive when needed (but leave room in your schedule to refresh and re-energize).

## Agreeableness

Look at your agreeableness score. Are you low, medium, or high? Those who are high in agreeableness have an optimistic view of human nature and value getting along with others and show concern with cooperation and social harmony. They are seen as considerate, friendly, helpful, and willing to compromise with others. Those who are low in agreeableness place a higher value on self-interest than in getting along with others. They are less concerned with other people's well-being. Agreeable people are better liked than disagreeable people. On the other hand, agreeableness is not useful in situations that require tough or objective decisions. Both ends of the scale can be an advantage or a disadvantage in leadership, depending on what is needed in the situation. If you know you are low on this scale, even though you can give tough feedback when necessary, you might spend time making sure you do not say things too bluntly or aggressively. If you know you are high on this scale, and know that you might have problems making decisions that will upset other people, you may need to switch mindsets from "being liked" to "being seen as fair." Do you have high agreeableness, low agreeableness, or somewhere in between? Do you agree or disagree with your score, and why? Think of some recent situations where this trait was in the forefront? Did it have a positive influence, negative influence, or mixed influence on the situation?

## Conscientiousness

Look at your conscientiousness score. Are you low, medium, or high? Conscientiousness scores reflect how much structure and organization a person wants in their life. Those with high scores on this trait tend to be purposefully planful, persistent, and reliable—all necessary ingredients for effective leadership. They can also be slow to make decisions, perfectionists, workaholics, and seen as stuffy or boring. Those low on conscientiousness can be seen as disorganized, unreliable, and having a lack of ambition. They can also make quick decisions, and be creative, and a bit zany. When participating in leadership, it is good to have some of both kinds of people (who are aware of their strengths and short comings in this area and are aware that it is good to have someone else working with them to balance them). Do you have high conscientiousness, low conscientiousness, or somewhere in between? Do you agree or disagree with your score, and why? Think of some recent situations where this characteristic was in the forefront. Did it have a positive influence, negative influence, or mixed influence on the situation?

## Neuroticism or (the Opposite) Emotional Stability

Look at your neuroticism score/emotional stability. Are you low, medium, or high? Those who score high on this scale tend to be more emotionally reactive in situations and tend to more easily feel anxiety, anger, or depression. Individuals high on this trait are less resilient in stressful situations and struggle to stay calm. They need to learn to temper their emotions and express their emotions in ways that others can hear them. Individuals who score low in neuroticism are less easily upset and are less emotionally reactive. They tend to be calm, emotionally stable, and free from persistent negative feelings. But too much poise can appear uninspiring or lacking in urgency. Which side of the scale are you on, or are you somewhere in between? Do you agree or disagree with your score, and why? Think of some recent situations where this characteristic was in the forefront. Did it have a positive influence, negative influence, or mixed influence on the situation?

## Openness to Experience

Look at your openness to experience score. Are you low, medium, or high? Those who are high on openness are seen as imaginative, and creative, while those who are low on openness are seen as down to earth and conventional. Those high on openness to experience are more individualistic and nonconforming, curious, and sensitive to art and beauty. Those lower on openness to experience have fewer interests and prefer the plain, straightforward, and obvious over the complex, ambiguous, and subtle. Those high on openness like to experience novel things. Those low on openness like to stick with the familiar. In leadership situations, you can be too innovative or complex, or you can be too conventional. Are you high on openness to experience, low on openness to experience, or somewhere in between? Do you agree or disagree with your score, and why? Think of some recent situations where this characteristic was in the forefront. Did it have a positive influence, negative influence, or mixed influence on the situation?

The takeaway from this section is that you can participate in leadership in any form, emerge as a leader, and be an effective leader, regardless of your personality. Personality is about preferences for behaving, thinking, and feeling in certain ways, not about how you actually choose to behave, think, and feel. When you participate in leadership, no matter what role you play, you can be yourself; there is no need to try to change your personality. Your personality will suggest situations where you are more comfortable than other situations and tendencies of acting, feeling, or thinking that can be both advantageous or disadvantageous. One key is awareness of yourself and what you bring to the table. A second key awareness is the realization that working with others who differ from you on personality traits (but are also self-aware) might be the most advantageous for leadership because they can balance you and you can balance them. The third key awareness is that you can learn skills that help you take advantage of your natural born traits, or where necessary tone down traits.

## Who Are You: Character Strengths

Before reading about character strengths, take the Values in Action (VIA) Character strengths survey on line: www.viacharacter.org/www/Character-Strengths-Survey. You can also take it here: www.authentichappiness.sas.upenn.edu/ (look under questionnaires). The VIA Survey is a reliable and valid instrument based on research that measures your response on 25 character strengths (Peterson & Park, 2009; Peterson & Seligman, 2004). Character strengths are core capacities for thinking, feeling, and behaving in ways that can bring benefit to yourself and others. You will need to register to take this instrument (at the time I am writing this, the registration is free on both websites). You will receive a free report with your top character strengths as well as other information on how to interpret and use your character strengths. Before moving on, what are your top five character strengths? As you read them, do you agree or disagree with your strengths?

Character is similar to personality. The difference is that people tend to believe that personality is something you are born with, while character is something you learn and develop over time (it builds from a combination of your personality and your life circumstances). What I like in particular about this instrument is that is concentrates on helping you discover your character strengths (rather than character flaws). Your character strengths are the positive parts of your character, which impact how you think, feel, and behave, and are the keys to you being you.

The 25 character strengths are divided into 6 larger virtues: cognitive strengths, emotional strengths, interpersonal strengths, civic strengths, strengths that prevent excess, and strengths that forge connections. See Table 5.1, which provides a summary of the categories and the character strengths.

The takeaway from this section is that you can participate in leadership in any form, emerge as a leader, and be an effective leader, regardless of your character strengths. As you can see from Table 5.1, at least one of your character strengths is important in just about any situation that you can think of, and you can probably use several of your character strengths in most situations. Like personality, character strengths are about your preferred way of behaving, thinking, and feeling, not how you actually choose to behave, think, and feel. In addition, similar to personality, realizing that different people have different character strengths and that they all bring something to the task is advantageous. In situations that call for leadership, everyone has character strengths that can be used. Finally, you have the potential to use any of these characters strengths if you are aware of them. For example, even if prudence is not in your top five list of character strengths, but you are aware that the situation is calling for a risk–benefit analysis, you can still practice prudence.

In summary, learning about yourself in terms of personality and character is useful to understand yourself better and how you uniquely express yourself in the world. You know a little bit more about what makes you, you. This knowledge clues you in to your general preferences about your behavior, the way you think, and the way you feel. But personality and character are preferences, not your destiny. If the situation calls for you to act differently from your preferences, you can and you will. You might find acting or thinking or feeling in ways that are different from your natural preferences to be a little more stressful, or a little more tiring, or you need to think more carefully about it before proceeding, but you can still do them and learn to do them comfortably.

**TABLE 5.1** VIA Character Strengths

| Virtues | Individual character strength | Description | Leadership situations that might use this character strength |
|---|---|---|---|
| Cognitive strengths entailing acquisition and use of knowledge: wisdom and knowledge | Creativity | You like to think of novel ways to think about and do things. You might be artistic. | Challenging situations that call for doing something in a different and creative manner or need a creative solution. |
| | Curiosity | You like to take an interest in experience for its own sake; you find all sorts of subjects and topics fascinating, you like to explore and discover. | Situations in which you need to acquire new information. |
| | Judgment | You like to think things through and examine them from all sides; you don't jump to conclusions; you change your mind in light of new evidence; you try to weigh all evidence fairly. | Situations that call for playing devil's advocate, or call for carefully considering pros and cons of alternatives. |
| | Love of learning | You like to learn new skills, topics, and bodies of knowledge; you add systematically to what you know. | Situations that call for learning and sharing new knowledge. |
| | Perspective | You are able to provide good advice to others; you have ways of looking at the world that make sense to yourself and to other people. | Situations in which a complex event needs to be considered from multiple perspectives, or in which you can offer advice (when asked). |

(continued)

**TABLE 5.1** *(continued)*

| Virtues | Individual character strength | Description | Leadership situations that might use this character strength |
|---|---|---|---|
| Emotional strengths involving the exercise of will to accomplish goals in the face of opposition | Bravery | You don't shrink from threat, challenge, difficulty, or pain; you speak up for what is right even if others don't agree; you act on convictions even if they are unpopular. | Situations in which you are called upon to speak up for an unpopular idea, or you need to report an injustice, abuse, blatant unethical practice, or abuse of power or resources to appropriate authorities. |
| | Perseverance | You finish what you start; you persist in a course of action in spite of obstacles; you take pleasure in completing tasks. | Situations in which you need to plan a big project and finish it. |
| | Honesty | You speak the truth and present yourself and act in a genuine way; you don't have pretense; and you take responsibility for your own feelings and actions. | Any situations that allow you to be authentic and honest, or situations that foster honest, forthright communication. |
| | Zest | You approach life with excitement and energy; you don't do things halfway or halfheartedly; You live life as an adventure and feel alive and activated. | Situations that call for a lot of engagement and energy. |
| Interpersonal strengths involving tending to and befriending others: humanity | Love | You value close relations with others, in particular those in which sharing and caring are reciprocated; you like being close to people. | Situations that call for exploring and appreciating the strengths of others; helping others use their strengths; celebrating. |
| | Kindness | You like doing favors and good deeds for others; you like helping and taking care of others. | Situations that call for sharing, helping, and encouraging others. |

| | Description | Situations |
|---|---|---|
| Social intelligence | You are aware of the motives and feelings of yourself and of other people; you know what to do to fit into different social situations; you know what makes other people tick. | Situations that call for listening and understanding others; emphasizing; being agreeable and being harmonious. |
| **Civic strengths underlying healthy community life: justice** | | |
| Teamwork | You work well as a member of a group or team; you are loyal to the group; you can be counted on to do your share. | Any situation that calls for starting a group, working together as a group, or facilitating a group. |
| Fairness | You treat all people the same according to notions of fairness and justice; you don't let personal feelings bias decisions about others; you give everyone a fair chance. | Situations that call for you to encourage equal participation of everyone involved in a discussion or activity, especially those who feel left out. |
| Leadership | You encourage groups to get things done, and at the same time maintain good relations within the group; you like to organize group activities and see that they happen. | Situations that call for organizing an event, or for mediating between conflicting parties, or any situation in which an individual is expected to stand in front of others. |
| **Strengths protecting against excess: temperance** | | |
| Forgiveness | You forgive those who have done wrong; you accept the shortcomings of others; you give people a second chance and are not being vengeful. | Situations in which you need to work with others who some how offended you, or where mistakes were made. |
| Humility | You let your accomplishments speak for themselves; you don't regard yourself as more special than others. | Situations in which you or the team finds yourselves in the spotlight. |
| Prudence | You are careful about your choices; you don't take risks; you don't say or do things that you might regret. | Situations that call for visualizing the consequences of decisions or for risk-benefit analyses. |
| Self-regulation | You are disciplined; you easily control yourself and regulate your feelings and behavior. | Any situations that call for setting goals and sticking to them. |

(continued)

**TABLE 5.1** (continued)

| Virtues | Individual character strength | Description | Leadership situations that might use this character strength. |
|---|---|---|---|
| Strengths forging connections to the larger universe and providing meaning | Appreciation of beauty and excellence | You notice and appreciate beauty, excellence, and/or skilled performance in various domains of life, from nature to art to mathematics to science to everyday experience. | Any situation in which you can notice or help others notice and appreciate the beauty of life around you; appreciating the beauty in the work that you are doing. |
| | Gratitude | You are aware of and thankful for the good things that happen; you take time to express thanks. | Situations that call for expressing gratitude to the people you work with and to people outside your team; situations that call for being mindful of all the people who are supporting your work in some way. |
| | Hope | You expect the best in the future and work to achieve it; you believe that a good future is something that can be brought about. | Situations calling for optimism in the face of adversity, difficulty, or setbacks; situations in which you and others need to be inspired. |
| | Humor | You like to laugh and tease and bring smiles to other people; you see the light side of life. | Situations in which a balance is needed between taking things seriously enough and not taking them too seriously; situations in which it would be helpful to find the fun and lighter side. |
| | Spirituality | You have beliefs about the higher purpose and meaning of the universe and you know where you fit in; you have beliefs about the meaning of life that shape how you act and feel and this provides comfort. | Situations in which it is helpful to remember how you and others fit into the larger scheme of things; situations that call for being mindful of your place in the larger context of life. |

*Source:* Modified from Peterson, C. & Seligman, M. E. P. (2004). *Character Strengths and Virtues: A Handbook and Classification.* New York: Oxford University Press and Washington, DC: American Psychological Association and www.viacharacter.org/resources/ways-to-use-via-character-strengths/.

In the next section, we switch from the general to the specific: In particular, what is your readiness to learn? This is important, as knowing your general readiness to learn as well as your readiness to learn leadership in particular is helpful for you to know as you develop yourself as a leader. Unlike personality and character though, your readiness to learn is more malleable and you can learn to manipulate it.

## Readiness to Learn

Recall from Chapter 2, learning processes are triggered by pressures, demands, challenges, and opportunities that affect individuals such that they cannot continue what they are doing in the same way and be successful. When and how an individual notices triggers for learning and responds by learning depends on their readiness to learn. Readiness to learn is how individuals recognize when triggers for learning are occurring and that they need to change accordingly: they must learn something in order to accomplish their task and then actually make a decision to take some sort of action. Readiness to learn has three dimensions. First, you need to believe that you can learn and change. Second, you need to persist in your learning—learning and development takes a long time. And third, you need to be motivated to learn (here you will address your motivation to learn leadership).

### *Openness to Learning*

Before reading about openness to learning, take the Learning Goal Orientation Scale (Button, Mathieu, & Zajac, 1996) below (Table 5.2). The Learning Goal Orientation Scale is part of a larger survey and is a reliable and valid instrument based on research. What is your score on this instrument? Did you score as high (scores between 4 and 5), medium (scores between 2 and 4), or low (scores between 1 and 2) in learning goal orientation?

As stated in Chapter 2, individuals vary in their belief that intelligence and abilities are something they can change and develop through experience and effort. Individuals that score high on this scale tend to believe that effort is the way to develop the ability they need for mastering a task, and they are more likely to exert effort to learn than those who score low on this scale. This is important for learning and developing leadership. If you believe that leadership is something that can be learned, you will challenge and push yourself to learn and develop it (Culbertson & Jackson, 2016). Conversely, if you believe that leadership is a trait, characteristic, or talent that a person is born with, you probably aren't going to expend much effort—you are either a leader or you are not. However, your learning goal orientation is changeable. You can manipulate it. For example, you can be more specific regarding what you want to learn. Rather than "learning leadership," you can decide that you want to "learn how to run a meeting" or something else more specific.

**TABLE 5.2** Learning Goal Orientation Scale

| 1 | 2 | 3 | 4 | 5 |
|---|---|---|---|---|
| Disagree strongly | Disagree a little | Neither agree nor disagree | Agree a little | Agree strongly |

1. _____The opportunity to do challenging work is important to me.
2. _____When I fail to complete a difficult task, I plan to try harder the next time I work on it.
3. _____I prefer to work on tasks that force me to learn new things.
4. _____The opportunity to learn new things is important to me.
5. _____I do my best when I'm working on a fairly difficult task.
6. _____I try hard to improve on my past performance.
7. _____The opportunity to extend the range of my abilities is important to me.
8. _____When I have difficulty solving a problem, I enjoy trying different approaches to see which one will work.

To score this instrument, *average* all 8 items. Add your response for each item then divide by 8. Strong agreement (an average between 4 and 5) with these items indicates a strong desire to perform challenging work, learn new skills, and develop alternative strategies when working on a difficult task (i.e., a strong learning goal orientation). Low agreement (an average between 1 and 2) suggests little concern for mastering tasks or gaining competency. Scores in the mid range (higher than 2 and less than 4) indicate a moderate learning goal orientation.

*Source*: Reprinted with permission from Button, S. B., Mathieu, J. E., & Zajac, D. M. (1996). Goal orientation in organizational research: A conceptual and empirical framework. *Organizational Behavior and Human Decision Processes 67*, 26–48.

In addition, individuals with a higher learning goal orientation are more likely to seek feedback and advice on how they can improve than those with a lower learning goal orientation (Culberston & Jackson, 2016). As stated earlier, feedback is one way to learn more about yourself. If you know that you aren't the type to seek feedback, start by asking for "how to" advice from other students and mentors who have done something you would like to try. Once you are more accustomed to asking for advice, trying out the advice, and getting insight on the advice, the next thing you know, you may then be going back and asking for feedback on how you did based on that advice.

Before moving on, do you agree or disagree with your learning goal orientation score? Why or why not? Interestingly, if you score low on this scale, and are made aware of your tendencies as well as made aware of the possibility that there are other ways to think, this mindfulness may help you develop a learning orientation. Also, once you begin encouraging yourself to learn smaller skills that you think you can learn (e.g., how run a meeting) and once you begin to ask for advice (telling your mentor you want to learn how to run a meeting and will they help you figure it out), you will find that your learning orientation will develop.

## Persistence

Before reading about persistence, take the Grit Scale (Duckworth, Peterson, Matthews, & Kelly, 2007). The Grit Scale is a reliable and valid instrument based on research. It can be found on this website under the questionnaires tab: www.authentichappiness.sas.upenn.edu/. It is 12 items long. At the end of the survey, you will receive your score. It will be a number between 1 and 5. This page also includes a comparison of your score to others by such demographics as gender, age, occupation, education level, and zip code. If you can, print this page. If not, note down your score. What did you score? Were you low on grit (a score between 1 and 2), medium on grit (a score between 2 and 4), or high on grit (a score between 4 and 5)?

Grit is the tendency to sustain interest in and effort toward very long-term goals and entails working strenuously toward challenges, maintaining effort and interest over years despite failure, adversity, and plateaus in progress (Duckworth et al., 2007). Here is a great TED video on YouTube by Angela Duckworth on grit: www.youtube.com/watch?v=H14bBuluwB8.

Individuals who score higher on this scale are more likely to sustain interest in and effort toward long-term goals and are willing to stick with those goals than those who score lower on this scale. This is particularly important for leadership learning and development. As stated in Chapter 3, you are never done learning and developing your leadership. Your identity continues to change and develop, the way you think about leadership continues to change and develop, new ideas about leadership emerge every few years and you need to familiarize yourself with those. And even your leadership skills and competencies continue to change and develop from novice to expert (then experts have to continually modify skills to stay up to date). In addition, as you will find out later in this book, you will probably fail (and sometimes fail epically) along your journey. Grit helps you stay the course.

Before moving on, do you agree or disagree with your grit score? Interestingly, if you score low on this scale, and are made aware of your tendencies as well as made aware of the possibility that there are other ways to behave, this mindfulness may help you develop grit.

## Motivation to Learn Leadership

In this section, you will determine your motivation to learn leadership by assessing whether you have leadership goals, and whether you think you have what it takes to lead.

## Leadership Goals

Before reading about the importance of having leadership goals to help motivate yourself to learn and develop leadership, take the Leadership Goals Scale (see Table 5.3). I developed this scale for use in my own research. It does not have the same research behind it to determine reliability and validity as other assessment instruments in this chapter.

When people want something, they set goals for themselves to help them get what they want. As a college student, what do you want to be or do when you graduate? If you have already decided (set your goal), you may then be in a major that will help you learn what you need to get you there as well as engaging in other career oriented activities, jobs, or clubs. If you have not yet decided, you may have a goal of exploring a few majors by taking classes in a few different subjects. Before reading this book, did you have goals to be a leader or to participate in leadership in some way? Had you ever thought about it? Now that you are reading this book, are you beginning to see the merit in preparing yourself to be a leader or to participate in leadership in some way? Scores on this scale can change easily. If this is the first time you are thinking about being a leader, you may have scored low on this scale. Some of you reading this book may have decided beforehand that you are not interested in becoming a leader and thus scored low on this scale. But as you proceed through this book, you may discover that leadership is much different than you imagined and that yes, in fact, you do want to learn and develop your leadership. Your goals may change. Before moving on, do you agree or disagree with your leadership goals score?

**TABLE 5.3** Leadership Goals

| 1<br>Disagree<br>strongly | 2<br>Disagree<br>a little | 3<br>Neither agree<br>nor disagree | 4<br>Agree<br>a little | 5<br>Agree<br>strongly |
|---|---|---|---|---|

1. _____My main goal professionally is to achieve a leadership position in my field of study.
2. _____I have plans to develop myself as a leader during college to achieve my professional goals after college.
3. _____I plan to be in a leader position in college in the near future.
4. _____I do not see myself in charge of others in my future.*
5. _____I see myself continuously furthering or advancing in the development of my leadership throughout my life.

To score this instrument, you'll first need to *reverse-score* the asterisked (*) item. To re-code this item, you should subtract your score from 6. For example, if you gave yourself a 5, compute 6 minus 5 and your recoded score is 1. That is, a score of 1 becomes 5, 2 becomes 4, 3 remains 3, 4 becomes 2, and 5 becomes 1. Then, you will create a scale score by *averaging* all 5 items. Add your response for each item then divide by 5. The maximum score on this scale is 5 (you have a goal to be a leader), and the lowest scale on this scale is 1 (you do not have a goal to be a leader). Scores in the mid range (higher than 2 and less than 4) indicate that you may have some goals to be a leader in place, but this is not strong.

## Leadership Self-Efficacy

Before reading about leadership self-efficacy, assess yourself on the following scale (Table 5.4) (Bobbio & Manganelli, unpublished, updated from Bobbio & Manganelli, 2009). The Leadership Self-Efficacy Scale is a reliable and valid instrument based on research.

Self-efficacy is an individual's belief that they have some measure of control over their own functioning and their environment (Bandura, 1997). The more confident an individual is in their ability to do something, the more likely they are to do it. Leadership self-efficacy is a specific form of self-efficacy around an individual's beliefs on whether they can be successful accomplishing leadership tasks. If you believe that you can be successful participating in leadership, or doing a leadership task, or taking on a leadership role, then you will be more likely to do so. If you have never thought about it, never done it, or think you weren't very successful last time you tried and aren't sure about your capabilities in doing leadership, then you are less likely to step up when an opportunity presents itself. Before moving on, do you agree or disagree with your leadership self-efficacy score? Similar to goals in leadership, your score on this instrument can change as you gain more experience. And as you become more confident (and your scores get higher on this scale), you will find yourself looking for and engaging in more opportunities. As your confidence grows, so will your readiness to learn and develop leadership.

Look over your results on the four readiness to learn scales. Taking all the scores into account (learning goal orientation, grit, leadership goals, leadership self-efficacy), what is your readiness to learn leadership? If your learning readiness is high, you will be more attuned to and ready to recognize opportunities for leadership learning and development in the environment when they present themselves. In fact, if your learning readiness is really high, you may interpret many situations as opportunities to learn and develop your leadership—you may have to pick and choose which ones to participate in. If your learning readiness is low, you may not notice opportunities to learn and develop leadership. In my work with college students, I have often had two or more students in the same situation, some of whom saw great opportunity to develop, some who stated that an opportunity never appeared, and some that stated that leadership wasn't even occurring and are disappointed by the whole experience. These students probably differ in their readiness to learn and develop leadership.

## Leadership Competency Assessment

The final way of assessing yourself in this chapter is by assessing yourself on your leadership skills and competencies. There are many possible leadership competencies that you need to develop yourself in. The instrument I am providing here (see Table 5.5) includes only a few basic competencies. Some or all of these may apply to your circumstances.

**TABLE 5.4** Leadership Self Efficacy Scale

| 1<br>Absolutely<br>False | 2<br>Quite<br>False | 3<br>Somewhat<br>false | 4<br>Neither<br>true nor<br>false | 5<br>Somewhat<br>true | 6<br>Quite true | 7<br>Absolutely<br>true |
|---|---|---|---|---|---|---|

1. _____ I can usually change the attitudes and behavior of group members if they don't meet group objectives.
2. _____ I am able to set a new direction for a group, if the one currently taken doesn't seem correct to me.
3. _____ I am able to change things in a group even if they are not completely under my control.
4. _____ I am confident in my ability to choose group members in order to build up an effective and efficient team.
5. _____ I am able to optimally share out the work between the members of a group to get the best results.
6. _____ I would be able to delegate the task of accomplishing specific goals to other group members.
7. _____ I am usually able to understand to whom, within a group, it is better to delegate specific tasks.
8. _____ Usually, I can establish very good relationships with the people I work with.
9. _____ I am sure I can communicate with others, going straight to the heart of the matter.
10. _____ I can successfully manage relationships with all the members of a group.
11. _____ I can identify my strengths and weaknesses.
12. _____ I am confident in my ability to get things done.
13. _____ I always know how to get the best out of the situations I find myself in.
14. _____ With my experience and competence, I can always help group members to reach the group's targets.
15. _____ As a group leader, I am usually able to affirm my beliefs and values.
16. _____ With my example, I am sure I can motivate the members of the group.
17. _____ I can usually motivate group members and arouse their enthusiasm when I start a new project.
18. _____ I am able to motivate and give opportunities to each group member in the exercise of his/her tasks or functions.
19. _____ I can usually make the people I work with appreciate me.
20. _____ I am sure I can gain the consensus of group members.
21. _____ I can usually lead a group with consensus of all members.

To score this instrument, you will create scale scores by *averaging* all 21 items. Add your response for each item then divide by 21. Your score should be between a 1 and a 7. If you scored between a 1 and 3, then you have low leadership self-efficacy. If you scored between a 5 and 7, then you have high leadership self-efficacy. Scores in the mid range (higher than 3 and less than 5) indicate a moderate level of leadership self-efficacy.

*Source*: Reprinted with permission from Andrea Bobbio, University of Padova, Department of Philosophy, Education, and Applied Psychology.

**TABLE 5.5** Leadership Competency Assessment

**Directions**

1. If you have never demonstrated a particular competency, write "none" and leave blank (you may have a few of these).
2. In column 1: Describe a recent situation where this competency was demonstrated by you.
3. In column 2: Describe your behavior—like it was a videotape only using words (avoid judgments).
4. In column 3: Describe the impact the behavior had on you, others, the situation: What you and others experienced as a result of your behavior.
5. In column 4: On a scale of 1 (early in development for a college student) to 5 (very advanced in development for a college student), rate yourself on each competency (you may give yourself all 1s. Few if any of college students will realistically have 1 or more competencies that they can realistically rate as a 4 or a 5).
6. In column 5: Pick three competencies that you might like to target right away to learn and develop; 2 you are good at and 1 you want to develop.

| Competency | Definition | Recent situation[1] | Behavior | Impact | Assessment | Three to target first |
|---|---|---|---|---|---|---|
| *Foundational competencies* | *Knowledge and skills needed in order to develop leadership competencies* | | | | | |
| 1. Communication | Effectively write, read, view, visualize, speak, and listen. | | | | | |
| 2. Critical thinking | Distinguish between fact and opinion; ask questions; make detailed observations; uncover assumptions and define terms; and make assertions based on sound logic and solid evidence. Demonstrate the ability to use a wide range of cognitive skills to reach informed decisions. Analyze and synthesize information objectively. | | | | | |

*(continued)*

**TABLE 5.5** (continued)

| Competency | Definition | Recent situation[1] | Behavior | Impact | Assessment | Three to target first |
|---|---|---|---|---|---|---|
| *Foundational competencies* | *Knowledge and skills needed in order to develop leadership competencies.* | | | | | |
| 3. Effective citizenship | Demonstrate skills, knowledge, and habits of citizenship, be informed, involved, and engaged in issues of relevance to communities. | | | | | |
| 4. Commitment to life-long learning | Recognize importance of continuous learning in self and others. Critically assess self and how others see you. | | | | | |
| *Leadership competencies* | *Knowledge and skills needed to participate in or carry out leadership tasks* | | | | | |
| 5. Ethics/values | Adhere to an appropriate and effective set of core values and beliefs during both good times and bad times. Is aware of and acts and talks consistently with own values and code of ethics. Understand how own values and code of ethics fits (or doesn't) with the larger community. | | | | | |
| 6. Big picture (perspective) | Look toward the broadest possible view of issues/challenges. Discuss multiple aspects and impacts of issues and projects them into the future. Envision the interconnectedness, conflicts, and ambiguities present in complex issues. | | | | | |

| Leadership competencies | Knowledge and skills needed to participate in or carry out leadership tasks |
|---|---|
| 7. Strategic agility | Anticipate future consequences and trends accurately. |
| | Articulate credible pictures and visions of possibilities and likelihoods. |
| | Create innovative and breakthrough strategies and plans. |
| 8. Results orientation | Steadfastly push self and others for results. |
| | Set plan of action, follows through, and attains goals. |
| 9. Community building | Demonstrate capacity to bring diverse individuals together to work towards and implement common goals through dialogue. |
| | Recognize own personal perspective. |
| | Understand and appreciate others' perspectives and interests. |
| | Find common ground and respect disagreements with civility and diplomacy. |
| 10. Inspiring and engaging others | Communicate a compelling and inspiring vision or sense of core purpose. |
| | Make vision sharable by everyone. |
| | Create milestones and symbols to continually rally support behind the vision. |
| | Make each person feel his or her work is important. |

The instrument asks you to think of critical incidents of yourself exhibiting the competencies, then asks you to rate yourself on how well you did. This assessment (and others like it) will help you begin to understand what skills you have begun developing and which ones you might want to target for development. Knowledge of what you want to develop next will actually help your readiness to learn because you will begin to notice where these skills and competencies are needed. Your ratings of yourself on skills and competencies should change as you learn and develop. Plan to assess yourself on skills and competencies on a yearly basis. If you have the opportunity to participate in other assessments of your skills and competencies, take them; there are many skills and competencies that you can develop and any one instrument cannot capture them all.

Based on your assessment of yourself on this instrument, what are your current competency or skill strengths? What competencies or skills would you like to develop in yourself next?

## Reflection Exercise: What My Instruments Tell Me about My Leadership

In the final exercise in this chapter, you will do an informal self-assessment in which you pull together everything you have learned about yourself in this chapter into a description of who you are as a leader. This exercise works best if you have a partner to help you get started. This could be an adult, such as a parent, an advisor, or a mentor. It could also be another student who is doing this exercise as well. If at all possible, it helps to have two sets of eyes and two people interpreting all the instruments you take in this chapter. If another student helps you do this, return the favor and help them interpret their own scores. Have at hand this chapter (specifically you will need the information on how to interpret your scores) and the scores on all the above instruments. If you have other instruments that you have taken for other courses or programs, you can add those too.

With your partner, look over all the instruments you filled out. What themes do you see when you look across all instruments together?

Here is an example of some themes arising from my own assessments:

1.  *I love learning.* This is probably my strongest theme. Maybe the following explains why I am a professor, why I study learning, and why I am writing a book to help students learn and develop their leadership:

    a.  According to the BFI, I am open to experience.
    b.  According to the VIA, my top five VIA strengths include curiosity and love of learning (which both fall under the cognitive strengths entailing the acquisition and use of knowledge).
    c.  I have a very high learning goal orientation.

2. *I am conscientious.* I work hard! And I stick with it. For example, this book has been a multi-year project for me. My idea for this book began many years ago. When I was ready to write, the first publisher I approached turned me down. The professionals who evaluated my book didn't like my first proposal. And it took me over a year to write it.

   a. According to the BFI, I am conscientious.
   b. According to the VIA, my fourth highest strength is perseverance.
   c. According to the Grit Scale, I am very gritty.

3. *Although leadership is low on my VIA strengths, I am comfortable in a leadership role.* I have goals to be a leader and I have high leadership self-efficacy. My interpretation of this is that I might not be quick to assume a leader role, but if the opportunity is right, I am comfortable doing so. In addition, I can help participate in leadership whether I am in a leader role or not.

Those are the themes that stick out to me when I look over my assessment and I share them only to give you an idea about how to look for your own themes. Your themes should be very different from mine!

In your leadership journal, describe yourself as a leader:

- Give a general description of yourself, drawing from all the instruments. Tie these together into themes rather than talk about each instrument separately.
- What are your strengths?
- What do you need to develop in yourself or watch out for?
- What kinds of people would you work best with, what kinds of people might you need help dealing with?
- What situations might be best suited for you? What situations may be more difficult for you?

Throughout this reflection, use concrete examples of yourself exhibiting these characteristics and competencies—both from the past and currently.

## Summary

- Assessment is discovering information about yourself: who you are, what your current level of behavior or performance is, what your strengths are, and what development needs are important in your situation. Assessment also provides a benchmark of where you are so that you can compare yourself in the future and see if you have changed.
- You can assess or receive assessment about many things about yourself: personality, character, values, abilities, skills, and competencies, behavior, performance, and results of your behavior and performance.

- There are many different ways of assessing yourself. You can self-assess, you can receive feedback from others, you can go through a simulation, you can participate in an assessment center, or you can receive an individual psychological assessment.
- In this chapter, you had a chance to self-assess: your personality and character, your readiness to learn in general and your readiness to learn leadership in particular, and your level of a few foundational leadership competencies.

## References

Bandura, A. (1997). *Self-efficacy: The exercise of control*. New York: Freeman.

Bobbio, A. & Manganelli, A. M. (2009). Leadership self-efficacy scale: A new multidimensional instrument. *TPM 16*, 3–24.

Button, S. B., Mathieu, J. E., & Zajac, D. M. (1996). Goal orientation in organizational research: A conceptual and empirical foundation. *Organizational Behavior and Human Decision Processes 67*, 26–48.

Culbertson, S. S. & Jackson, A. T. (2016). Orienting oneself for leadership: The role of goal orientation in leader developmental readiness. *New Directions for Student Leadership 149*, 61–71.

Duckworth, A. L., Peterson, C., Matthews, M. D., & Kelly, D. R. (2007). Grit: Perseverance and passion for long-term goals. *Journal of Personality and Social Psychology 9*, 1087–1101.

Greenwald, A. G. (1980). The totalitarian ego: Fabrication and revision of personal history. *American Psychologist 35*(7), 603–618.

John, O. P., Donahue, E. M., & Kentle, R. L. (1991). *The Big Five inventory: Versions 4a and 5a*. Berkeley, CA: University of California, Berkeley, Institute of Personality and Social Research.

John, O. P., Naumann, L. P., & Soto, C. J. (2008). Paradigm shift to the integrative Big-Five trait taxonomy: History, measurement, and conceptual issues. In O. P. John, R. W. Robins, & L. A. Pervin (Eds.), *Handbook of personality: Theory and research* (pp. 114–158). New York: Guilford Press.

Peterson, C., & Park, N. (2009). Classifying and measuring strengths of character. In S. J. Lopez & C. R. Snyder (Eds.), *Oxford handbook of positive psychology* (2nd ed.) (pp. 25–33). New York: Oxford University Press.

Peterson, C. & Seligman, M. E. P. (2004). *Character strengths and virtues: A handbook and classification*. New York: Oxford University Press and Washington, DC: American Psychological Association. www.viacharacter.org

Taylor, S. E. & Brown, J. D. (1988). Illusion and well-being: A social psychological perspective on mental health. *Psychological Bulletin 103*, 193–210.

Toegel, G. & Barsoux, J. (2012). How to become a better leader. MIT Sloan Management Review. www.researchgate.net/publication/291729320_How_to_Become_a_Better_Leader

# 6

# THE FIRES OF EXPERIENCE

## Challenging Experiences

In this chapter, I begin to describe the various key events that serve as triggers for learning for student leaders. Specifically, this chapter focuses on key events that are challenging experiences. The other chapters in Part II describe additional key events including key events involving other people, key events in the classroom or training session, and key events involving hardships.

Challenging experiences are experiences that stretch your ability to work outside of your comfort zone. When you are pushed out of your comfort zone, are unfamiliar with a task or situation, and find the situation either intense of meaningful but are not sure what to do next, your activation level increases. As discussed in Chapter 2, this activation level stimulates your learning processes.

What is it about challenging experiences that cause learning processes to be activated? What are the characteristics in the environment that are necessary to trigger leadership learning processes? Five characteristics are likely to make experiences into leadership learning triggers (McCauley, Ruderman, Ohlott, & Morrow, 1994). These are: dealing with unfamiliar responsibilities, higher levels of responsibility, creating change, working across boundaries, and managing diversity.

When you are in a situation with *unfamiliar responsibilities*, you may need to exhibit new knowledge, skills, behaviors, or feelings that you have not needed before. When you have *higher levels of responsibility* than you have encountered before, you may need to juggle more (and more important) initiatives than you have had to in the past. In addition, these initiatives may involve multiple parts (for example, when managing a large event, you need to oversee, coordinate, and manage other students who are involved in procuring the location, the technical set-up, the finances, the program, etc.). Sometimes, you may discover that some sort of *change is needed*. This includes fixing a problem that you discover, changes in the way your club is run, or changes in your own or others' behavior. Sometimes, you may need to *cross boundaries*, such as when you need to convince your school administration to support a proposal or work with another club or clubs to put on an event. And finally, you find that you are *leading a group of others who differ* in many different ways including culture, gender, race, ethnic, age, year in school, major, living arrangements (on or off campus), etc. In each of these cases, you may be called on to think critically about the situation, identify underlying causes and consequences of problems, and process new and ambiguous information. You may need to experiment with new ways of influencing people who are different from you. Finally, you may need to figure out how "things work around here," why they work that way, and if needed, how to change them.

Challenging experiences are one of the best ways for up and coming leaders to learn leadership (Sessa, Morgan, Kalenderli, & Hammond, 2014). Of the 180 key events student leaders discussed in my research, half of the events mentioned were challenging experiences encountered in the institutional context through jobs on and off campus and participation in athletics, co-curricular clubs, associations, and Greek life. Some student leaders recalled leadership lessons that they learned in non-leadership roles. Some student leaders recalled leadership lessons from major hands-on, action oriented leadership roles with real bottom lines including their first formal leadership role (that they were elected into, or were selected into), moving up in an organization to a higher leadership position that expanded their scope and scale, and moving to another organization that required changing their approach to leadership. Finally, some student leaders recalled volunteering for or taking on a project. Others recalled starting a club or association from scratch, that is, creating something new from nothing or almost nothing. In this chapter, I will describe the kinds of challenging experiences that stood out to the student leaders in my study and the kinds of lessons they said they learned as a result.

## Non-Leadership Roles

Out of the events student leaders discussed, 10 percent were experiences in roles they held that were not formal leadership roles. These included being a member of organizations, task forces, project teams, or committees. Although students were not in leadership roles in these events, they were not merely passive members who attended the occasional meeting or event. They were involved and they worked hard, which pushed them out of their comfort zones. These events were often first debuts to the campus that generally happened early in a student leader's college years during orientation or during their freshman year (or during the first year that they transferred). These experiences set the stage for future challenging experiences.

*I feel that the first big event that made an impact on me and developed me into a leader was my freshman year when I joined a service fraternity on campus. During the first semester of my college experience I wasn't very active on campus. I was kind of shy. I was kind of reserved. And joining the fraternity, although I didn't hold leadership position immediately, I was extremely involved. It helped me to break out of my self and it helped me to get on the path towards becoming a very active person on campus, towards meeting new people, getting involved, being less shy, being less reserved to being able to take part in more activities. So I joined in the spring semester of my freshmen year, and I have been extremely involved in it since then. It was an excellent group of people who were all very motivated, very involved on campus. I guess seeing them kind of inspired me to be more like them.*

Student leaders said that they learned three main lessons from experiences in these non-leadership roles (when a non-leadership role was mentioned, these lessons were mentioned at least 25 percent of the time): communication, task skills, and taking initiative (see Table 6.1).

**TABLE 6.1**  Lessons Learned from Non-Leadership Experiences

*What Is Leadership?*

*Identity*

- Self-identity
- Leadership identity

*Personal or Self-Awareness*

- Professionalism
- Balancing roles

*Learning and Reasoning*

- Big picture perspective
- Decision-making
- Learning to teach/learn

*Individual Competencies*

- Accountability and responsibility
- Adaptability and flexibility
- Resilience, persistence, and hard work
- **TAKING INITIATIVE**

*Support Systems*

- Developing and using support systems
- Being a support system

*(continued)*

**TABLE 6.1** *(continued)*

*Working with Others*

- **COMMUNICATION**
- Teamwork
- Dealing with conflict
- Dealing with diversity
- Delegation
- Inspiring and motivating others

*Getting the Job Done*

- **TASK SKILLS**
- Organizational savvy

## Communication

Student leaders said they learned how to communicate in these roles. This included the value and importance of everyone in the club, organization, or committee having and using their voice, and learning how to communicate more effectively, which included talking and listening to others as well as developing speaking skills and presenting to groups. You will see communication pop up again and again as being related to challenging events here and in other chapters. Communication was one of the most commonly mentioned lessons across the board in my research. This may be because communication is a foundational skill—that is, learning to communicate is not an end in and of itself. Although each and every one of us will need to continue to improve our communication skills throughout our lives, communication is also a necessary and important skill that will affect the successful development of many other skills. Not surprisingly, other research on college students has also found that participating, even in a non-leadership capacity, does lead to the development of communication skills (Pascarella, & Terrenzini, 2005).

## Task Skills

Students learned task skills by participating in these roles. Task skills include learning how to organize self, projects, and programs; how to plan; how to budget; and time management. Each of these task skills is made up of multiple components. For example, as a member of a project team, a team member participates in setting up a plan, putting a plan into action, tracking the progress of the plan, meeting deadlines, and keeping paperwork organized. Like communication skills, task skills are foundational. In the project example, it helps to know and have practiced all these steps before attempting to lead a project team and guiding all the members in getting these steps accomplished. You will see learning task skills mentioned in almost all the challenging events in this chapter. But learning task skills is not a commonly mentioned lesson learned through challenging people, leadership courses and programs, or hardships. You need to participate in challenging events to learn task skills.

## *Taking Initiative*

The third lesson, taking initiative, is the first step in a series of actions that are needed to take charge. When you take initiative, you demonstrate a willingness to get things done. Joining and actively participating in a role or an event helped even shy and reserved students learn that they can take initiative. They also discovered in taking initiative that there is a complex and rich organization supporting the university structure with many opportunities that they would not have been aware of and many interesting people that they would not have met otherwise. Joining and participating in a non-leadership role opened doors.

Some students began taking initiative and approached clubs they were interested in joining before they started school their freshman year. Others needed a bit of convincing:

> *What triggered that realization (I needed to get involved) was the first day of classes, my university isn't too good at scheduling freshman students, so though they are good for scheduling your first class at 8:30 am, they schedule your next class at 3 pm. Back then, they had these parking decks where you could find parking and it was fend for yourself in trying to find a space—so leaving and coming back wasn't an option. I got out of my first class and I went out and sat outside on the fence and knew no one and did nothing for about six hours. And the second day I came back and it was the same set up but it was worse. I had a class at 10 o'clock and my next class was at night. At 11:15 when I got out of class there was nothing to do, I knew no one, and I sat in the library, asleep in the library. I got woken up by a librarian—I'm lucky I made it to class. After that second day, smack, like all right, you really have to get involved if you want to do something here because that's what your life looks like for the next four years. Something's got to give. The first thing I said was, you know, let me go and find something to do.*

In a nutshell, participating in non-leadership roles is important. It helps you develop foundational skills such as communication and task management skills. And it opens doors into a rich and complex system full of opportunities and people that many who attend college don't even know exists or realize is an important part of their college learning experience.

Every one of the events that the students described in this section fall under co-curricular activities. These are a vital part of college student learning experiences. Co-curricular opportunities occur in the institutional context and include activities, programs, and experiences that complement in some way what you are learning in the academic context of your college education. Co-curricular activities are separate from academic courses; they are ungraded; and they are non-credit earning (however, in most schools, you do pay a fee to support these activities). You often need to use what you are learning in classrooms to do and be successful at co-curricular activities and programs.

Co-curricular activities include the following options:

- *Student government*: Students can become involved in college or university student governance organizations. To get into these organizations, students are typically elected by the student body to function as the "official voice" of students to university administration. Some of the duties that student governments perform include allocating funds to other organizations, planning programs, providing forums for student issue discussion, and helping to build and sustain a vibrant campus community. The most common organization is the Student Government Association. Additional examples of campus governance organizations include residence hall councils, honor councils, which seek to enforce a university's honor code, and judiciary boards, where students hear disciplinary cases and render verdicts.

- *Athletic teams and organizations*: Almost every college and university offers some type of on campus athletic organizations and teams, including both intercollegiate and intramural athletics. Intercollegiate sports teams compete with other universities and colleges while intramural sports teams compete within the college or university.

- *Academic and professional organizations*: Academic major and professional organizations help members acquire additional knowledge and experience in their chosen occupational field and can also aid in job searches. Students meet, plan and attend lectures, invite and meet with people who are already working in the field, and discuss topics and issues related to their field of interest as well as learn job-related skills. Professional organizations typically focus on one career area of interest. Examples include marketing clubs or psychology clubs.

- *Volunteer and service-related organizations*: Volunteer and service-related organizations plan and conduct programs and activities designed to help improve the local and sometimes worldwide communities. Some options, such as an alternative spring break program, occur during a defined period of time such as the college spring break. Additional service organizations function throughout the year or even over multiple years, including the Bonner Leaders program or Americorp, and promote service and volunteerism throughout the college years. Service-learning courses offer students an opportunity to contribute to their community and to critically reflect upon their service experiences.

- *Multicultural organizations*: Multicultural organizations and the activities they plan and conduct focus on increasing awareness and understanding of various cultures and ethnic and racial backgrounds. Activities may include festivals, concerts, lectures, and discussions that promote multicultural awareness. Examples of multicultural organizations include Black Student Union, Lambda (a gay, lesbian, bisexual, and transgender student organization), Muslim Student Association, and Chinese Students' and Scholars' Organization. In some cases, these organizations are combined with other groups such as the Asian American InterVarsity, which is both multicultural and religious, or the Black Law Students' Association, which is multicultural and professional.
- *The arts*: Almost every college and university offers some type of arts opportunities in which students can actively participate (or attend). Activities include plays, musicals, and dance concerts, marching band, jazz band, orchestra, and singing groups.
- *Other on-campus organizations*: There are other organizations as well, here are a few more. Honorary organizations recognize student scholars, often in a particular academic discipline, who maintain a specific grade point average. Religious organizations offer students an opportunity to meet with students of similar religious backgrounds. Media organizations include print (newspaper or alumni magazines), television stations, and radio stations. Those involved in these activities may write or take pictures for the school newspaper, serve on the yearbook staff, host a talk show for the campus TV station, or work as a disc jockey for the campus radio station. Individuals interested in politics may join the College Republicans, College Democrats, or College Libertarians. Students who enjoy planning campus-wide events may participate in the Homecoming or Parents' Weekend committees. Greek organizations (fraternities and sororities) offer many social opportunities while also promoting service and leadership.

However, many students do not take advantage of these co-curricular opportunities to expand their educational opportunities while in college. Less than 12 percent of students across the nation live on campus (Bishaw, 2013); 46 percent of students do not participate in co-curricular activities (with another 34 percent only involved 1–5 hours per week) (Buckley & Kinzie, 2005); and 2 percent of students participate in Greek life (Chang, 2014). These are all related—those who live on campus are also more likely to be co-curricularly active and/or involved in Greek life. Students who do get involved in co-curricular activities also tend to be more engaged in school and tend to complete their degree (Pascarella, & Terrenzini, 2005). In addition, as stated above, they learn foundational leadership skills and find doors they didn't know existed open into a world of opportunities and people willing and interested in working with them.

## Major Leadership Roles

Many leaders believe that the best way to learn leadership is to do leadership: "Leaders are formed in the fires of experience" (Ghosn & Ries, 2005: 152–153). In these positions, leaders must get results through working with others rather than doing it all by him or herself. And the leader is accountable, not only for their own actions but also for the actions of those on their team (and perhaps members of the whole organization) and for the outcomes of the organization. Close to one quarter of the events discussed by student leaders in my research were about stepping into major leadership roles: moving into the first leadership role, moving to higher level leadership roles within an organization and the increases in scope and scale that accompany moving up, and changing leadership roles by moving into another organization. Some 9 percent of the key events discussed included first leadership positions, 8 percent were about moving into a higher leadership position in the same organization that was larger in scope and scale, and another 6 percent included switching from a leadership role in one organization to a leadership role in another organization.

### First Leadership Role

A student's first leadership role, through appointment, selection, or election, can be daunting as well as exciting. Students discover that there is more to leading than anything they have read or watched or done themselves. Moving from being a team member to your first leadership position in which you are in charge is one of the biggest and most difficult transitions in developing yourself as a leader. Although there is a lot to learn, you are expected to hit the ground running when you take on your first official leadership role.

> *I joined the National Collegiate Scholars society at the end of my Freshman year and ran for an eboard position. Beginning my sophomore year, I became secretary on an eboard of seven people. The presidents were seniors. It was intimidating to join a group like that because the club is enormous. On paper there are 900 members, but 200 active members. It is intimidating to have the responsibility of helping run a body of over 200 members and also being under someone who has been doing it for a long time. As well as their expectations, because they know what they should be doing and they expected me to know what to do too. Obviously, you watch and learn and do a lot by yourself. I was secretary, but again I don't do well with not saying anything if I feel like something is amiss or there is an idea to be said. So I tried to immerse myself into it and didn't just take notes. Along with the other members I had a lot of responsibility placed on me. Although my job was to take minutes there was a seven-member eboard and the*

*work was spread across all of us. So I picked up slack wherever it was and helped people out. In doing that I think I learned a lot about how your title isn't necessarily your job. I think that was an important step, knowing that I signed up to be secretary, but by signing up to be on an eboard in general I was already taking responsibility . . . If work needs to be done it is going to come to you first and then someone else. So that year was a big growing year. It wasn't just joining an eboard, it was joining an eboard and being tossed into a well to learn how to swim.*

Student leaders said that they learned six main lessons from first leadership experiences (when a first leadership experience was mentioned, these lessons were mentioned at least 25 percent of the time): Self-identity, accountability/responsibility, communication, teamwork, task skills, and organizational savvy. Interestingly, these lessons are similar to what adult leaders in organizations say they learned as they moved into leader roles (Paese & Wellins, 2007) (see Table 6.2).

**TABLE 6.2** Lessons Learned from First Leadership Experiences

*What Is Leadership?*

*Identity*

- **SELF-IDENTITY**
- Leadership identity

*Personal or Self-Awareness*

- Professionalism
- Balancing roles

*Learning and Reasoning*

- Big picture perspective
- Decision-making
- Learning to teach/learn

*Individual Competencies*

- **ACCOUNTABILITY AND RESPONSIBILITY**
- Adaptability and flexibility
- Resilience, persistence, and hard work
- Taking initiative

*Support Systems*

- Developing and using support systems
- Being a support system

*(continued)*

**TABLE 6.2** *(continued)*

*Working with Others*

- **COMMUNICATION**
- **TEAMWORK**
- Dealing with conflict
- Dealing with diversity
- Delegation
- Inspiring and motivating others

*Getting the Job Done*

- **TASK SKILLS**
- **ORGANIZATIONAL SAVVY**

## Self-Identity

Your leader identity is part of your larger self-identity. Self-identity is how you understand and define yourself as a whole (not just as a leader but of course the two are related) and your relationship to the world. In my research, students talked about personal characteristics like self-confidence, personal boundaries, and how they behaved. They often talked here about a realization that led to making changes. In this instance, a young athlete was asked by her coach to be team captain:

> *I became team captain in my junior year. I was caught off guard, because I look at a captain as someone vocal, someone that you can come to, and someone able to help with problems. I feel like I am an approachable person, but I didn't think my team-mates looked at me that way. I was like "Wow, I can't believe I am captain, I am so quiet, why would she choose me?" I don't talk a lot in practice and as captain you have to be very vocal and I did not see myself as that type of personality. When I sat down with my coach and she told me all the positive things I do and do it without talking, and how if I was to speak up that much more how much it would help the team and it made me want to be more outgoing, made me want to talk. Having the title and having to own up to it. Thinking I need to be the best captain that I can made me want to lead better . . .*
>
> *I learned it was never too late to change. How I opened up to my teammates my junior year. It's never too late to change and if you are more open and comfortable talking to people it is a lot easier.*

## Accountability and Responsibility

When you are responsible and accountable for something, you are required or expected to accomplish it and you are answerable for how well it is done or not done. These lessons centered on learning to take responsibility for self, your roles, and others. They dealt with being up front with responsibilities, setting expectations for self and others, being upfront about responsibilities and holding self and others accountable.

> *I was asked to be in my first leadership positions by the university ombudsperson. I remember him coming up to me and saying I have this group that meets called the Brotherhood. We want to get a charter for organization. I see you came to the meetings a couple of times. Would you mind taking a leadership position and taking initiative to be able to charter this organization and make something out of it, make it have a successful run? That is when I said, all right, I agreed, and I went on to work. That was my first real leadership position on campus as far as an executive board type of position. I went on and worked with the Brotherhood . . .*
>
> *Definitely, I would say responsibility. I was one of those kids, I never had a pet. What did I have to be responsible for was myself, staying alive, and whatever school work that I had to do. I never really had to be responsible for the actions of others, or the actions of a whole eboard, or even my own actions as a leader. It definitely made me a more responsible person. Kept me in order. And I had to learn how to deal with responsibility. Because I didn't know that. Because eventually I have to be responsible for a career, and supervising someone under me. Or when I get married, I have to be responsible for a family.*

## Teamwork

Student leaders learned that they had to work collaboratively together with others to achieve their team's goals and objectives. Here they mentioned such lessons as learning to value teamwork, learning to be a team player, learning how to bring the team together, and maintaining the integrity of the team. In this example, the new RA realizes that not only is she responsible for 50 residents in her own right, but she is also part of a team of other RAs that she must work together with to maintain the integrity of the whole residence hall.

> *I started thinking about leadership as a group thing. And learning how to be a team player because you have the other RAs, who you're leading with. So that's actually where it [leadership] starts, in the central meeting. That we all have our own little leadership areas but all the RAs have to come together as well when we are leading the whole building.*

## Organizational Savvy

Students learned about the larger university and how to work within it. Organizational savvy is an understanding of how individuals, clubs and organizations, and the university function, how they intertwine, and how to react appropriately within and between those systems. Lessons here include learning about the university environment, learning about the structure of the club or organization, the resources available to them in the organization, and the organization in general. It also included lessons about how to run an organization (within the larger university) including regulations, policies, and operations. Finally, it includes learning about the position, where the position is "placed" in the organization and the university, and realizing there is more to the position than they thought. It is worth noting here that the three main places that students indicated learning organizational savvy is in this first leadership position, when they moved into a higher leadership position that increased their scope and scale (discussed next), and when they started up a club (discussed later in this chapter). This is one of those important lessons that can only be learned in the fires of experience.

> *I became an orientation leader. It's a group of about 50 students that work through the summer and winter welcoming incoming students whether they are transfer or freshmen. We acclimate them to the school and how the programs are run. We make their schedule with the help of some advisors. We also speak to their parents and answer and questions that they have on the student experience at the university. We are like the sales people of the school. It was good experience for me to meet new people . . .*
>
> *It was a good experience for me to get to know the school and the resources. If I didn't know an answer to something, I had to know where to point and which department would have the answer.*

## Communication

Not surprisingly, communication was again an important lesson to be learned in assuming a first leadership position. In fact, it was one of the most commonly mentioned lessons students learned across the board. Like I stated above, communication is a competency in its own right. It is also a foundational skill that you need in order to develop many other skills. And you can learn about it and how to do it from many different events and circumstances.

## Task Skills

Similar to communication, learning task skills was a commonly mentioned lesson students learned in many different events and circumstances. Learning task skills was an important lesson to be learned in a first leadership positions.

One of the best ways to learn leadership is to do leadership. A first leadership position was a rich learning event for many of the student leaders in my research that led to lasting change in how they lead. Within these events, they learned more about themselves as a whole, they learned how to be responsible and accountable, they learned how to work with others including communication and teamwork, and they learned how to get their job done through the development of task skills and organizational savvy.

The events that students described in this section fall under both co-curricular activities and on-campus jobs. In terms of on-campus jobs, students mentioned campus recreation positions, residence assistants (RAs), peer leaders, orientation leaders, commuter student coordinators, and writing tutors. There are many more on-campus job possibilities and these vary by college. While some of these positions are voluntary, some positions on campus are paid or have a stipend.

In today's world, many students must work to pay the costs of attending college. And research does consistently show a moderate amount of work while in college has benefits. For example, retention rates are higher for students who work a modest number of hours per week (10–15) than they are for students who do not work at all or those who work more than 15 hours per week. Research also shows increased academic success for students working on rather than off campus (Perna, 2010).

For those who must work in a paid position in order to attend college, it is worth considering a position on or near campus. While a first leadership position can occur anytime and anywhere, doing it in a university setting may offer some benefits not readily available elsewhere. College is one of the last gates before entering into the working adult world. People who work within the college setting generally do so because they are interested in the learning and development of young adults. Therefore, it is easier to find a support structure (which I will talk about more in Chapter 11) to help and advise you in your first leadership position. In addition, everyone within the university follows the same rhythm or flow of the university life—professors, administration, and other students alike are aware of and also part of semester beginnings, midterms, and finals. They know that you can do more work at certain times of the semester and less at others as they are dealing with the same issues themselves.

How did students get into these positions? In some cases, students were self-initiated in looking for these positions: they ran for and were elected for positions, or applied for and were selected for positions. Some took on these first leadership positions because friends were doing it, because friends recommended they take on a position, and in one case, a student leader said,

> *Freshman year, I moved in next door to my friend from home and we go to hall council. He kinda forced me into position of RHA (Residence Hall Association) representative. He was the RHA treasurer at the time. He told me I had to get involved in something so I should just do this. So I was like whatever and got involved.*

Finally, some students took on leadership positions because someone in charge, a professor or a school administrator took notice of them and either recommended a position to them or asked them to take on a position of leadership.

## Increases in Scope and Scale

Another common event students mentioned that changed the way they did leadership was taking on a new leadership role that was a leap in scope and scale from their previous leadership role within the same club, association, or job area. When your role changes in scope, you generally have an increase in responsibility that is both broader and different from what you did before. When your role changes in scale, you have an increase in responsibility over larger numbers—larger numbers of people, bigger sums of money, etc. When your role increases in scope and scale, you cannot perform the same way that you did in your past, "simpler" position. At this juncture in their leadership development, these student leaders had to rethink their roles and how to accomplish them:

> This would definitely be becoming an intramural coordinator for campus recreation. This is definitely a step up from just officiating for the program. Once I gained this position, I, along with five or six other intramural coordinators, run the entire program. We are managed by our boss, who oversees the entire program. We schedule all the games, we hire all the workers, we train all the workers, if we have to we let the workers go if they are not up to our standards. We also teach the workers to use this job as a basis for how it will be out in the workforce after they graduate, so it's our job to make sure that they're learning from this program and it's not only just officiating the games but it's about time management skills and customer service, coming to work on time and prepared to work. Also, my job requires me to work 15 hours per week by contract, however I do work overtime so the past 3 years I have been working overtime maybe between 15–19 hours a week but I don't get paid for that. That's because I was hired to do a job and if it was not finished then I would have to stay overtime to finish that or come early beforehand. It is harder on me since my job technically ends at 11 but we don't ever get out till 11:30, or I have to come in at 6 to get something done, or later on in the season we have games sometimes from 4–11 so I have to come in earlier. So I always find myself coming in between class to access our shared file that is only accessible from our office, which is an inconvenience because my classes are on the other side of campus.

Student leaders said that they learned seven main lessons from increases in scope and scale (when a role that was an increase in scope and scale was mentioned, these lessons were mentioned at least 25 percent of the time). Several of these lessons were similar to what students learned in their first leadership role. These were: self-identity, accountability/responsibility, communication, task skills, and organizational savvy. In addition, two more important lessons were also discussed: professionalism and developing and using support systems (see Table 6.3).

**TABLE 6.3** Lessons Learned from Increases in Scope and Scale

*What Is Leadership?*

*Identity*

- **SELF-IDENTITY**
- Leadership identity

*Personal or Self-Awareness*

- **PROFESSIONALISM**
- Balancing roles

*Learning and Reasoning*

- Big picture perspective
- Decision-making
- Learning to teach/learn

*Individual Competencies*

- **ACCOUNTABILITY AND RESPONSIBILITY**
- Adaptability and flexibility
- Resilience, persistence, and hard work
- Taking initiative

*Support Systems*

- **DEVELOPING AND USING SUPPORT SYSTEMS**
- Being a support system

*Working with Others*

- **COMMUNICATION**
- Teamwork
- Dealing with conflict
- Dealing with diversity
- Delegation
- Inspiring and motivating others

*Getting the Job Done*

- **TASK SKILLS**
- **ORGANIZATIONAL SAVVY**

## Self-Identity

Self-identity (along with communication and task skills) was one of the most commonly mentioned learnings by the students in my research. So you will see this learning pop up as a result of several challenges. And this is not surprising. It is well known that the college years are a time of significant growth and change for students. There are entire books written on your identity development during these years (see for example, Jones & Abes, 2013). Your college experience, in total, can be seen as a huge triggering event for lessons in self-identity as you regularly confront new ideas and experiences that challenge what you thought you knew and believed. Your self-identity will shift as you face challenges in college in general, and leadership challenges in particular.

## Professionalism

These lessons were about the proper way to act in a leadership role when dealing with others. They dealt with how to present themselves well, represent their organization well, interact with others in a polite manner, as well as, lessons in which they learned that they no longer just represent themselves but that they also represent their organizations wherever they go. For example, here is one of the lessons from the example above:

> There are so many times, I cannot even count, that I'm on campus, not even at work, and people come up to me asking about the program because I am a representative of the intramural program no matter where I go. I can never take myself out of it. People know me as the intramural girl because I've been working there for four years. They know me, they know who to come up to if they have questions.

## Developing and Using Support Systems

One of the big lessons students learned as their jobs increased in scope and scale is that the job was now impossible to do on their own or with their immediate team (as they learned in their first leadership role). As leader roles become more complex to accomplish due to their scope and scale, they require the leader to reach out to a larger array of people. Here student leaders learned to ask others for help and for resources. They consulted with others, both inside and outside the university on how to do things they did not know how to do. And they learned both the importance of and how to network. Finally, they learned that developing and using support systems were not distractions from their "real work" of leading, but were actually at the heart of their new roles.

> I became RA second semester of my freshman year. Now I am the NRHH (National Residence Hall Honorary) President. It is a sister organization of RHA (Residence Hall Association).
>
> RHA is very well known on campus and NRHH usually gets caught in the shadows of it. So we wanted to make sure people on campus know the difference between RHA and NRHH because they do completely different things. For me, the way to start was top administration. If they know the difference, they are usually the ones that confuse us and it trickles down. From a business perspective,

*if administration understands the difference between us, then that could aid in the future years. I started talking to a lot of different administrators. I would go to professional staff meetings and talk about what we do and how they can get involved or how to collaborate with different things. I started talking to a lot of different professional staff members and I just started talking to different departments too and if there was anything we could do that would be beneficial for the organization type things, I would just go and do it and a lot of the networking. Personally now I know a lot of people from different offices. I know the Dean of Students office really well, because I worked with them on many different things. I worked with people in academic advising, campus residences, I know a lot of upper administration.*

The student leaders in my study realized that to do their jobs and do them well, they needed to develop and use support systems. The idea of "networking" took on real meaning, it was a legitimate part of their job.

Taking on a new leadership role in the same club or organization that is larger in scope and scale is a challenge. The leadership is broader, deeper, and more complicated. And when things get more complicated, new skills are needed. First, not only did they learn that they needed to develop and use support systems to accomplish their work but they also realized that developing and using support systems was PART of their work. The student leaders continued to learn about themselves as a whole, but with a new dimension; they became aware of how others saw them as well and realized that that was something that they had to think about and manage. When they were walking across campus or attending a social function, or networking, they were seen by others not just as their individual self, but as the face of the organization they were leading as well as the university as a whole. From this point of view, accountability and responsibility have more nuanced meanings as students began realizing that holding themselves and others responsible and accountable was necessary not only for their own success but for the success of their program or their organization. Finally, the student leaders learned more about communication, and more about getting the job done through the development of task skills, and organizational savvy.

As these leadership roles were a progression from previous roles in the same organization, these events tended to happen a bit later in the student leaders, lives (late in their sophomore year at the earliest and more often in their junior and senior years). Interestingly, while most of these events occurred on campus in clubs or on-campus jobs, some students also mentioned off-campus jobs. One student had been working in an ice cream shop since high school, worked her way up, and was now the night manager in charge of closing the store. Another had been working in her community theater in various roles and was now assistant stage manager. A third started in high school as an attendee at a summer leadership conference and was now one of the counselors. As I stated above, many students find that they must work to pay for college expenses. While you may not be able to participate in a leadership role when you first start these positions, even if these jobs are not something you want to pursue a career in, you may have leadership opportunities as you grow within these jobs (even if you don't have an official title).

## Organizational Switches

A third major leader role students mentioned that changed the way they did leadership was moving from a leader role in one organization to a leader role in another organization. New organization, new role, new rules, new people—their leadership practices and the leadership lessons they had learned before didn't necessarily work or work the same in this new position. This student gives a history of both increases in scope and scale as well as an organizational switch as he is currently Vice President of his fraternity as well as President of Greek Council:

> *Basically Greek Council is 34 organizations, but the reason I talk about Greek Council is because I am also in a fraternity. I joined a fraternity in my freshman year and I have been in several different leadership positions in that fraternity. I was President, Vice President, and Treasurer of the fraternity. I am currently Vice President of my fraternity, but I am also President of the Greek Council, which means I am president of 34 Greek organizations. I feel like being involved in Greek Council is the hardest leadership role that I'm in, but the most productive one because it goes from financial, running meetings, Robert's Rules of Order, learning how to conduct and talk to people, doing paperwork, just being organized, I actually have an office, so it's pretty cool. The main thing about being involved in different positions is that you have to do different things. As far as being president, you're the head of the organization. What you do is seen and the members follow everything you do. That's leadership in itself, because you want to be a leader that does what you say because you don't want to be hypocritical in anything that you do. You also have to meet with other people in high-leadership positions, other presidents. And that builds on your leadership because you listen and you learn from them. And also as Vice President, you actually control meetings. In Robert's Rules of Order, the vice president is the person that speaks whereas the President is the head of the organization. When I am vice president that's when I really got a chance to apply my leadership by running meetings, meeting with other organizations to set up co-sponsorships. Even as Vice President of my fraternity dealing with stuff such as members going through emotional stress, or school work, you get to practice just being the peer leader.*

Student leaders said that they learned seven main lessons from these organizational switches (when an organizational switch was mentioned, these lessons were mentioned at least 25 percent of the time). Some of these lessons were similar to those learned in other challenging events including communication, developing task skills, and professionalism. But there were some important new ones as well. When these leaders took on their new positions, they also had to learn about managing and balancing different roles, adaptability/flexibility, being a support system, and dealing with diversity (see Table 6.4).

**TABLE 6.4** Lessons Learned from Organizational Switches

---

*What Is Leadership?*

*Identity*

- Self identity
- Leadership identity

*Personal or Self-Awareness*

- **PROFESSIONALISM**
- **MANAGING AND BALANCING DIFFERENT ROLES**

*Learning and Reasoning*

- Big picture perspective
- Decision-making
- Learning to teach/learn

*Individual Competencies*

- Accountability and responsibility
- **ADAPTABILITY/FLEXIBILITY**
- Resilience, persistence, and hard work
- Taking initiative

*Support Systems*

- Developing and using support systems
- **BEING A SUPPORT SYSTEM**

*Working with Others*

- Communication
- Teamwork
- Dealing with conflict
- **DEALING WITH DIVERSITY**
- Delegation
- Inspiring and motivating others

*Getting the Job Done*

- **TASK SKILLS**
- Organizational savvy

---

## Managing and Balancing Different Roles

Student leaders, especially those who have worn or are currently wearing multiple hats, find that they have different roles depending on who they are standing in front of and what they are doing. These roles require different behaviors and this needs to be understood and managed both within the person and between the person and the others they are dealing with. Here students dealt with differentiating between personal relationships such as roommates and friends with professional responsibilities, being a leader in this organization (and the expectations that come with it) and being a leader in another organization (and different expectations that comes with it), and between being a student and being in a leader role. Here's an example of a football player who saw himself first as a mentor to other team members and to his fraternity and then taking on an RA position:

> *[I learned] how to balance two different loyalties. Being a football player and being an RA are polar opposites. Being an RA you are very structured with the rules, you have protocols, you have all these things where you may question them, but you still have to follow them. I don't always agree with the policies, but it is my job to enforce them. Being a football player your ideology is "me, a football player first. I am a caveman. Anything that bothers my way of life bothers me." I've had teammates who have been documented by RAs. I've even had to document my own teammates/little brother in my fraternity because of something he'd done. So it helped me develop a way of balancing the two and making myself understand that sometimes you have to pick one or the other and sometimes you can balance the two. That was extremely important to me in that aspect.*

## Adaptability/Flexibility

In this lesson, students learned they needed to change their behavior, method of approach, or style to meet the needs of a new situation. They made adjustments and used different tactics and strategies on the fly, and tried not to get stressed while doing so. In this situation, a pre-med student moved from being an orientation leader into a new position that tied together the leadership skills he learned as an orientation leader with his medical interests:

> *We have a department called the Center of Prevention and Outreach. They work with anything from drugs and alcohol with students, suicide, depression, and sexual assault. They have a peer education program that's called CHILL. This program specialized in mental health students. My growth as a student and a leader came from that. We're dealing with very heavy issues, with regards to stress, suicide, and depression. That's uncomfortable to talk about in general. You don't bring that kind of stuff up in a conversation. But we had to. We were the Center of*

*Prevention Outreach's spokespeople. A student isn't going to go to a professional staff member. They might go to a friend and tell them that they feel completely bummed out. You see signs like that. It was our job to notice these things, but we can't diagnose these things. We can only make a suggestion that not many people would suggest, something like CAPS which is Counseling and Psychological Services or student services . . .*

*You have to be prepared with anything. You need to have a tool belt of things on your mind. Anything may come to you and you have to be prepared with that tool belt. That was definitely the most growth I ever had on campus.*

## Being a Support System

In this lesson, students realized that it is not enough to create, maintain, and use your own support system. They realized that they had to be that support as well for others. These lessons are about being a part of someone else's network, being seen as a resource, and helping others. It includes learning to mentor, coach, and role model. In this example, this person who has held a number of different leadership roles on campus runs for and is elected homecoming king:

*Aside from some of the things I've done on campus I think that the cherry to top it off was when I ran for homecoming king. I wasn't going to do it, but the resident hall director from my RA job suggested it over the summer. She kept pushing and other friends made the suggestion and I bought it up to my orientation leader friends, my peer education friends, and my student health advisor leader friends. I ran and that was the best way for me to express my growth on campus, as a student leader and as a person because it was me expressing my support for everyone else. I felt like crying in happiness the entire time that I went through it. I was scared. It was almost like a beauty pageant. I had to stand in front of a panel of judges with the audience in the back asking questions and I had to then perform some creative school-spirited performance. Then three days later they tell you who won. That opened me up so much more because now I became the representative for the whole school and now more people knew who I was. Now even more so I had to maintain that image. If I believe in something, I need to express it. If I want to help the world for the better, I need to make myself that agent of change. If you want to change the world, you need to start with yourself. That to me was a great opportunity to manifest my morals and my beliefs into myself as a person. This to me was like a catalyst and it exploded and people were coming up to me and I didn't even know them. You're asking me a question or about other things on campus and I need to know the answer so I can put you in the direction . . .*

*[I learned] it pays off big time when you really invest your time in people. Even if it's just a two-minute conversation that you have with somebody, it makes a*

*really, really big difference in their life, whether it's advice you give them or a new insight on a different perspective and you open up their spectrum of understanding and they now become more empathetic and go on with a more positive attitude with whatever issue they were having. This expanded even more so into personal and professional relationships. People would come to me with these questions and I just had to be more empathetic or get more of a bird's eye view of life. This gave me the bigger picture of all the leadership activities that I've done. This was the very top of everything else I've done on the ladder. Now I can see down the ladder and see everything around it.*

## Dealing with Diversity

In this lesson, students learned to work across differences and using those differences to move the team forward or towards its goal. These lessons centered on learning about, valuing, and appreciating others' differences and opinions. Differences here included things like personalities, skills, communication styles, leadership styles, perspectives, cultures, and demographics. Here is an example of an RA who has held several different positions on campus:

*Understanding that things that you may see as right might not seem right in other people's eyes. You have to be adjustable to what's in other people's minds and what they are thinking. Because everyone doesn't have a mind like me or everyone doesn't have a mind like you. I wish that could be possible so that other people could see where I'm coming from, but that doesn't happen. Everyone is different, which makes us unique. So I've worked on being open to other people. Especially when roommate conflicts come up. And they're arguing about she had her stuff over by my area. They're arguing about that, and I'm like why can't you guys just work this out real quick and then it could be settled and done? But I just have to work on knowing that other people see wrong in other people then they get upset about the simple things, which I don't. So being open to that.*

Switching from a leadership position in one organization to another organization is a challenge. What worked in the past may not work in the current position or may need to be modified adding to the complexity of learning leadership. Just when you thought you knew something to be true, you need to re-learn, change, and adapt again. New lessons are needed. The students in my study realized that to do their new jobs well, they needed to change. They added additional individual competencies to their tool belt and learned to be flexible and adapt to changing circumstances. In some cases, they were now in more than one leadership role and they had to learn to manage and balance their different roles. They became aware that support systems have two sides—the one looking for support and the one providing support. Many of these students had already had the benefit of supportive others in their leadership development and realized that it was time to give back, to be that mentor, coach, or role model themselves to a new generation of college students. And while they continued to add to their skills in working with others through communication, they also learned that they needed to understand and appreciate others who are different from them.

Interestingly, every one of these events occurred within the university system. In many of these events, students moved from a position of leadership in athletics, clubs, or the Greek system into a Residence Assistant position. Students often become Residence Assistants later in their college years. In the case of the student leaders in my research, they often had some other leadership experience already under their belt. Many students become interested in an RA position because you get a room on campus and get paid. However, they soon learn that being a Residential Assistant is a rich leadership experience that is full of challenges. It generally starts with a selection process and rigorous training program. RAs are expected to work with other RAs to build a community in their halls, in their entire buildings, and in the entire residence life system through the development and delivering of programming. They are there on the first day helping students move in and on the last day helping students move out. They are expected to be a first resource for students with academic or institutional questions or issues, as well as a counselor for personal problems and roommate disputes. Finally, they enforce university rules and policies. While doing this, RAs need to learn to balance their schedules and priorities with the needs of the residents they are supporting. Finally, as RAs have highly visible positions within the university, they are expected to behave professionally and be a role model to the students they are serving. This challenging job alone could provide the opportunity to learn many leadership lessons, given a student with a high readiness to learn leadership.

## Self-Initiated Challenging Events

Student leaders were involved in two additional challenging leadership roles that were different enough from the ones listed above to merit another category, and similar to each other in three respects: in both of these challenging experiences (11 percent of the events), the students took something on because they wanted to and ran with it, they were loosely supervised by university faculty or administration, and they had to convince others to help them do it. Four percent of the key events discussed stepping up and volunteering to lead a task force, project team, or committee. What was key about this role is that it had an expected goal or outcome and was short-term with a defined start and end date. The second challenging leadership role in this category was starting a club from scratch (7 percent of the events fell into this category). What was key here was students created something from nothing. They built a club from the ground up.

## Serving as a Leader of Task Forces, Project Teams, or Committees

People tend to place the success or failure of a committee, project team, or task force squarely on the shoulders of the leader, making it quite a challenging experience, especially the first time a person volunteers to take it on. In the beginning, the leader needs to set the direction by clearly stating the purpose or goal of the committee (for example to put on an event). Next, the leader needs to find and persuade volunteers to contribute, often many hours, throughout the entire process. Then, the leader needs to manage the entire process, often orchestrating the jobs of the volunteers or even subcommittees of volunteers. In most of these events, students who volunteered to lead or even created new committees were part of an organization, either in a leadership role already or a contributing member. They volunteered to take these projects on, or developed them, and took them from idea to fruition.

> *I took on an event called the Halloween funfest. This was the first big event I chose on my own to head off. It was just brought up in a meeting where we were assigning events to people and this one came up and I knew I could so I just volunteered for it. I don't know what made me volunteer for it, and I kinda worried after volunteering for it. We put together an event with a bunch of little stations for the kids in the community. The athletes host it and we give them candy. I was in charge of that event and I think putting that event on and realizing how much work goes into it, gave me a huge appreciation for a lot of people in my life who have to do things like that. It also seemed that it was successful and that I was responsible for it and that really made me believe in myself more. I think it was with that event that I started thinking okay I can to do this. After seeing that I could do it and it worked out well, I started seeking out more.*

Student leaders said that they learned seven main lessons from leading task forces, project teams, and committees (when this event was mentioned, these lessons were mentioned at least 25 percent of the time). Some of these lessons were similar to those learned in other leadership roles. Not surprisingly, communication and developing task skills were again mentioned. And they learned to be adaptable and flexible. They learned about self-identity, but this time they also learned more about their leadership identity. What is particularly key here is that they had to learn how to convince other people, volunteers, to do things they didn't have to do. They learned that not only did they need to develop and use support systems but they also had to learn delegation (see Table 6.5).

**TABLE 6.5** Lessons Learned from Leading Task Forces, Project Teams, and Committees

*What Is Leadership?*

*Identity*

- **SELF IDENTITY**
- **LEADERSHIP IDENTITY**

*Personal or Self-Awareness*

- Professionalism
- Balancing roles

*Learning and Reasoning*

- Big picture perspective
- Decision-making
- Learning to teach/learn

*Individual Competencies*

- Accountability and responsibility
- **ADAPTABILITY AND FLEXIBILITY**
- Resilience, persistence, and hard work
- Taking initiative

*Support Systems*

- **DEVELOPING AND USING SUPPORT SYSTEMS**
- Being a support system

*Working with Others*

- **COMMUNICATION**
- Teamwork
- Dealing with conflict
- Dealing with diversity
- **DELEGATION**
- Inspiring and motivating others

*Getting the Job Done*

- **TASK SKILLS**
- Organizational savvy

## Leadership Identity

Leadership identity is a subset of self-identity and pertains directly to who you are as a leader. When students talked about learning about their leader identity, they learned that they could be a leader, how to be a leader, the kind of leaders that they wanted to be, could be, or never wanted to be, and what they were good or bad at in leading. As stated in Chapter 3, developing a leader identity is important in your leadership development. How you identify as a leader shapes how confident you are as a leader, how you act in a leadership role, how you relate to others (either as a leader or as a follower), and how motivated you are to seek out challenges and opportunities to continue to build and hone your leadership skills. In the example below, the leader realizes two things about her identity: (1) what she does not want to be like as a leader (someone who yells); and (2) also that perhaps she already has a leadership identity that includes mutual respect, which cuts across her leadership roles.

> I directed eight 9- and 10-year-olds in Alice in Wonderland this summer and I was in a theater company that gave me full permission to do basically whatever I wanted to. I'm like, well I'm 19 years old and I have this opportunity, this is great. I had a vision for it. I tore the script apart. I did something different from the norm. It was my own thing. We did a kids bop version and I thought that would be better and it involved more kids. I blocked everything myself. I hired my best friend as the music director, hired my other friend to be the scene manager. I had interviews for a bunch of other positions, filled them, then had auditions. I think working with those kids and working with the producer and working with my fellow staff members did light years for me. I grew so much that summer. I can't even tell you. I was working with a staff of half my friends and half people I didn't know. So, working with friends is hard, I actually had to confront my best friend because I was like listen you're not doing what I need you to do. You need to get your stuff together and he was like okay yeah. We were yelling at each other. Then after a while we passed that point and I was like listen I am not trying to hurt you, I'm just trying to help you. And then we did fairly well towards the end. I think working with that and working with a producer who was crazy, the craziest woman I have ever met in my entire life. She would say you can't do one thing one minute and then you can the next. She picked one person who she could yell at all the time to make her feel better and that was me.
>
> I learned that I don't ever want to lead like the producer. I want to be somebody that people respect. I enjoyed the fact that people felt they could come to me if they had an issue and that I would take care of it in the best way possible. Having that reinforced in a different environment, not SGA or not in the things that I have always been in where I have the reputation I have and yet still I created that reputation there too. Maybe that means that I lead this way whatever I do.

## Delegation

Student leaders needed to learn to persuade others to help them accomplish their goals, and then needed to entrust them with a task or responsibility while following up to make sure that they did what they said they were going to do. Students needed to learn the importance of delegating as well as how to delegate to volunteers that they did not have any control over.

> *Our chapter was selected to host the national convention and I took lead on that. I pledged as a freshman and learned the ropes my sophomore year. My junior year I took the responsibility as President and lead the initiative to host the national convention. That was a time where I brought the knowledge I learned from the pledge process into light and the real world. It was difficult only working with a committee of five individuals to plan the convention for over a hundred brothers who attended. We had to book accommodations for the brothers, find caterers, and really plan for the whole convention. This was done through weekly meetings over the phone with the national council. I was the one taking lead and I put a lot of responsibility on myself.*
>
> *One thing I learned through my mistakes was how to delegate, the importance of delegating, and how to utilize other's knowledge. As a president I thought I had to do it all. But essentially, I had to lead a team, which was difficult because the individuals on the committee were all older than me. They felt that they knew more than me and really didn't have to listen to me because I was junior. It was HARD.*

Leading a task force, project team, or committee is hard work. These are usually short-term projects with an expected outcome at the end. The most common outcome with the students in my research was some sort of event, but other outcomes could be a decision, a product, or a service. Students volunteered to take these roles on because they wanted to do it. Then they had to convince others to join them and help them do the work. Thus their roles included both people management and project management. They learned a lot from these short-term projects. They learned task skills. They learned about their identities—who they are as a person and who they are as a leader. They learned to be adaptable and flexible. They learned about the need for strong support systems and how to delegate. And they learned communication. That's a lot of leadership learning potential packaged into a short-term project.

## *Starting a Club from Scratch*

Executives report that one of the toughest assignments they have ever faced in their careers is to start something from scratch, to build a business or department out of nothing (McCall, Lombardo, & Morrison, 1988). Some of the students in my research decided, on their own, to pursue this challenging event during college. And they often did this early in their college career so they had little prior knowledge of the university and how things were done. They had to design a club, which included both figuring out internal processes as well as university policies, rules, and procedures, and they had to convince people to join the club and remain involved as they figured out all the details.

*My friend and I decided to start a club. We were on the varsity riding team together and at school we only have an English team. Intercollegiate riding is both English and Western riding; it's two different styles of riding. We didn't have a team here for the Western because there has never been an interest before. The girl that I started the club with learned how to ride Western and it was new for her. She was more aware of the Western showing and how things happen and it was fun and she wanted to start a club. She got us to help her. There were a number of hiccups that we came across the way. First was that we wanted to make it part of the current varsity team such that the varsity shared the money, shared the resources. All the girls that were on English could also ride Western. It was determined in a team meeting that wasn't necessarily the way that the coach and the captain wanted to go. As that happened, we realized if we want to start this up, it needs to be separate from the current team, girls then started to drop out. I admit I was one of those girls that at the very end when I was looking around, it was just me and that one other girl and I told her I would hate to break it to her, but maybe this wasn't a good idea or maybe it's not going to go through. She asked me how could I do this. She was counting on me. If anyone was going to go through with it, she knew I was going to do it. I agreed to do it. That was the first hiccup in trying to get started. We couldn't go with the team. After that, we started doing the club sport stuff, and I remember we had to have a meeting with the head of athletics and the head of club sports, and head of student dean too. Part of it was we had bad email communication and we didn't realize all the rules. They were not forthcoming with some of the rules and we were not finding out about the rules. We were trying to do things that we were not allowed to do and were like why can't we do this, you're not telling us the rules behind why you can't do it? It was messy the way it started, but for the second half of the year, she and I were able to start. We can't start a club sport for two people. We can't give you money for a club sport if you have only two people. You have to have more people. At that point we had to recruit people. Some were English girls, but the majority of them were not. There are a surprising number of people on campus that would like to ride horses but they don't want to compete. We just had to convince them to come out, it'll be fun, for the majority of it you can take lessons and there will only be two days possibly throughout the year that you would have to commit into showing. We were able to fill a sport card, so about seven people including us. Unfortunately, it was all our friends. That's fortunate and unfortunate because over the years they graduated and keeping the club going has been a little difficult as well.*

Student leaders said that they learned three main lessons from starting a club from scratch. The big lesson was organizational savvy. But they also learned adaptability/ flexibility and communication (see Table 6.6).

Starting a club from scratch is exciting but a lot of challenging work. The students were passionate and energetic about their vision and saw a need for a new club in the university, but had no advisor, no money or resources, no membership, and little knowledge of either what is needed for a club (for example, charters), or the inner workings of the university and how to get things accomplished including paperwork, procedures, rules, regulations, policies, and politics. As they moved through the process, they had to be

**TABLE 6.6** Lessons Learned from Start Ups

*What Is Leadership?*

*Identity*

- Self-identity
- Leadership identity

*Personal or Self-Awareness*

- Professionalism
- Balancing roles

*Learning and Reasoning*

- Big picture perspective
- Decision-making
- Learning to teach/learn

*Individual Competencies*

- Accountability and responsibility
- **ADAPTABILITY AND FLEXIBILITY**
- Resilience, persistence, and hard work
- Taking initiative

*Support Systems*

- Developing and using support systems
- Being a support system

*Working with Others*

- **COMMUNICATION**
- Teamwork
- Dealing with conflict
- Dealing with diversity
- Delegation
- Inspiring and motivating others

*Getting the Job Done*

- Task skills
- **ORGANIZATIONAL SAVVY**

flexible and adapt to better fit into the organizational structure and to attract more members, and they had to communicate to the administration, to the student government association, and to their peers who they wanted to join the club.

## Overview of Challenging Experiences

Joining and participating, first leader roles, increases in scope and scale, organizational switches, leading a task force, starting a club—what did these challenging experiences have in common? In all of these experiences, the student leaders in my research were pushed out of their comfort zones, they were unfamiliar with the task or the situation, they didn't know what to do or how to proceed: they were stretched. No one mentioned a stable, predictable, and comfortable position. They were all in the fire of experience and they had to learn new skills on the run, learn to do things when stakes were high, learn to work with and through other people, and learn to cope with a lot of work on top of their main university focus—their academics. They learned and developed leadership skills and competencies because they had to in order to succeed. While you may be able to learn leadership in many different ways, you will find that the richest and most valuable lessons you can learn are when you push yourself to the edge of your own leadership capabilities then leap. Table 6.7 summarizes the lessons learned in challenging events and it is an impressive list. In the following chapters, you will see there are other ways to learn leadership and other lessons to learn, but it is clear that challenging experiences were major sources of leadership learning for the student leaders in my study.

Seeing these results might tempt you to think about development in oversimplified ways: I need to join a club, I need to get on an eboard, I need to move up on the eboard, then I need to move to another organization, maybe become an RA. Maybe I should lead a task force along the way. And start a club. Check, check, check—look, I've learned leadership. What is key here is not ticking off the experiences on the list. What is key is that you put yourself into positions that stretch you, into new places that you have no experiences with, into experiences where you don't already know what to do.

As each student reading this book is on their own leadership learning trajectory, what might be a challenging next step for one person might be an easy comfortable step for another. And what might be challenging for one person for one reason, might be challenging in an entirely different way for another. For example, for some shy students or for some students with many responsibilities outside of school, joining and participating in a club, or committee, or project team might be a big stretch, while for others, well that's what they do. As another example, many students mentioned the RA position. One student said that it was

**TABLE 6.7** Summary of Lessons Learned in Challenging Events

*Identity*

- **SELF-IDENTITY** (first leadership experiences, increases in scope and scale, leading a project team)
- **LEADERSHIP IDENTITY** (leading a project team)

*Personal or Self-Awareness*

- **PROFESSIONALISM** (increases in scope and scale, organizational switches)
- **BALANCING ROLES** (organizational switches)

*Individual Competencies*

- **ACCOUNTABILITY AND RESPONSIBILITY** (first leadership experiences, increases in scope and scale)
- **ADAPTABILITY AND FLEXIBILITY** (organizational switches, leading a project team, start-up)
- **TAKING INITIATIVE** (non-leadership roles)

*Support Systems*

- **DEVELOPING AND USING SUPPORT SYSTEMS** (change in scope or scale, leading a project team)
- **BEING A SUPPORT SYSTEM** (organizational switches)

*Working with Others*

- **COMMUNICATION** (all challenging events)
- **TEAMWORK** (first leadership experiences)
- **DEALING WITH DIVERSITY** (organizational switches)
- **DELEGATION** (leading a project team)

*Getting the Job Done*

- **TASK SKILLS** (all challenging events, except start-ups)
- **ORGANIZATIONAL SAVVY** (first leadership experiences, increases in scope and scale, start-ups)

no big deal (he casually mentioned that he used it as a launching pad for bigger challenges). For some students it was a first leadership position; for others it was an organizational switch.

Students might find themselves in challenging situations not mentioned in this book. For example, a few challenging events described were about turning around a failing club into a success. I didn't mention it above because it wasn't mentioned often and it was difficult to discern what lessons were learned. Students might find that they learn different lessons than the main lessons associated with challenging experiences in my research. You could certainly learn more about your leadership identity or how to delegate in your first leadership experience, for example, if that's what you needed to learn to succeed in that role.

Finally, although the student leaders in my research mentioned positive leadership learnings, in certain experiences, you might learn a lesson that is right for that instance, but might need to be re-learned. For a hypothetical example (but one I think some have encountered), you might learn in a challenging event that you have to do it all yourself and that you can't count on others . . . all experiences and all lessons need to be reflected on. And be aware that a lesson learned now will continue to be changed, tweaked, and modified as you grow and mature.

In the next chapter, I describe a very different kind of event that led the student leaders in my research to change the way they thought about or practiced leadership. Instead of describing an experience or role, they described another person or persons. These people were bosses, peers, or younger students. What they learned from these people and how they learned it was different from what I have described in this chapter.

## References

Bishaw, A. (2013). *Examining the effect of off-campus college students on poverty rates.* Report by US Census Bureau, Social, Economic & Housing Statistics Division, Poverty. www.census.gov/hhes/www/poverty/publications/bishaw.pdf.

Buckley, J. & Kinzie, J. (2005). Profiles of student engagement in co-curricular life: Lessons from research. Presentation at the annual ACPA Convention Nashville, TN. http://nsse.iub.edu/pdf/conference_presentations/2005/acpa2005_profiles.pdf.

Chang, C. (2014). Separate but unequal in college Greek life. The Century Foundation. https://tcf.org/content/commentary/separate-but-unequal-in-college-greek-life/

Ghosn, C. & Ries, P. (2005). *Shift.* New York: Currency Doubleday.

Jones, S. R. & Abes, E. S. (2013). *Identity development of college students: Advancing frameworks for multiple dimensions of identity.* San Fransisco, CA: Jossey-Bass.

McCall, M. W. Jr., Lombardo, M. M., & Morrison, A. M. (1988). *The lessons of experience: How successful executives develop on the job.* New York: The Free Press.

McCauley, C. D., Ruderman, M. N., Ohlott, P. J., & Morrow, J. E. (1994). Assessing the developmental components of managerial jobs. *Journal of Applied Psychology 79,* 544–560.

Paese, M. & Wellins, R. S. (2007). Leaders in transition: Stepping up not off. www.ddiworld.com/DDIWorld/media/trend-research/leaders-in-transition-stepping-up-not-off_mis_ddi.pdf?ext=.pdf.

Pascarella, E. T. & Terrenzini, P. T. (2005). *How college affects students: A third decade of research, Volume 2.* San Francisco, CA: Jossey-Bass.

Perna, L. W. (2010). Understanding the working college student. American Association of University Professors. www.aaup.org/article/understanding-working-college-student#.V8iB6GWRu6V

Sessa, V. I., Morgan, B. V., Kalenderli, S., & Hammond, F. (2014). Key events in student leaders' lives and lessons learned from them. *Journal of Leadership Education 13,* 1–28.

StateUniversity.com (n.d.) College extracurricular activities: Impact on students, types of extracurricular activities. http://education.stateuniversity.com/pages/1855/College-Extracurricular-Activities.html

# 7

# WHEN OTHER PEOPLE MATTER

## People Who Significantly Impact Your Leadership Learning

In the previous chapter on challenging experiences, it was clear that the leaders had to work with and through other people to be successful in their roles. There wasn't any choice; they wouldn't have accomplished their work without them. In these challenging experiences, the leaders learned about communication with others, delegation, teamwork, and dealing with diversity. They learned about developing and using support systems, and being the support system for others. Other people matter in leadership and they always will. As I stated in Chapter 1, *all* people participate in leadership—in setting direction, in alignment, and in commitment, even if one person has the title of "leader" and others do not.

But not all learning about other people comes from challenging experiences and roles. Some 28 percent of the key events in my research featured being challenged by a specific person or persons rather than some sort of experience. At the center of these events were people who had a significant impact in their own right, and were more important than the particular event happening. The person or persons triggered the learning, something they did or how they interacted with the student leader pushed the leader out of their comfort zone right into some sort of intense situation. The purpose of this chapter is to discuss how a student can learn from the people that they may encounter during college. The student leaders in my research mentioned four ways that being challenged by people had triggered their learning. These included receiving some sort of feedback or recognition, being challenged by role models and mentors, being challenged by peers, and being challenged by others who considered them to be role models and mentors.

But don't forget. In order to be exposed to people that might have an impact on you, you do need to get out there. You need to join, participate, take on leadership roles, and work and interact with other people. In doing so, you will be more likely to get feedback and recognition for the work you do, you will meet senior people who will be mentors or role models, as well as junior people who want you to be their mentor and role model, and you will work closely with a broad array of peers.

## Feedback and Recognition

The most often mentioned challenge from other people that led to a lasting change in the student leader's leadership was receiving some sort of feedback or recognition. Of the events mentioned, 11 percent included receiving feedback or recognition. Students here mentioned feedback (both positive and negative) and recognition related to their performance, as well as pivotal conversations.

Here is a story and image about feedback. Feedback was a term first coined by Norbert Wiener in the early part of the twentieth century. Wiener was a child prodigy who entered Tufts University in 1906 when he was 10 years old. He received his PhD from Harvard at age 18. For 41 years he taught at MIT and studied the analogy between human brains and machines, and how people, animals, and machines control and communicate information. Wiener created the word cybernetics to describe this analogy from the Greek word kybernitis, for the person who steers a boat. This person sits with a hand on the rudder and watches over the prow to see where the boat is headed. If the boat is aimed a little to the right, he or she turns it slightly to the left. When the boat finally overshoots, the steersman corrects to the right again, and so on. The steersman constantly compares the actual direction with the intended direction and applies a correction—one that opposes the error. That is where the concept of feedback originally came from. Feedback is the information sent to an individual or a group about their prior behavior so that the individual/group may adjust their current and future behavior to achieve the desired result. Although a leader must give feedback to their followers or to their team to stay on course, that leader also needs to receive feedback to stay on course as well. And the student leaders in our study made it quite clear how important receiving feedback was to their own learning about leadership.

Here I give an example of positive feedback a young man received from a teacher based on his active participation in class his freshman year. This feedback was unexpected but helped reset this student's leadership learning trajectory into high mode. And I give a heart-wrenching example of "developmental" feedback given to a student leader by her entire eboard as president of her club.

*The second key event in my leadership development I have to say is being rec-ognized as a leader by one of my professors. I had never really been told I was leader. I never saw myself like that. And so, at the end of the class, at the end of my first semester, she made us come to the class to pick up our term papers. And she told me, you know I really admire the way you participated in class, the way you had input, you didn't have to do that. It was a freshman class, so everybody stayed quiet, no one really talked. I was pretty much the only one that was talking. She said, I see a lot of qualities in you, that you are going to be successful, that you are going to do good. Stay in the game and you'll be all right. We had an hour-long conversation and I was telling her where I was from. And she was saying, now I can see you are even more of a leader because you made it out, you are doing good for yourself, so keep on the right path and you'll be all right. I think that conversation was probably the second most important conversation I've had at this university. With her telling me how I would succeed and do good things if I stayed focused.*

This feedback example was harder to hear, the leader persevered and listened:

*I thought everything was going well with the [name] Club. At least in the public eye, it was going phenomenal. There was demand for events and everything was going well. As far as the eboard we definitely looked like a happy family. We never fought, at least publicly or privately, but I definitely noticed that there was a change and a split in the eboard. I know that three out of the five eboard members were acting differently. They were talking among themselves, a lot of inside jokes. I just thought it was ok, that they had gotten really close, they definitely weren't friends before. There were times that I did feel excluded even in a social setting, not eboard things, but a social setting. I felt like I was being ignored. Ok, we don't have to be best friends, that's not what this leadership position is about, being best friends. There's that question, would you rather be liked or respected, that they use in all the interviews if you want to be an RA or whatever, and that comes to my mind while I'm seeing this. I just felt it, a lot of unhappiness going on at the recent eboard meetings.*

*I do so much for the club, more than I feel that I need to. I do above my job. I'm not trying to get an award for that or anything, I do it because I love [what the club stands for]. I love helping people. It's my passion. I feel like I saw the potential in it and now I see where it has grown. I love it.*

*So I enter the eboard meeting. A lot of looks going on. I first run the entire eboard meeting because as president that's what you do. So we have the beach cleanup coming up, what should we do about that, then we're going to the senior citizen home for game night, then our multicultural fashion show fundraiser coming up. Just stuff like that. And as usual, this is the usual case, I throw out an idea and there's never a response from them. As leaders, just because someone's the president and you're the VP doesn't mean you don't have a voice and I made sure that everyone would have a voice but on their part, they never, and this has been for a while now, like ever respond to me. So the meeting ended and everything was just kind of quiet.*

*I'm like ok, if anyone else has anything to say we could end this, and our advisor was at the meeting and she knew what was going on because they had spoken to her and I had spoken to her because I felt that something's going to happen and they had told her that they weren't happy with the way things are running. No one at the moment spoke up and for me I didn't feel the need to, because like if they really feel that they're being wronged right now they would speak up because that's what you do. Especially as a leader you are a leader elected to this club. As a leader you know that your voice, that's like the number one thing as a leader, your voice and your voice being heard. So she's like, ok, the advisor's like "wait everyone, as eboard members of this club you reflect on this club and the way you interact with each other will reflect on how the club is being run, so if anyone has anything to say please say it right now." Then one of the board members raises her hand and she's like "Yeah I have a problem with her." And I'm sitting right next to her, like not awkward at all! That's when it started and it was, there's just no better word than bashing. At the same time I feel like I was trying to be the responsible leader. Yeah this was bashing and this was horrible, but at the same time this is how they feel. They wouldn't make this up, this is how they feel. And I'm going to listen to how they feel and then we'll see how things go from there. She felt like I was telling her what to do instead of asking her what to do. Then another eboard member accused me of not participating in the events. At those events I don't get to participate because as president I decided that there has to be that one person who oversees everything and that's how we make sure things run smoothly and that's the way we've been successful. The whole event was kind of my idea. I don't know, I didn't say that, but I was thinking I'm just gonna let them speak. And then another board member had a bunch of things to say like your tone of voice with me is very rude. So I kind of just took it all in and I kind of got, I didn't cry in front of them but I got kind of teary. I was like, to each person individually, I know that I made you feel that way and I don't want to deny your feeling but it was never my intention. Like for one member, it was never my intention to tell you what to do, that wasn't my intention and I apologize if it came out that way it's just that in the pressure of all the things that go on I may have slipped and raised my voice or stuff like that. To every person I tried to, I understand that you feel this way.*

Student leaders said that they learned one main lesson from feedback and recognition. It is an important lesson that is not commonly mentioned with any other event: they learned to understand others' perspectives and as a result see the bigger picture. Anais Nin (a famous author) said, "We don't see things as they are, we see things as we are." Feedback from others gives you a glimpse of another person's perspective. More feedback gives you an even broader perspective.

In a leader role, decisions have to be made, things need to be done. You lead by exercising your authority and expertise, and others follow. Right? These student leaders learned that life and leadership are not so simple. And maybe there is a better way. They learned that it is important to see other people as fellow human beings, and engender an attitude of respect towards them, even if they disagree. And in doing so, they come to understand values and assumptions leading to their own perspectives and that of others. Further, seeing an issue from multiple perspectives gave these leaders a broader understanding of the issue (see Table 7.1).

**TABLE 7.1** Lessons Learned from Feedback and Recognition

*What Is Leadership?*

*Identity*

- Self-identity
- Leadership identity

*Personal or Self-Awareness*

- Professionalism
- Balancing roles

*Learning and Reasoning*

- **BIG PICTURE PERSPECTIVE**
- Decision-making
- Learning to teach/learn

*Individual Competencies*

- Accountability and responsibility
- Adaptability and flexibility
- Resilience, persistence, and hard work
- Taking initiative

*Support Systems*

- Developing and using support systems
- Being a support system

*Working with Others*

- Communication
- Teamwork
- Dealing with conflict
- Dealing with diversity
- Delegation
- Inspiring and motivating others

*Getting the Job Done*

- Task skills
- Organizational savvy

*I was gone from the newspaper at this point, and another woman had taken over the newspaper as editor-in-chief. She came up to me personally and asked me to rejoin the paper, and I said "No, I haven't seen any proof that this organization has solved the flaws that I saw in it, so no." And she sat me down and we ended up talking. In the conversation, I asked how the newspaper was going and she said, "Well that's actually what I wanted to talk to you about. I'm thinking about succession planning" and this previous editor had burned many other bridges besides me so there was a dearth of people my year there. The new editor in chief had done a good job of rebuilding it, there were a lot of freshman and sophomores on the newspaper, but there was no one ready for a leadership position. She said I want you to come back to the paper and I want you to run for editor in chief. And I said you are out of your mind. You are absolutely out of your mind. Why would I do this? She sat there, we sat there, I think we got lunch, and we were there until closing. She talked about why I would be a good fit for this position. You know, she wasn't pulling out that I had run this organization or run that organization, although that was part of it, but she was talking about how people talked about me on campus, that I wasn't someone who took a lot of nonsense, which is important for an editor, that I was someone who worked well with a lot of people, important for an editor. I had good relationships with administration and faculty, again important. So she was pulling out all of these things that she had observed about me, and we weren't particularly good friends but she knew enough about me and she had looked into me and she had picked these things out that had made her want to work with me for eight months to the point where I could take over as editor. I ended up accepting and joined the paper and then ran and then won. Her faith in me and her observing of me taught me a lot about what it takes or I guess, what people are looking at.*

*It taught me that the smaller things matter too. There are always people watching you, they're always evaluating you. Performing well every day and going out there and giving your best to everyone, even if they don't seem important, you don't know what opportunities that's gonna open up later on . . . You know, the conversations that you have with the dean and then when someone's looking for someone and mentions you . . . conversations with professors we had in common and she had heard about me there. The conversations with people who you don't expect are going to continue to be part of your lives, you know, the freshman you gave directions to ends up recommending you to someone else, you know it gave me an appreciation for that interconnected web.*

In every single one of these events, the students were participating, they were trying, they were doing something that other people noticed—for good or bad. In order to receive feedback or recognition, you need to put yourself out there for others to see and evaluate. As a result of their actions, the students in my study received feedback. And in experiencing and hearing what others thought, their activation levels increased and learning processes were stimulated. They learned, not because the event challenged them, but because they heard something about themselves that challenged their own views and beliefs about themselves. This could be in the form of a conversation, a "bashing," some sort of recognition, or even a nomination.

There are two important pieces of information that are important to remember when you are receiving feedback. First, feedback from another person (you included) is information. It is not necessarily "true" or "false." A key factor to remember about feedback: it is one opinion coming from another individual's unique perspective. They are trying to correct the way that your boat is headed *from their point of view*. Second, feedback is often misunderstood as being a one-way communication between the feedback giver and the feedback receiver when in fact it is the process or overall *interaction* between the two including the change that occurs as a result of the feedback. You have done something, or behaved in some manner, or communicated some sort of message. Someone has observed or been the recipient of your actions and they respond. For the student leaders in my study, this response tended to be verbal feedback, though you could also get written, non-verbal (for example, a smile or a grimace), or even behavioral feedback (someone who previously was a friend suddenly won't answer your phone calls or texts). This response gives you an idea regarding how your message was received or your behavior was interpreted and whether you should modify it by changing it completely, by doing less of something, or by doing more of something.

## Mentors and Role Models

The student leaders in my research learned from three categories of people who changed the way that they did leadership. In this section, I discuss people who were senior to or supervisors of the student leader: Role models and mentors. In the next section, I discuss people who were at the same level as the students—their peers. And in the final section, I discuss people who are younger or came after the student leaders, these students look up to the leaders as role models and mentors.

Tryon Edwards, a theologian from the nineteenth century said, "People never improve unless they look to some standard or example higher and better than themselves" (Edwards, 1908: 56). Adopting successful people higher than you as mentors and role models is a powerful way to develop yourself as a leader. Mentors and role models were mentioned in 9 percent of the events that student leaders learned from and changed the way they did leadership. Some of these mentors and role models were remembered fondly, with students wanting to emulate them. And some of the interactions with mentors and role models gave students lessons in how NOT to lead. Below, I give an example of both.

## Mentors and Role Models to Emulate

*I met him in the second week of my freshman year. He lived in a completely different building and it was absolute chance that I ran into him and introduced myself and he took me under his wing. We had a lot in common, we exchanged numbers and we started a friendship from there. He was president of the National Honors Society at the time and also RHA. He told me great things about the university, how I could get involved, introduced me to the honor society that I am now on the eboard for, got me involved with a bunch of things on campus, we started a marketing club, tried to get me involved with the Campus Involvement Project, which is another leadership aspect to this campus. That was really the first thing that started to shape me was my introduction to him and him bringing me through things. He was my mentor until he left, he graduated last year. He is absolutely one of the people who shaped who I am right now. He was an environmental studies major and I am a marine bio major. By the end of the year I joined RHA as a representative and at that time he was the president, which means he sat on the eboard, which means he was always there. So we talked and got close and that is when he nominated me for NRHH.*

*He took a lot of kids under his wing. I know several people that I still talk to that owe him a lot of stuff. He is very passionate about this school. One of the things I took from him is to leave this school a better place than when we found it. It was just his thing to take people and motivate them. He is a great talker and a great motivator.*

## Role Models and Mentors Not to Emulate

*I had missed a weekly staff meeting because it was finals time and my schedule got all screwed up. It was a Tuesday night. Wednesday morning I called my boss, "Really sorry, finals, life got in the way. Let me come up to the office and you can run me through what the meeting was" and the answer I got was a very aloof, "Come up to the office tomorrow and we'll discuss this." I go up to the office, and it's my immediate supervisor and his boss, sitting in the room, closed door. You know, really intense here, talking to me about what a disappointment I was and how it's not appropriate for me to be missing meetings, and this is going in my permanent record, you know my employee record, and just really, really, heavy-handed, "I'm disappointed in you. How could you do this?" This was the first meeting I had missed in the three semesters I had worked for them and the weekend before that I had spent 18 hours in one of their offices to help them with an emergency that had come up that weekend. From my experience, I was doing everything they asked and then doing more and I had missed one meeting because finals studying had gotten in the way. And I felt their reaction to it was way, way over the top. Way over the top. In that conversation I pointed out that this was the first time I'd missed anything. And he goes "Well, you know, we're just getting you ready for the fall and we don't want anyone to think they can slack off and we have some people who don't bring 100 percent to the table" and I sat there thinking "But I'm not one of them. You had issues with other people on the staff and nothing direct you can say to them. Why am I the one who's getting this heavy-handed approach?"*

*It was one of those conversations where my relationship with the people involved hasn't been the same since. It was the last term where I worked for Residents Life. That position asks a lot of you. They asked us to give up our fourth of Julys and give up our Fridays and stay there until 11:00. They're asking a lot. It's just a very clear display that they were not following that up with the support that you needed to succeed in that. The situation, their reaction, was way out of proportion to what I had done, and I felt like they were not looking at me as an individual, they were looking at me as a member of their staff and if we don't come down hard on all of the staff there will be a rebellion or something.*

*I was very quiet, and I listened and I nodded, and that unnerved them more than anything because they knew me and they knew how I should be reacting to this and my boss goes "Do you have anything to say to this? What do you think of this?" And I said, "If you think that putting the fact that I missed one meeting down in my record is an appropriate reflection of the work I've given you, then you're my boss and that's your decision, I don't have to approve of it." That was it, and I ended up leaving the office and I felt better about giving that "I'm very not happy about this but I'm going to be professional about it" response, that felt better than raging or getting upset.*

Students learned two lessons from their mentors and role models (when a mentor or role model was mentioned, these lessons were mentioned at least 25 percent of the time): taking initiative and communication (see Table 7.2).

## Taking Initiative

In the previous chapter, I mentioned that students who joined clubs learned on their own to take initiative. But you can learn to take initiative in a very different way: through your mentor or role model. Sometimes, seeing someone you respect and admire demonstrate a willingness to get things done convinces you that you should and could do the same. Sometimes, you need someone to encourage you to take initiative, to boost your confidence that you can and should step up. And sometimes, you need to practice taking initiative with people. Role models and mentors can do all of these things. Here, a young man is talking about his mentor and how speaking up in his relationship with his mentor gave him confidence to say what was on his mind in other situations:

*He was my backbone for the year and it was really important to me. Having that support was important. [I learned] not to be afraid to say what was on my mind. I could say anything to him. He would get angry sometimes, but I knew what I said was in confidence and he would give me his opinion on anything. I was never afraid to express something I didn't like. It helped me to open up to other people. I am like a rock. I don't like to express emotions, it is not like me at all. I am straightforward and blunt. I just want to get things done. He opened me up and broke me out of my shell a bit. Before I would never talk about emotions, but I am more likely to now.*

**TABLE 7.2** Lessons Learned from Mentors and Role Models

---

*What Is Leadership?*

*Identity*

- Self-identity
- Leadership identity

*Personal or Self-Awareness*

- **PROFESSIONALISM**
- Balancing roles

*Learning and Reasoning*

- Big picture perspective
- Decision-making
- Learning to teach/learn

*Individual Competencies*

- **ACCOUNTABILITY AND RESPONSIBILITY**
- Adaptability and flexibility
- Resilience, persistence, and hard work
- **TAKING INITIATIVE**

*Support Systems*

- Developing and using support systems
- **BEING A SUPPORT SYSTEM**

*Working with Others*

- **COMMUNICATION**
- Teamwork
- Dealing with conflict
- Dealing with diversity
- Delegation
- **INSPIRING AND MOTIVATING OTHERS**

*Getting the Job Done*

- **TASK SKILLS**
- Organizational savvy

---

## *Communication*

Similar to taking initiative, some people learn this lesson by doing it because the event demanded it. They are put in a situation that required that they speak before a large crowd . . . and they did it. Another way to learn communication is by watching and modeling your role model or mentor and emulating their behaviors.

> *I guess the first event in my undergraduate experience here was when I first sat down with the head of our center for leadership and service. I told her that I would really like something to do outside of college. To go out into the community to volunteer, to do some sort of community service that was in some way connected to school and to stuff I did in the past. She said, "okay, I think the perfect organization would be [name], a local community based non-profit. And so we kind of played email tag for a while. Just kind of confirming—making sure that that was something indeed that I wanted to do or that I was interested in somehow. Not that it was a perfect fit per se but it some how matched my interests. And constantly engaging, just checking in with me, "Is that okay." "I'm going to do this." [He goes on to talk more about the organization he eventually joins.]*
>
> *[I learned about] really listening to someone, the willingness of someone to hear you out, to really listen to what are the things you want to do, what are your values, what are your goals and to help connect that to a real experience. I use an almost "monkey see, monkey do" approach, a modeling behavior. I was able to see what her actions were and able to replicate that in my own life and my own leadership experience. [When I work with others] I really listen to what are their values, what are things that they are doing, what do they want to do. What are their struggles, their hopes, their fears about it and to help challenge some of those fears. To help challenge some of those idealistic thoughts of what could happen as well. Then offering different steps for them. And with the stuff that they choose, helping supporting them through it, checking in as well, and then eventually letting them just do it on their own. So building them up on their own so you can get them to the point that you can let them go. But then constantly checking in with them and reflecting with them and asking them "How did it go?" or just challenging them at where they are at.*

When your role models and mentors challenge you (either in a positive way or a negative way), often learning happens in one of three ways. First, their encouragement may prompt you into putting yourself in a challenging situation. Second, you can practice skills with them before you try them in the larger world. And third, you can learn vicariously. Vicarious learning is a generative learning process (as discussed in Chapter 2). By watching your mentor or role model and how he or she behaves, and seeing what impact this behavior has on the situation, themselves, and others, you decide to behave in that way (or decide not to behave that way) as well.

The students in my research considered faculty, bosses, administrators, coaches, and other students to be their role models and mentors. All of the role models and mentors that the student leaders in my research mentioned were within the university setting. Having role models and mentors within the university setting is important. Most who work in the university take their jobs as educating and developing students seriously and like working with college students. In addition, they know the college system and where great opportunities for learning and development exist. However, there are a wide variety of people in your life that you may discover are also role models and mentors. Some may be in the university system, but depending on your activities, they may also be outside the university including parents, older siblings, teachers from high school, ministers, and bosses to name a few. In addition, some role models and mentors may only be there momentarily in your life, for example, a professor you interact with for a single semester. Others may last your entire college career and even beyond.

## Peers

Peers were mentioned in 7 percent of the challenges that student leaders learned from which led to a change in the way they did leadership. Interestingly, research shows that peer interactions significantly impact student learning across the board while in college: "The student's peer group is the single most potent source of influence on growth and development during the undergraduate years" (Astin, 1993: 398). Your interactions with peers impact your academic learning, cognitive growth and intellectual development, your persistence in pursuing your degree, changes in your attitudes, morals, values, political views, and your leadership learning (Pascarella & Terenzini, 2005).

> *The university is very diverse, I'm sure as everybody knows, and you're being in classes and hearing experiences from other people, and participating in the game "If you really knew me," I realized I'm grateful for what I have and for who I am and the experiences I've had in my life. Hearing stories from other people who are much less fortunate, it was just incredible to see that people were still being leaders after having a past that is much worse than mine. To elaborate on that, there are some other leaders on campus whose past was unfortunate. Things did not go the way that they should have, but you would never know by looking at them. Everyone has that*

*potential to be a leader no matter what the past was. It was a huge thing that stood out just because it was really a culture shock as well that there are people who have been raped or their parents . . . they come from these horrible backgrounds that to me is just completely foreign but they still stand out as leaders and they go out and they give back to the world. That's been a huge thing. That proves that no matter what your background is you can still give and be a leader and good things will eventually come to you.*

In terms of leadership learning, often the research findings are general, "Peer interactions leads to leadership development." Less attention has been paid to determine what it is that students learn about leadership when they interact with peers. The students in my study shed some light on this. In my research study, students indicated that they learned four main lessons in their interactions with peers (when a peer interaction was mentioned, these lessons were mentioned at least 25 percent of the time): self-identity, adaptibility/flexibility, developing and using support systems, and dealing with conflict (see Table 7.3).

**TABLE 7.3** Lessons Learned from Peers

*What Is Leadership?*

*Identity*

- **SELF-IDENTITY**
- Leadership identity

*Personal or Self-Awareness*

- Professionalism
- Balancing roles

*Learning and Reasoning*

- Big picture perspective
- Decision-making
- Learning to teach/learn

*Individual Competencies*

- Accountability and responsibility
- **ADAPTABILITY AND FLEXIBILITY**
- Resilience, persistence, and hard work
- Taking initiative

*Support Systems*

- **DEVELOPING AND USING SUPPORT SYSTEMS**
- Being a support system

*(continued)*

**TABLE 7.3** *(continued)*

*Working with Others*

- Communication
- Teamwork
- **DEALING WITH CONFLICT**
- Dealing with Diversity
- Delegation
- Inspiring and motivating others

*Getting the Job Done*

- Task skills
- Organizational Savvy

## Self-Identity

As I stated in the previous chapter, students are expected to and do develop their identities while in college. In the last chapter, as students engaged in various challenging experiences, they learned more about who they were and their relationship to the world. They learned about their personality, their values and attitudes, and their behaviors through these experiences. The students in my research also learned about who they are through challenging interactions with their peers. Here, though, the lessons were more relational; as they interacted with others, they saw themselves reflected back to them through their peers' eyes and gained an understanding of who they were as others saw them, which led to lasting change in their leadership.

> I am in a sorority. I held the position of Bursar, which is just a fancy word for treasurer and that included a lot of responsibility with the budget, time management, and communicating with the sisters about financial issues. There were a lot of experiences where I dealt with as part of that where I think I grew as a leader. There was an instance where a girl was not happy with what I was doing. If girls wanted to order things through the sorority they had to go through me because I am pretty much responsible for billing. I think she thought I was attacking her at one point and I didn't even realize. Maybe she was sensitive or it was a combination of both. I sent her a private email and she forwarded it to the sorority with a reply. Instead of going back at her and going what are you doing, what are you thinking, I calmly asked her if she wanted to meet. After she kept avoiding me, I tracked her down and tried to hear her point of view and tried to figure out how we can work through and past it and not dwell on the past, so we could move forward.
>
> For some people, not explaining why I need something in a certain way I may [come across] as too rigid. If I could go back I would have sucked it up or just changed

*it instead of asking her to keep reformatting it in the way I wanted. In certain cases, be more lax with some people and doing a bit more of the leg work myself if they are feeling like I am attacking them.*

## Adaptability/Flexibility

Student leaders learned to be adaptable and flexible in challenging experiences because they had to meet the needs of new situations on the fly without getting too stressed about it. They also learned about how to be adaptable and flexible through challenging experiences with their peers. You probably have long since learned the lesson that when you are interacting with your peers and your friends, you will not always get your way. You might get your way sometimes and graciously let a friend get their way another time. And you can negotiate, compromise, and modify plans or relationships so both are happy with the results. But the student leaders in my research also discovered that their peers responded in different ways to similar situations and that there were multiple and equally correct ways to handle similar situations. They did this by watching and talking with their peers. Once they understood that their way wasn't the only way, or necessarily the best way, or that there perhaps is no best way, they could be open to being adaptable and flexible themselves.

> *I think talking with all of my friends who were also leaders on this campus especially this year, because two of my best friends are actually president of their Greek organizations. Another one of my friends is president of the Up 'Til Dawn organization that we have on campus and I think just kind of talking things out with them and kind of sharing our different leadership ideas and stuff like that made me grow more as a leader because it made me see there is another way to do this because sometimes I don't always, it's hard to see a different leadership example from someone in your own club group or organization but looking at an outside organization and then kind of taking back on what you learned from there is helpful I think in a sense.*
>
> *There are definitely different outlooks on how to do things. There's not always one way to do something and that's definitely something that I learned from my friends and looking at how they handle a problem in their organization or how they change something in their organization or club.*

## Developing and Using Support Systems

In the last chapter, students indicated that they learned that when the complexity of their job increased, they needed to develop and use support systems. They needed to consult with others, both inside and outside the university on how to do things they did not know how to do. And they learned both the importance of and how to network. Finally, they learned that developing and using support systems were not distractions from their "real work" of leading, but were actually at the heart of their new roles. However, through challenging interactions with their peers, they learned how to make these connections work, learned benefits of having connections, and that having these connections was not just important but also a gratifying and even fun way to get work done.

> *I would say being a student ambassador. I know the girl who was in here before me is in all of these things too. Student ambassadors is a very selective group from campus and one thing I learned at [the university], you have 20,000 people. Then you have people that don't care, people that do care. All of the sudden you get involved with one person and people who care, you see it's all the same people involved in everything, literally. I know you and you're involved in six different things, and then my roommate is involved in one of your six things . . .*
>
> *A few people are in everything and it's really cool because then we all learn networking. We learn how to make those connections work. I was proud of myself last night because I was trying to get information, and I was texting people who I thought might know. I was using my connections. [A club] and student ambassador are groups of 13 and 22 on this campus and when you're selected out of everyone else, important people notice you. Once some important people notice you, many other important people notice you. I just got the chancellor's award for excellence from the student chancellor. Because I handed in my application there, the person who is in charge nominated me for another award I'm getting. It's a very big domino effect here. Student ambassador, who I got to be, involved with the assistant dean of students, but then you work events with admissions, and then you get to meet admissions people. Then I use to use these contacts for my other project. These people in admissions know who I am. They don't know everybody on campus. They say hi to me and I say hi to them.*

## Dealing with Conflict

In the business world today, a great deal of work is accomplished in teams. And these teams are increasingly diverse, the members are multicultural (if not global), and represent multiple functions in the organization (for example, marketing, finance, production). Conflict is a fact of life in teams. Members clash on team products or services and how to accomplish work. Some team members will not like each other. When team members are diverse, the differences in ways of thinking about and approaching tasks and work grow. For example, in an organization, while the sales team member may want to promise a customer that they will deliver the product quickly, the production team member may argue that it is not possible to produce in that short amount of time, while the financial team member may be worried about price.

As organizations have increased their use of teams, they are calling upon universities to prepare students to work in teams and be effective team players (NACE 2015), including learning about conflict management. In my research, learning this important leadership competency was most commonly associated with challenges when working with peers. When student leaders spoke of learning to deal with conflict, they included the importance of confrontation and how to do it effectively, creating and enforcing boundaries, how to manage conflicts with others, how to manage conflicts between third parties, and how to act during arguments.

> *My first event occurred my freshman year. I was very close to my RA, she happened to be from the same town as myself. And she was completely stressed about our floor. We had a heinous floor. It was just so bad. But the thing is that we were all really close friends and that made it 10 times worse for her, because you can't really choose who is to blame for situations. There was just one night, and everyone was just acting up. People were piling furniture through the walkways and everything. And she started crying, it was just too much for her. And she had a test the next day—it was a Sunday night. I like flipped out because I personally felt sorry for her and the fact that she hadn't done anything. She isn't the type of person who reprimanded, really like "I'll write you up" and stuff like that. So I reprimanded my whole floor. It wasn't as though everyone hated me after. This was the first time I was ever so assertive to people who I wasn't very close with, the fact that I was a freshman and in the same position as everyone else.*
>
> *If you address a certain situation a certain way, people will respond a certain way. And the way she addressed things, usually by threats and stuff like that, I feel that people don't respond. Especially if the person is fairly, almost the same age of you. It's kinda like who are you actually threatening? So I learned that you act in some way you get a certain response, you act another way and you get another response.*

Interacting with, communicating with, working with, studying with, or even just hanging out with your peers can be a rich learning experience. And college is a great place to do this. For many traditionally aged college students, during these years you are increasingly growing independent from your parents and increasingly focusing on peer relationships. In college, you are surrounded by others who are engaged in similar experiences, yet may be diverse in terms of age, how they were raised, culture, ethnicity, sexual orientation, and many other factors. You can learn valuable knowledge, ways of thinking, and skills from your peers. As you interact with people who are experiencing the same situations that you are (but may have a different background), you tend to do three things. First, you watch how your peers behave and the effect that it has on you, others, and the situation. If it works well, you might try it yourself. If it doesn't, you realize that perhaps you should try something different. Second, as you behave in certain ways, your peers react. You learn to see yourself through their eyes. If they react positively to something you do or say, you will repeat it. If they react negatively, you tend to question, modify, or change your behavior (or change your peers). Third, when you have open and frank conversations (and reflections) with your peers, you co-construct your knowledge, ideas, and interpretations of events together. Interacting with your peers can help you learn in many ways as I mentioned above. It can impact your academic learning, your cognitive growth and intellectual development, and your persistence in pursuing your degree. You may find your attitudes, morals, values, and political views changing. And it aids in your leadership development, in particular through developing your self-identity, by helping you become more adaptable and flexible in the way you approach the world, by helping you develop and use support systems, and helping you learn how to deal with conflict.

While you may have peers and friendships in many different areas of your life, research shows that it is important to form peer attachments at the college or university that you are attending. Students with friends at school, who are going through the same experiences, have better academic, emotional, and personal adjustment to school, and are more attached to their school (so are likely to stay in school) (Swenson, Nordtrom, & Hiester, 2008).

The college environment is generally an easy place to meet people and make friends. You are surrounded by thousands of others who are interested in meeting others. And there are many activities that are designed to help you get introduced to other students. Here are some ideas: (1) Depending on your school and program, there may be social networking groups set up. Join, scope out the members, see if there are discussions regarding meeting up (or start your own). If you see people on campus later that you think are on the social networking group, strike up a conversation asking if they are on the social networking site. (2) Attend pre-session or information sessions before classes start. While most of these may be for freshmen or transfers, perhaps there are additional ones for returning students. One big benefit of these events is that they are typically run by more senior students. Part of their job is to make everyone feel comfortable and included. If you are not sure what to do at these events, start by introducing yourself to the students running the event and ask them to introduce you to others. (3) If you live on campus, hang out in the common room of your residence hall and try to get to know everyone on your floor. (4) It's a bit more difficult to meet people if you live off campus. In fact, my commuter students have told me that you need to be "aggressively social" to meet people as a commuter. But it is worth it. Don't leave immediately after your classes are over. Check out the commuter lounge. Check out the local coffee house. And strike up a conversation. This is accepted within a university setting, especially at the beginning of semesters. (5) Classes are a great way to meet people. Think of group assignments as more than an assignment but also as a way to meet and get to know people. Chat with the students in front, next to, and behind you (as we tend to sit in the same seat repeatedly, you will be with them all semester). Set up a study group before a test. Ask to borrow notes if you miss a class and ask if the other student wants to borrow your notes if they miss a class. (6) I would be remiss if I didn't remind you of a key way to start your leadership development journey—join clubs, associations, student government, sports teams, there are any number of opportunities on campus. (7) Get a part-time job on or near (where other college students hang out) campus.

## Being a Mentor and Role Model to Others

Although this did not occur as often as other challenging experiences involving other people (it was only mentioned as a challenge 3 percent of the time), I am including it because at some point, you may realize that you are "that person" to another developing leader. Someone is considering you to be their mentor or role model.

> *I joined the peer leadership program. It's pretty much the students who run new student orientation for the students that come in in the fall. I joined that actually because it was a lot of fun at the school I had transferred from. And just the role that I had as an upperclassman to the new students coming in. It gave me a chance to be an upperclassman role model for the new students coming in. It was their first connection at the university before they made any friends here. Throughout the summer, we contact the students through email, let them know if they have any questions, let me know. Being a student here, I can tell you anything you really need to know about being at school. It was that first connection that they made, so it was when they got here, they had an upperclassman that they could turn to for whatever, be it personal or school related, anything. It was that kind of connection that you made with the students to let them be more comfortable around, getting accustomed to being in college now.*

In my research study, students indicated that they learned six main lessons in their as a role model or mentor (when being a mentor or role model was mentioned, these lessons were mentioned at least 25 percent of the time). Some of these were similar to lessons they learned in other challenging interactions with others such as self-identity, adaptability/flexibility, and communication. They also learned professionalism, being a support system, and diversity (see Table 7.4).

## Professionalism

Similar to learning professionalism through taking on a new leadership role in the last chapter, these lessons were about the proper way to act in a leadership role when dealing with others. They dealt specifically with how to present themselves

**TABLE 7.4** Lessons Learned from Being a Mentor and Role Model

---

*What Is Leadership?*

*Identity*

- **SELF-IDENTITY**
- Leadership identity

*Personal or Self-Awareness*

- **PROFESSIONALISM**
- Balancing roles

*Learning and Reasoning*

- Big picture perspective
- Decision-making
- Learning to teach/learn

*Individual Competencies*

- Accountability and responsibility
- **ADAPTABILITY AND FLEXIBILITY**
- Resilience, persistence, and hard work
- Taking initiative

*Support Systems*

- Developing and using support systems
- **BEING A SUPPORT SYSTEM**

*Working with Others*

- **COMMUNICATION**
- Teamwork
- Dealing with conflict
- **DEALING WITH DIVERSITY**
- Delegation
- Inspiring and motivating others

*Getting the Job Done*

- Task skills
- Organizational savvy

---

well and how to interact with others in a polite manner. The young woman in the example above learned that she needed to be concerned with how she showed herself to both the incoming students as well as their parents.

## Being a Support System

Interestingly, there has been a great deal of research on peer mentoring. Students who *have* a peer mentor, that is, the mentees, receive emotional and social support, enhanced academic performance, and are more likely to stay in school (Kiyama & Luca, 2014). Less attention has been paid to being a support system. The students in my research who served as mentors and role models needed to learn how to be a support system. They need to learn what is expected of them, how to act in this role, and about important boundaries.

> I am the first of my family to go to college, the first of all of my cousins on my dad's side and the second on my mom's side. Everyone knew after I graduated [high school] that I would be going to college. I had two places I was applying to. I got into both. That was a big leadership thing for me and I had my whole family, cousins, looking up to me saying "Well, if she can go to college then I can go to college." There was a lot of pressure there as far as trying to be a good role model. Once I moved in, cousins wanted to come and visit and find out how they could get into college, what I needed, and what my grades were, and what my essay was about. And as they started applying, they are asking me to help them write this or that. They see me doing well in school and want to know how its done. Being that 'go to' person and being that role model for them has been a really big thing.
>
> I learned that it's hard to be a role model that's for sure. It's definitely . . . constantly . . . you have to, not always be available, but definitely be available for them. You have to be there for them when your cousins or family members need you. You can't be like "Oh well I'm sorry I can't really help you." You want to set up a good example, that's something that I learned.

## Diversity

Another lesson that students learn from being a role model and mentor is how to deal with diversity. Lessons centered on learning about, appreciating, and learning to role model, mentor, and give guidance to people who are different from you in many different ways. Differences here included things like personalities, skills, communication styles, leadership styles, perspectives, cultures, and demographics.

> The second event was the commuter assistance program. It's a mentoring program where you get trained and then you get partnered up with incoming freshman and transfer students. You help them adjust to university life. It is like a mentoring process. You ask them if there are any questions, if they have any issues. You're their peer-to-peer to make their transition easy. With that program I got partnered off with 7–8 partners. I did that entering my sophomore year. I was three years in that program. In every year I got different people for the year.
>
> The fact that you have so many different people really made you understand there are many different people out there and how to deal with them. It helped you put

> *yourself in their perspective like "I was living on campus and now I want to move back home." You have to understand what their needs are and how to help them make a more comfortable transition. That was really beneficial.*

Mentoring and role modeling is an important challenge in your leadership development and has many important lessons associated with it. When you are the role model or mentor, your mentee will look up to you for the appropriate way to behave and will learn vicariously through watching you. First, leaders set the tone of the situation: If the leader acts in a supportive and caring manner, his or her followers tend to act in a supportive and caring manner. If the leader acts in a hostile and divided manner, again, others follow suit. Leaders set the norms, standards, and rules—how to communicate, how to treat others, etc. Second, leaders can motivate, inspire, and encourage others to attempt new challenges or they can discourage and demotivate. Third, leaders help others develop new skills and behaviors by encouraging others to practice new behaviors with them before trying them in the broader arena.

The students in my research were considered to be role models and mentors by younger or newly arrived students as well as by family members. Some were in formal peer mentoring programs within their colleges and universities while others were in more informal roles either within or outside of the academic setting. Stepping into a role modeling or mentoring role brings with it a number of important leadership lessons. Students mentioned that they learned more about themselves; they learned how to behave appropriately; they learned that they needed to be flexible and adaptable; they learned that they needed to be a support system for someone else as well as how to be a support system for others, they continued to hone their communication, and they learned to work with others who were different from themselves.

Many colleges and universities offer formal peer mentoring and peer leadership programs. These typically utilize upperclassmen to help ease freshmen and transfer students into the university. In these programs, there is generally a rigorous selection system and then you receive considerable training in how to assist incoming students to adjust to the university and help them persist in their attainment of their educational goals.

## Overview of Challenging People

Receiving feedback or recognition, being challenged by role models and mentors, being challenged by peers, being challenged by those who consider you to be their role model and mentor—what did each of these have in common? In each of these, the students were interacting with others in significant and meaningful ways. In some cases, the interactions were positive but powerful. In other cases, the interactions and outcomes were difficult, even painful, but powerful nevertheless. As a result of these interactions in which student leaders were working for, with, or through others, they learned and developed leadership. Table 7.5 summarizes the lessons learned through challenging others. The two major themes of learning through challenging others are (1) You learn about yourself—but differently from challenging assignments, you learn particularly who you are in the eyes of others; and (2) You learn how to better work with others—utilizing support systems, communicating, dealing with conflict, and dealing with diversity.

While much good advice suggests that we shouldn't define ourselves by others' opinions or accept the labels others give us, seeing yourself through others eyes is something different. Comedian Ellen DeGeneres said, "Sometimes you can't see yourself clearly until you see yourself through the eyes of others." This is called metaperception (your perception of how you are viewed by others) and developing this perspective is helpful in navigating social relationships. Humans want and need to fit into a social universe. We want to be accepted, to authentically connect with others, and to reap the satisfaction that comes with that acceptance and those connections. Developing your metaperception skills helps facilitate making connections with others. Although you see yourself in one way, realizing that others may be seeing something different, allows you to decide whether you want to continue behaving in a particular manner or that perhaps you can change, modify, or tweak your behavior. For example, I once participated in a group discussion. I

**TABLE 7.5** Lessons Learned Through Other People

*Identity*

- **SELF-IDENTITY**(peers, being a mentor)

*Personal or Self-Awareness*

- **PROFESSIONALISM**(being a mentor)

*Learning and Reasoning*

- **BIG PICTURE PERSPECTIVE**(feedback)

*Individual Competencies*

- **ADAPTABILITY AND FLEXIBILITY**(peers, being a mentor)
- **TAKING INITIATIVE**(mentors)

*Support Systems*

- **DEVELOPING AND USING SUPPORT SYSTEMS**(peers)
- **BEING A SUPPORT SYSTEM**(being a mentor)

*Working with Others*

- **COMMUNICATION**(mentors, being a mentor)
- **DEALING WITH CONFLICT** (peers)
- **DEALING WITH DIVERSITY** (being a mentor)

thought I was acting in a reasonable manner, but another team member was clearly growing aggravated with me for some reason. I was mystified. I thought back through what I had said and could find nothing offensive. Fortunately, the interaction had been videotaped and the team watched the videotape together. This team member pointed out to me exactly where she began becoming aggravated. It turned out that my words together with a particular hand motion suggested to her that I was excluding her and a few other teammates. When I saw and heard myself from her point of view, I understood why she was aggravated. Now I try to be aware of both my words and my non-verbal behaviors.

Similarly, developing social or people skills also facilitates and eases making connections with others. Learning how to make and use and be part of support systems, communicating, dealing with conflict, and dealing with diversity are all helpful in connecting with others. Participating in leadership (either as the person in charge, a follower, or in a group that is doing this together) assumes at least a minimal capability in making connections. And the way to learn these lessons is to interact with others in intense and meaningful ways, which leads to a rise in your activation levels. This triggers your learning processes.

In the next chapter, I describe yet another kind of event that led the student leaders in my research to change the way they thought about or practiced leadership. Instead of describing a challenging experience or role, or another person or persons, they learned within some sort of leadership development experience. In some cases, they took a leadership class, in others they participated in a leadership development program either on or off campus. What they learned from leadership development programs and how they learned it was different from what I have described in either this chapter or the previous chapter.

## References

Astin, A. (1993). *What matters in college: Four critical years revisited.* San-Francisco, CA: Jossey-Bass.

Edwards, T. (1908). *A dictionary of thoughts: Being a cyclopedia of laconic quotations from the best authors of the world, both ancient and modern.* Detroit, MI: F. B. Dickerson.

Kiyama, J. M. & Luca, S. G. (2014). Structured opportunities: Exploring the social and academic benefits for peer mentors in retention programs. *Journal of College Student Retention 15*, 489–514.

NACE (2015). Job outlook 2016: Attributes employers want to see on new college graduates' resumes. www.naceweb.org/s11182015/employers-look-for-in-new-hires.aspx

Pascarella E. T. & Terenzini, P. T. (2005). *How college affects students: A third decade of research.* San Francisco, CA: Jossey-Bass.

Swenson, L. M., Nordtrom, A., & Hiester, M., (2008). The role of peer relationships in adjustment to college. *Journal of College Student Development 49*, 551–567.

# 8

# LEADERSHIP COURSES AND FORMAL LEADERSHIP DEVELOPMENT PROGRAMS AS KEY LEADERSHIP LEARNING EVENTS

Colleges and universities generally believe that leader development should be part of their responsibility for preparing individuals to participate in a democratic and progressive society. As a result, many colleges and universities across the nation provide their students with leadership courses, curricular programs, and co-curricular programs that are designed to develop students' formal knowledge about leadership as well as opportunities and experiences to develop students as leaders. Close to 10 percent of the key events the student leaders in my research discussed were experiences they encountered in leadership courses, on-campus leadership development opportunities, and off-site leadership conferences. Of the 180 key events that student leaders mentioned, courses and formal leadership development programs were seen as events leading to lasting change in a student leader's leadership a total of 17 times. This is in line with what researchers found in the classic study conducted by the Center for Creative Leadership on organizational leaders. In that research also, about 10 percent of the events mentioned that led to lasting change in how the executives did leadership were leadership courses or programs of some sort.

However, I also need to note that the only two of the schools that participated in my research had curricular leadership programs. There are many rigorous curricular programs in existence, including the Buccino Center for Leadership Development at Seton Hall University, which was named the top program nationally among educational institutions in 2015 and 2016 (see www.shu.edu/leadership-development/). This four-year curricular leadership development program requires an application to get in and is quite intensive with diverse academic and experiential learning as well as executive mentoring and coaching. Had I interviewed some of the students in this program, I believe I would have had more events in this category, with plenty of lessons associated with them.

Although less often mentioned in my research than challenging events (about 50 percent of the events mentioned) or other people (28 percent of the events), the lessons students learned in the classroom or in formal leadership development programs were important ones, and not often mentioned in other challenging experiences. The purpose of this chapter is to discuss leadership courses and formal leadership development programs, both curricular and co-curricular, and both on and off campus, and the valuable lessons students learned from these.

## Learning in the Classroom

The International Leadership Association's website (www.ila-net.org/Resources/LPD/index.htm) lists over 1,000 undergraduate leadership certificates, minors, and majors from Adonai International Christian University in Sacramento, CA to Wright State University in Dayton Ohio. The National Clearing House for Leadership Programs (https://nclp.umd.edu/resources/CurricularPrograms.aspx) also provides a listing. Some colleges and universities list multiple leadership degree opportunities, such as the University of Worcester in the United Kingdom which lists four: a BS in Outdoor Adventure Leadership and Management, a BA in Business Leadership and Entrepreneurship, ABA in Business Leadership and Human Resources Management, and an BA Honors in Leadership. These listings are probably an underestimate as these are the programs that have requested that their programs be included in the ILA and NCLP websites. In addition, many colleges and universities have one or more leadership courses even if they do not have a formal degree program. There is no listing available for individual courses.

In courses, certificates, minors, and majors, students learn about formal theories of leadership as well as receiving assessments, skill and competency development, and experiential opportunities. Students often meet with organizational executives for coaching, mentoring, and networking opportunities. Assuming that you are already in a college or university as you read this book, if you are not familiar with what is offered at your school, look through the course catalogue, check out your school's website, ask your advisor, ask your teachers, and ask your peers for courses, certificates, minors, and majors. Here is an example of a student in a freshman leadership course, which led to her also getting accepted into another academic leadership program:

> When I was a freshman I was in my Leadership 101 class. I was so excited because it was one class that wasn't like a biology class. In high school I was involved in everything, president of everything, the principal gave me a super special award. I loved that school. So I came to this campus and thought, oh my god, I am like a small fish in this huge pond. It was overwhelming and the leadership class allowed it to be smaller, it allowed me to create a community, allowed me to feel like I belonged to something. Once I got more involved in the class, my teacher said, "I think you

*would be great for this program called the college fellows program." That was my freshman year, I got to be a college student fellow. What that entails was a semester of learning basic skills of how to deal with students in certain situations in terms of drugs and sex and giving them advice about college, because you have experienced it [during second semester freshman year]. We helped TA a Leadership 101 class the following semester [during first semester sophomore year]. So that semester I learned all these different skills and about leadership and what leadership is college. In HS you are given a position and it is fun, but this is college, it's more official and you have more of a sense of responsibility. So becoming a college fellow was the first thing that opened the door to everything else.*

## Learning in Co-Curricular Programs

In addition to leadership courses, certificates, minors, and majors, many colleges and universities offer co-curricular leadership development programs. The National Clearing House for Leadership Programs has a partial listing of these (https://nclp.umd.edu/resources/CoCurricularPrograms.aspx). Similar to curricular programs, you might be introduced to formal theories of leadership, receive assessments, have opportunities to develop leadership skills, and be exposed to experiential opportunities to practice leadership. In addition, some of these programs offer opportunities for mentoring, coaching, networking, and job shadowing with organizational executives.

Here is an example of the Blue Hen Leadership Development Program, a multi-tiered leadership certification program offered at the University of Delaware (www.udel.edu/usc/ld/bhlp/). This program was the recipient of the 2014 Outstanding Leadership Program presented by the Association of Leadership Educators (see www.leadershipeducators.org/Resources/Documents/Awards/ALE%20Awards%20-%20Past%20Recipients-15.pdf for other award winning programs). According to their website, the Blue Hen Program's mission is to "build individual and organization leadership capacity and foster engagement and service by providing diverse opportunities to question, explore, understand and apply leadership in order to positively transform one's campus, career and community." Blue Hen has a program for incoming freshman (QUEST), a four-tiered leadership development program open to all students, a leadership development program for athletes, and alternative winter and spring breaks.

In addition, you often get leadership development training as part of becoming an RA or a peer leader, or any number of leadership positions on campus. If you are not familiar with what is offered at your school, check out your school's website, ask your advisor, ask at your school's career center and Centers for Student Development, ask your teachers, and ask your peers.

Here is an example of a formal on-campus leadership development program mentioned by a student in my research:

> *I applied and was accepted to the Diversity Professional Leadership Network, which is run through the career center. They basically make you a well-rounded leader while pushing you toward your career goals. For example, they help you with all the different aspects about being a leader like delegating, working with others, learning your personality and how to work with each others' personalities in different scenarios and everything. It also helped to push me toward how those applied to my future career goals and whatever I was interested in. Because I was interested in attending medical school in the future, they matched me with someone I could shadow. Through the shadow, I was able to make good contacts. I had to apply and was accepted. There was an application process and an interview, but the majority of leaders on campus I think are part of this organization or they show some traits of leadership. We applied for this and through the interview they decide if you are a good fit for this program. They select you and there are about 40 students for different areas, some are not leaders, but most are developing leaders or potential leaders. So that was a really nice program I was able to participate in.*

Finally, there are also off-campus leadership development opportunities for college students. Some of these are highly intensive semester long opportunities such as those offered by Outward Bound (www.outwardbound.org/classic/college-expeditions/). Others such as the National Society of Leadership and Success offer online opportunities and regional conferences (www.societyleadership.org). Many off-campus leadership development programs are associated with on campus co-curricular programs, Greek organizations, or leadership development programs. That is, these on campus organizations are part of a larger network, which hold regional or national conferences that offer leadership development. Here is an example of a student leader at an off-site leadership conference offered through a residence hall association:

> *I got the opportunity to go to conferences: the NRHH and RHA conference, because both organizations are sister organizations and tied under the same national organization. So we go to conferences and I represent our NRHH chapter and we also have people representing RHA here. When we go we talk a lot about business and NRHH and RHA stuff. Then there are also all these program sections like leadership development. Usually, I go to the NRHH focused ones, but this one time I went to one and it was about leadership development. I loved it because the national conference I went to was before I was President, but the regional conference I went to was after I had a month's experience with stuff as President. I learned a lot about how to interact with people and your eboard, things from delegation and macromanaging to micromanaging. It would help me do a lot of things, because I would see things and be like this really needs to be improved because I can't micromanage everything for you guys because this is your thing. Although it would be good for me*

*because I could ensure it would get done, I need you to do it on your own. I was able to learn that when I went to the conference because I was experiencing all these and now they were telling me ways to get through it. So being able to go to conferences like that was definitely an experience to help me continue to go on with my role, but to help me continue to develop as a person too.*

In my research study, students indicated that they learned seven lessons through courses and leadership development programs (when a leadership course or leadership development program was mentioned, these lessons were mentioned at least 25 percent of the time): what leadership is, self-identity, leadership identity, taking initiative, communication, teamwork, and diversity (see Table 8.1).

## What Is Leadership?

Words matter—a common language helps you connect with others. As I stated in Chapter 3, when you are aware of the formal knowledge, theory, and language about leadership, it gives you a better understanding of leadership, it helps you understand yourself as a leader, and it helps you understand how your skills and competencies relate to leadership. In addition, you can better discuss with others about leadership as you share a common language (for example, in a job interview, you can use common terms to discuss your skills and competencies and the levels of expertise that you have attained).

*The first experience that comes to mind is my freshman experience being involved with the emerging leaders learning community.*

**TABLE 8.1** Lessons Learned from Leadership Courses and Leadership Development
Programs

---

*WHAT IS LEADERSHIP?*

*Identity*

- **SELF-IDENTITY**
- **LEADERSHIP IDENTITY**

*Individual Competencies*

- **TAKING INITIATIVE**

*Working with Others*

- **COMMUNICATION**
- **TEAMWORK**
- **DEALING WITH DIVERSITY**

---

*It taught me a lot of different things, principles of leadership that changed my overall perspective when I came to the university. The experience taught us that a leader has different perspectives, principles, types of leadership that you can use in different situations. I felt like there is no wrong way to lead, but there is a better way to do it, and different sources you can use, and different information you can use to lead. For example, different cohorts dealing with different age levels. For me, primarily college students dealing with peers.*

## Self-Identity

Self-identity is who you are, combining your values, your experiences, and how you perceive yourself. As you are developing as a leader, you are also developing into adulthood. As you learn and develop as a leader, this is impacting and changing how you see and understand yourself. And as your self-identity changes, this is impacting who you are as a leader. In this example, you can see that this student is developing her self-identity by meeting and working with other passionate leaders at a national leadership conference.

*I went to the national Bonner Leadership Conference and that was a really huge event for me. I met Bonners from all over the country who were doing great things and were spreading awareness about hunger, homelessness, poverty, education and how it is failing in our country. Overall it was just such a great experience and to be able to get such an enriching experience was really wonderful.*

*[I learned that] having all these leaders from different places, and they're doing all these great things, it really does enrich you inside and it's not just about giving to people or being a leader, it's also self-enriching and it is finding out who you are and finding out what you can do for the world or for the community or just for yourself. So that's really what I learned, that it's not just giving to other people, or being a leader, or starting something or whatever, it is for yourself as well, which a lot of people miss.*

*For myself I realized that being a leader makes you a better person overall. You see college students going out and partying and, for example, littering, and not caring about animal cruelty, or that people are dying of hunger, or they are homeless. So having that, realizing that these are problems and that there is something that I can do about it is what was really enriching because throughout my life I was always like "that is something that we should really do." I should take a stand, do something about this to change it, and I got that I can really do something. I can make a difference. Whether it's just in my life and one other person's life or a community.*

## Leadership Identity

You have multiple sub-identities within your self-identity including your identity as a student, as a friend, as a romantic partner, as a child to your parents or care-givers, as a member of your community, and as a leader, to name a few. The more you think of yourself in each of these roles, the more likely you are to enact this part of yourself. In terms of leadership identity, the more you see yourself as a leader, the more confident you are as a leader and the more likely you are to take on leadership roles and to develop yourself as a leader. Seeing yourself as a leader motivates you to seek out challenges and opportunities to build and hone your leadership skills. How you see yourself as a leader shapes how you act in a leadership role and how you relate to others. In this example, you can see a student leader's leadership identity emerge for the first time. At the very end of the example, you can see that this newly forming leadership identity is now leading to the desire to take on another leadership role!

> *Working in my service-learning leadership class at the [local primary] school for their after school program. That was when I first knew that I was a leader and I wanted to do something with the skills that I have. I was there as a tutor and had a small group of students assigned to me that I was working with along with two other college students. And we were tutoring them and we had to go through and teach them according to this packet [given to them by the school program]. So from there, I knew that now that I'm here teaching them and I'm being a role model for them. That was exciting. As I went through the process and I was going through the packet they were really making a breakthrough. I was taking more of the teaching role where the other two college students were like, "Hey you're doing a great job." So I was really sort of in charge of [the kids] and the other two college students were sort of just helpers. That was really when I knew that I wanted to be a leader, it was something that came easy to me and I knew that I could be that leader and I was very comfortable with it. I was very comfortable just kind of taking the lead like, "You wanted me to do it and this is what I could do."*
>
> *That was when I first knew that I was a leader and I wanted to do something with the skills that I have. I had that epiphany that I'm comfortable in this role and with what I'm doing and being that leader.*
>
> *I learned that I was happy being a leader. But at the same time, on the other two students that were there, I kind of hoped they would step out and go further with being the leader. I thought they may have wanted to have the same experiences I would, so they would realize that they could be leaders too and take some initiative to go further and to step up and be a leader as well instead of just sitting back and relaxing, and they didn't.*

*I learned that I did really well as a leader, I got a really great evaluation and I did really well in my class and from there my professor recommended that I become a Bonner. So that was also what I learned, that I'm good at what I'm doing.*

## Taking Initiative

As I wrote in Chapter 6, taking initiative is the first step in a series of action, that are needed to take charge (of yourself, of others, or even of a situation). Students learned more about themselves through their leadership courses and their leadership development activities. As they learned more about themselves and who they are, they gained confidence and took initiative to bring their real selves to the leadership arena. They were more confident in saying, "This is who I am" and less concerned of what others thought of them.

*Being selected to the National Student Athlete Leadership Conference. It was over 300 student athletes (divisions I, II, and III) that got selected. It was a conference that helped student athletes become a better leader so that they can better their campus and teammates as a whole. Being able to know how to work with other people from different cultures and bring the student population together, and being more open and not just worrying about your sport getting to know people from other sports and just getting to know the whole student body as a whole. Doing different types of workshops and getting to know everyone and going through stereotypes and learning how you can't go off of stereotypes even though everyone knows that you still have a judgment in mind. Opening everybody else's mind up as student athletes and it was a good networking thing we got to do.*

*I had a problem with voicing my opinions because I was afraid of what others might think. I would say the first two years of being on the team I was never completely 100 percent myself. Then we did a DISC assessment and everything it said was exactly how I was deep down inside and I was like "Oh my God how does this thing know exactly how I am?" And I wanted to be like that with my teammates, but then because they only knew a certain side of me for the first two years I couldn't bring it out and say "Guys this is who I really am." So I was kinda forced to act who they say I was for the first two years, but after going to the leadership conference I was like "No, I can be who I really want to be." And I was more open to talking more to them and sharing more experiences with them. It really helped open me up as a person and it made me want to be more involved and more active in the community and on campus.*

You can also learn more about specific skills in leadership courses and leadership development programs. You get pointers, tips, and strategies. And you often have a chance to practice those skills in a fairly safe and risk-free environment. Students in my research mentioned learning more about three leadership skills involving working with other people: communication, teamwork, and managing diversity.

## Communication

Students again mentioned communication as a lesson they learned in classes and workshops. Remember, they often mentioned it within their challenging experiences (Chapter 6) and in working with others (Chapter 7). Communication is a foundational skill that is the basis for so many other skills, leadership and otherwise. You will hone your communication skills for the rest of your life, in all your sub-identities, including as a leader. Here, although students mentioned learning the lesson of communication, it was more about the formal aspects of communication. In the example below, the student learned about how to speak in front of large groups, about how to acknowledge and address his fears, and actually practiced speaking in front of a large group.

> *It was an event in which they did different types of seminars and things of that nature. But one seminar that stood out to me was talking in front of people. I really wasn't a fan of talking in front of people until I had to do it more and more and more. So I did it. I went to the seminar and I actually came out with a lot of good things that I needed to do to become a better leader. Because as a leader you are always put into positions in which you have to talk to people. Not all the time, but one time you might have to talk to someone in front of a crowd. And then, what do you do now? Do you be scared in going up there? Or do you face the fear of speaking and see what you got to say?*

## Teamwork

Students learned in their first leadership roles that they had to work collaboratively together with others to achieve their team's goals and objectives. They had to learn the importance of working together as well as how to do it as they were doing it. When the students mentioned learning teamwork while in a course or leadership development program, they learned about teamwork, and practiced it in a safer and more risk-free environment. That is, they learned formal knowledge about teamwork and they participated in team development activities. I'm sure the students who mentioned this lesson in this category would agree that having a little practice under their belts before having to do it in the real world helped immensely.

> *In the winter we have our [Greek organization] national conference. I went there and I decided to participate in our national leadership development courses. That series of leadership development courses really brought me to where I am today with*

*everything that I can say that I know about being a leader. I took a teamwork devel-opment course. It was interesting because I was with a bunch of people, we were all brothers in [Greek organization], but we didn't know each other at all. So I was thrown in with a bunch of people that I didn't know and I had to figure out how to work as a team to do . . . We played a lot of games, like, leadership development games and things like that. I learned a lot about teamwork there.*

## Managing Diversity

Students in my research said they learned lessons on managing diversity in a number of different ways. Some mentioned that they learned about managing diversity when they switched from a leadership position in one organization to a leadership position in another organization—people in the new organiza-tion differed from people in the previous organization and they had to adapt. Some students mentioned that they learned about managing diversity when they mentored others. They had to learn that not everyone thinks or acts like them and that that is okay. In coursework and leadership development pro-grams, the lessons on managing diversity centered on learning that diversity is an issue that they would need to consider, about what diversity is, and the importance of valuing and appreciating others' differences and opinions. In this example, a student leader talks about the formal training he participated in to become a peer leader:

*How to be more culturally aware of what's around you. We go through a whole workshop on it. All the different types of ethnicities that are around you and the cul-tures they are about and how not to shut it down but more like embrace it and bring it in to our community. It really taught me how to connect with everyone around me and embrace all of our differences.*

## Overview of Leadership Development Coursework and Leadership Development Programs

Leadership courses, on-campus leadership development programs and work-shops, and off-campus leadership development programs, what did these have in common? In each of these experiences, students were able to learn about leadership, about themselves as leaders and as individuals, and about skills that are important to leaders. They were also able to practice new leadership skills in a safe and less risky environment. Table 8.1 summarizes the lessons learned through these activities. Three main themes of learning through leadership courses and for-mal leadership development program are: (1) You learn about leadership; (2) You learn about and develop your identity, in particular your leader identity (which is less often mentioned in the other experiences; and (3) Timing is important.

It is mainly through coursework and leadership development programs that students learn formal knowledge about leadership, how to think about and understand leadership, how to think about and understand how your behaviors, practices, and attitudes are linked to leadership, and how to articulate this knowledge and understanding to others using words that are common to both of you. This is a crucial lesson for college students who will need to articulate their leadership learning and development to others who will be selecting them for jobs or for future educational opportunities. If someone asks you a question about transformational theory, or servant leadership theory, or authentic leadership theory, or any number of other theories, you will be able to know what they are asking and answer them knowledgeably and with clarity. If someone asks about your strengths and weaknesses, you will not only have all the assessments that you have taken in leadership courses and leadership development programs to draw from, but you will use words to describe your strengths and weaknesses that the other person is probably familiar with. And as you analyze your own experiences, you will be able to connect those experiences to the language of leadership—to both formal theories and to leadership skills and competencies.

Similarly, it is often only when attending a leadership course or a formal leadership development program that we have the time and luxury to focus on ourselves and who we are as leaders. As we learn about formal ideas and theories of leadership; take assessments to better understand ourselves and leaders; and reflect on the linkages between ideas, assessments, and our own behaviors—all with the help of a teacher or a leadership expert—it is then we begin to articulate our leadership identities. And once we give ourselves permission (or even receive permission from others) to embrace that label, "leader," then our leader identity begins to form. Once formed, it becomes a sub-identity within our overall self-identity and will continue to grow as we attach formal knowledge about leadership to it and attach our experiences to it.

The third theme that arose in leadership courses and formal leadership development programs was timing. The formal courses were often mentioned as being early in the student leader's development process. In fact, the course often launched the student's foray into leadership development. Within the course, they saw something in themselves or they were recognized by the teacher and encouraged to take a next step. The formal leadership development programs occurred at the right time. The medical student who made good contacts, the President of NRHH chapter who went to a conference before becoming president then another one a month after becoming president, the athlete who was afraid to be herself for two years—they all needed something and the leadership development program provided it—often it was just the needed nugget among the array of other workshops that the student leader attended.

Leadership development coursework and formal leadership development programs do not often substitute for challenging events learned in the fires of experience. Properly used however, they can start or enhance the leadership development journey and should be considered as part of everyone's leadership development journey. That said, I have two caveats to mention. First, remember that everyone is on their own leadership development trajectory, and it is a journey that will last your lifetime. If you are in a situation during college where your only option is to take a leadership course as an elective, or add a leadership certificate or minor, then it is still a great start. Second, as I briefly mentioned above, colleges and universities are starting to offer more and more challenging leadership certificates, minors, and majors, as well as leadership development programs. These may include within them the fires of experience and opportunities to learn from others, which lead to the powerful and plentiful leadership lessons. For those who are attending schools with these programs, you may find that these are more than enough.

In the next chapter, I describe the final key event that led the student leaders in my research to change the way they thought about or practiced leadership. Instead of describing a challenging experience or role, or another person or persons, or some sort of leadership development experience, the universe threw them a curve ball. Students encountered a hardship or a difficult situation in which they felt alone and had a lack of control over the event. They had to confront themselves, and they had to take appropriate responsibility to handle the situation. What students learned in these hardships were some powerful lessons, indeed.

# 9

# USING CHALLENGES THAT
# LIFE THROWS US

## Hardships as Key Learning Events

One of the surprising events from the original research conducted by CCL (McCall, Lombardo, & Morrison, 1988) was the extent to which hardships arose in the executives' minds as being important to their development as a leader. And the college students in my research were no different; they mentioned hardships as key leadership learning events as well. The purpose of this chapter is to discuss how hardships that students may encounter during college can be learned from.

Risk and failure is a fact of leader development. Challenging experiences that prompt learning and development are often marked by risk of failure, and sometimes actual failure occurs. When you interact with others, not all encounters are pleasant. You might even fail a test in your leadership course! But hardships are different from challenges, people, and coursework and programs, even if these were not successful. The above events have some degree of choice inherent in them. We know going into them that there is a possibility it won't turn out well. Hardship, we don't choose. It finds us. Hardship is a hard circumstance to endure, and it pushes us to the brink, sometimes even making us question our own survival. It includes suffering, and requires painful effort as we work our way through. It is disruptive; we can't go on with our routine and our life as we have in the past. And it is ambiguous: the path through it is not clear (Stoner & Gilligan, 2002). There is generally a sense of loss, a lack of control, and a feeling of aloneness. To overcome hardships, individuals must confront themselves.

The executives in the original CCL study mentioned six types of hardships that they learned from: (1) personal trauma threatening the health and well-being of themselves or their family; (2) a career setback involving demotions and missed promotions; (3) changing out of dead-end jobs and risking entire careers to do so; (4) business mistakes in which bad judgment and poor decisions led to failure; and (5) subordinate performance problems forcing the executive to confront people with issues of incompetence or with problems such as alcoholism (McCall, Lombardo, & Morrison, 1988). The college students in my research mentioned five similar types of hardship. Of the key events students mentioned in my study, 5 percent were: (1) personal illness and injury; (2) dealing with race or gender bias; (3) lousy jobs; (4) losing elections they thought they had as good as secured; and (5) problems with others.

Critical illnesses and injuries are significant life events. Although there has been a reduction in mortality from childhood and adolescent critical illnesses and injury due to advances within critical care (Manning, Hemingway, & Redsell, 2013), the hardship of the illness or injury and surviving it is traumatic. Another hardship involves situations in which a student experiences or witnesses bias, prejudice, or discrimination. Our students mentioned enduring events where their race and gender were front and center, but others may confront biases due to size, sexual orientation, religion, ethnicity, social economic status, and others. Some students reported jobs that were too tough for them. They were stuck in a situation where they couldn't perform well, couldn't figure out what to do, and couldn't figure out how to get out of the situation. Students assumed they were going to win an election or get a position and had their hopes dashed. And finally, some students spoke about having to work with people who were problematic in some way.

When we suffer from a hardship, we receive a wake-up call. We need to decide what really matters and become clear on our values and who we are. We may be stimulated to search for new meaning and understanding in our lives. And we get a dose of reality regarding the limits of what we can control. We learn that while it is not always possible to control our immediate situation, our environment or even our own destiny, instead our greatest realm of control is how we respond to situations as they occur and after they occur (Moxley & Pulley, 2003). Here is an example of a student who thought he had an election in hand, and didn't win. It was unexpected, it was disruptive, and he wasn't sure how to proceed though he considered quitting. He received a wake-up call but gained a sense of control in his own post-election actions and reached a new meaning and understanding about his leader development. A lot was packed into the losing of an election:

> This event was actually negative. I'm a brother of a coed service fraternity, I served with them in my freshman year and in my sophomore year, I decided I was ready to take on an eboard position. Up until the week before the election I was the only one running. I was so set on having this eboard position, I thought it was going to be great. The week before the election, two other people decided to run. I didn't

*think much of it because I had been talking to people about it all semester, kind of campaigning for it. I knew I had the qualifications.*

*I didn't win. I was destroyed because of that. I didn't get the leadership position. In the fraternity, our principles are leadership, friendship, and service. I knew I had already developed, well not to my fullest potential, but I had already been developing a lot in service and friendship and I really wanted to develop more in the leadership aspect and I thought that was the only way to do it. What I learned is that I was wrong. The week afterwards I didn't want to do anything, I was ready to quit. But I took a step back and realized that wasn't the right thing to do, and if I was really passionate about this whole leadership thing I had to stick with it and take it in potentially in other ways.*

Of all the key events, hardships are probably the most difficult to learn from. And if we do learn from them, there may be a significant length of time between enduring the hardship and extracting the lessons from it. We are tempted to distance ourselves from the hardship, or blame something or someone else. But there are rich lessons that can be learned if we endure the suffering and look inward. Student leaders said that they learned two main lessons from experiences in hardships (when a hardship was mentioned, these lessons were mentioned at least 25 percent of the time): self-identity, and developing and using support systems. In this chapter, I'm going to add two additional lessons that are commonly associated with hardships but weren't necessarily mentioned by the students in my research. Although students mentioned this less often (it was mentioned more than 20 percent of the time), one key lesson commonly associated with hardship is resilience and persistence. A final lesson commonly associated with hardship is compassion for others, but this was not mentioned by my students. However, I'm including a discussion of learning compassion in this chapter as well (see Table 9.1).

**TABLE 9.1** Lessons Learned from Hardship

*Identity*

- **SELF-IDENTITY**

*Individual competencies*

- **RESILIENCE AND PERSISTENCE**
- **COMPASSION**

*Support Systems*

- **DEVELOPING AND USING SUPPORT SYSTEMS**

## Self-Identity

Learning about the self arose as an important factor in many of the key events that students mentioned as impacting who they are as leaders. They learned about themselves in their first leadership experiences, when they took on positions that increased in scope and scale, when they led a project team, when they interacted with their peers, when they served as a role model or mentor to someone else, and through leadership programs and coursework. In fact, self-identity was one of the most commonly mentioned learnings across the board. And here too, students who endured a hardship also mentioned learning more about who they were as a result of the hardship. However, when the key event was a hardship, students first felt a loss of identity, which then led to the rebuilding of a new sense of identity as they made sense of who they were before and the new person they were after the hardship. In this example, the young woman emerges from her hardship with both the discovery of an internal drive she didn't know she had and a new identity that includes her old identity (a volleyball player), her new internal drive, an expanded identity (academics), with the idea that maybe there was even more she could do ("I was capable of more than what I was"):

> *A big event that came to my mind was when I was injured in volleyball, I had major arm surgery and I wasn't able to play for 10 months. This caused me to do a lot of internal reflection and I had to find strength from other areas. I had always relied on my physical strength and I was always defined as "the volleyball player." I didn't play for 10 months and for the first few months it was a really tough and painful recovery, and it was really slow. It was hard to stay positive and keep moving when I had to. I found this drive in me that I didn't know I had. I ended up doing better on all my rehab than they expected me to. I was really determined. I know I would come back from it and be able to heal from it, but found this inner drive and aggression, just a different side of me that I didn't know I had. I guess sometimes it just takes an experience like that to bring that out in you. I had to redefine who I was as a person because I was always a volleyball player and then I wasn't. All I did was go to class and work out a little bit and do my rehab. That experience made me focus more in the classroom, because I thought, ok if I can't be great at volleyball, which was what since early high school I prided myself on. So I couldn't do that, so I wanted to be great at whatever I could do. So I applied myself more in academics and I think that drive in pushing through that and pushing through rehab applied to my academics. I think that is when my GPA really skyrocketed from what it was. Then the following year when I was able to play volleyball again, I maintained that. So, the experience sparked something in me that I was capable of more than what I was.*

## Developing and Using Support Systems

Students learned that social support plays a pivotal role in dealing with hardships. They discovered that they couldn't go it alone and didn't have to. They turned to family, friends, co-workers, advisors, and coaches for encouragement, to help them deal with the hardship, and for advice. In this situation, the student was dealing with a problem person, as well as dealing with the fact that many others quit rather than having to deal with this person and left her with many more responsibilities than she had signed up for. She discovered, though, that she could get support from the problem person, those who she felt had abandoned her, and her larger network to help her work through the situation successfully.

> *I was stage-managing for Theater second semester of my sophomore year where we ended up having some trouble with the director. Three set designers quit, a lighting designer quit, all the seniors by the way. I was a sophomore; my production manager was too. My assistant stage manager was a freshman and our producer was a senior, but had never done tech before and decided half way through that he wasn't good at it and tossed most of it on me and the production manager. I don't know if that was the best example of leadership for me or from the other sides. It was definitely a very stressful time and ended up with me taking on a lot more responsibilities than I thought I signed up for.*
>
> *Initially I felt abandoned by the upperclassman, felt thrown to the wolves. But one of my close friends called and said that even though they couldn't make it through dealing with the director that they were there for advice. So, I made sure that I was still going to some of the upperclassman for advice, talking to our advisor, and whatnot. Asking for help from them to learn what to make it go as smoothly as possible. I wasn't getting along with the director either and I knew that wasn't going to be productive, so setting up a meeting with her. Find out what she needs, what the cast needs, and putting it all together.*

## Persistence and Resilience

In hardship events, students mentioned a lesson that was not commonly mentioned with any other event. They learned to be resilient and persevere. Given that perseverance is defined as steady persistence in a course of action, especially in spite of difficulties, obstacles, or discouragement (http://dictionary. reference.com/browse/perseverance) and resilience is defined as the capacity to recover quickly from hardships (http://dictionary.reference.com/browse/ resilience), this is not surprising! In fact, resilience is only something you realize you have (or can develop) after a hardship. Those who are resilient and persevere understand and accept their current reality, believe that life, and the current situation, is meaningful, and improvise solutions with whatever resources they have (Coutu, 2002). In this situation, freshman year, this student witnessed a racist act directed at a friend of his. And no one outside their association seemed to get it or care. His group took the bias incident, thought about appropriate and meaningful ways to publically respond, and came up with a solution. In the end, it didn't matter to this young leader that others didn't get it; he had no control over that. What mattered was that he did get it and that he did something about it.

> We were preparing for Soundfest, a showcase for Greek organizations. The person who was running for Soundfest chair received a very offensive message posted on her dorm room door. Someone had drawn a noose around her flyer. And she was African American. So it was one of those situations where you don't know why a person did it. Are they targeting just her, or the whole organization, or general population of African American students? It was the first time I really experienced such offensive behavior. I was a freshman so it was, like, welcome to college!
>
> During the actual Soundfest, we were supposed to perform. Instead of performing, we sat down on the stage and the vice president of the organization spoke and she generalized our feelings about the situation and told people that while we are not saying that we are going to blame everyone on campus, or every Caucasian person on campus, people are responsible for their actions. It caused a lot of commotion because everybody was like, "So what is the point of this sit down?" No one really responded to this by saying "Oh sorry," just people kind of blew it off, and were like "Oh well, it's that group complaining again." At the same time, it brought attention to the situation.
>
> I learned that I can't allow these sorts of situations to bring me down. My favorite quote is "To be successful, you must be resilient." And I feel like it was a really harsh situation but what can you do to bounce back from it was more important than dwelling on it.

## Compassion

A final lesson that I would like to include is compassion, although this was not mentioned by the students in my research. Compassion is a feeling of deep sympathy and sorrow for another who is stricken by misfortune, accompanied by a strong desire to alleviate that suffering (http://dictionary.reference.com/browse/compassion). Research shows that people who have had more, and more severe, hardships in life, such as loss of a loved one at an early age or threats of violence or consequences of a natural disaster were more likely to empathize with others in distress. And they were more likely to donate money or donate their time to help others (DeSteno, 2015).

While compassion can be seen as selfless, it may actually be a strategy for those suffering a recent or past hardship to regain their own footing. For example, in the aftermath of a very bad hurricane in my town, I had the option of either staying home in my dark and cold house or doing something. About the only thing to do in a town full of water was to help others who were in worse shape than I was. I helped the elderly at shelters get their prescriptions filled and other elderly and disabled who stayed in their homes get food and water, I helped sort food and emergency supplies, I did whatever was needed. Along the way, I met many other volunteers in the same situation who decided they would rather help than sit and feel sorry for themselves. One of the best predictors of well-being is social relationships, and although the volunteers all wanted to help, we were also enhancing our bonds with others during our own times of hardship, and ultimately enhancing our own well-being.

## Overcoming Hardships and Extracting the Lessons

Learning from hardship differs from learning from challenges, learning from other people, and learning in courses and programs. When the students in my research spoke of learning from challenging experiences, they were learning on the run, they were learning as they were doing, they were learning because they had to in order to accomplish their work and succeed. When the students spoke of learning from others, they received information and perspectives about the situation and about themselves that was either different from their own perspectives or confirmed their own perspectives. This information and perspective had an impact on themselves, their work, and their relationships, if not immediately, then soon after. Participating in courses and programs was all about learning. In each of these situations, the time between the trigger to learn (the event) and the activation of learning processes was short.

Hardships differ for two reasons. First, hardships may or may not be a learning experience. Some people face a hardship with resolve and courage, and rise above it, eventually turning the experience into a learning and growth experience. Others do not, and can become stuck, or bitter, or lose hope. Second, the lessons from hardship are usually learned in retrospect—sometimes long after, through reflection. Researchers Youssef and Luthans (2007) explain that the individuals who go through a hardship and then learn from it need to take the time, energy, and resource investment to recover, rebound, and return from the hardship before moving on.

What do those who rebound and learn from hardships do differently than those who do not? A social scientist, Professor Charles Stoner, and the CEO of a company, John Gilligan, joined forces to find out (Stoner & Gillian, 2002). They interviewed 35 CEOs and other top executives and found that they all followed a fairly consistent path as they worked through their hardships. It turns out that the path they discussed is actually similar to the learning model that I introduced in the second chapter, with the inclusion of an additional stage between the triggering event (the hardship in this case) and the activation of the learning processes. They found that after the hardship, the executives discussed a disillusionment stage before entering into the learning processes of transformational learning through reflection and through conversations with others, which resulted in change.

During and after the hardship, the executives were disillusioned. They were down, hurt, and confused. But even within this darkness, they understood two things. First, they realized that this disillusionment and these emotions were a natural reaction to the hardship. Second, they realized that this disillusionment and these deeply felt negative emotions were only temporary and would pass. With this understanding, they committed to "working through" their disillusionment. They did not try to simply "get through" the hardship; they took an active role in moving through this stage. One way they did this, like the students mentioned above in my research, is that they turned to significant others. But not just any significant others: these others helped them, uplifted them, and encouraged them rather than encouraging wallowing or self-pity, or reinforcing the idea of defeat.

It is at this point that the executives moved into the learning model I outlined in Chapter 2. Once the executives suffered from a hardship and worked through the disillusionment and dark emotions that they knew were a normal reaction to the hardship, then learning processes were activated, specifically transformational learning through reflection and through interactions with others. The executives in this study spent time in introspection, in examining their own thoughts and feelings. They spent time thinking about their perceptions, thoughts, feelings, and behaviors. They tried to understand their assumptions and biases. And as a result made meaning of their life circumstances in a way that allowed them to move forward. In addition, they engaged in transformative learning through others. They continued to turn to trusted others, and through conversations and interactions were able to gain perspective and continued to make meaning of their circumstances, which continued to allow them to move forward. What is key here is that they reflected rather than ruminated. The executives came out of this stage with four main learnings: (1) rediscovering significance in their lives and what really counts; (2) realizing or reaffirming core values; (3) understanding and accepting limits; and (4) recognizing that there are some things they can affect and some things that they are unable to control.

Here were some of the changes that they made as a result. First, they courageously made changes to their life and their work and carried this courage with them as they moved forward. This courage was not bold or dramatic, or even self-assured. Instead it was the decision to take the next step even when risk is present and error is probable. For example, one of the managers in their study who had a business crisis said, "You keep trying things. Some of them, maybe even most of them, fail. But a couple of them work. You just keep trying." Second, they reframed the hardship that they had suffered into a challenge that they had overcome. And if they could overcome a challenge of this magnitude, why then, the next challenge would be surmountable as well! Third, they came to better understand what they could control and what they could not control. Moving forward, they could now "turn loose" what they could not control and instead concentrate their energies on what they could have an impact on. And finally, they gained a firm understanding that you can't go it alone and you don't need to try. They had turned to significant others, family, friends, business colleagues, and peers in the midst of the hardship and it worked. This was now the process that they would engage in whether in another challenge or not.

## Summary

None of us are exempt from hardship. Many students reading this book have already encountered tremendous hardship in their lives: personal trauma that threatened the health and well-being of themselves or their families, being the victim of a crime, dealing with biases, dealing with big mistakes, dealing with big let downs, and dealing with problematic others. Others may have been lucky so far. But everyone is handed hardship in some capacity in their life—no one will be immune. In this chapter, I have discussed some ideas about how to turn those hardships into life and leadership lessons.

Learning from hardships does not happen the same way as other key events; it requires time to deal with the hardship and the negative emotions that naturally emerge. During this time, you need to devote your attention and your energy to "working through" this stage, giving yourself space to process what happened but also knowing that you want to and will move on. The length of the time needed in this stage will depend on the hardship and the person. While we may wallow, and feel victimized, self-pity, and defeated for a while, we realize that these feelings are natural and temporary and that we need to work through them. Once you have worked through this disillusionment stage then the learning processes can begin, namely transformational learning through reflection and interactions with others. I discussed some lessons that you may learn above: self-identity, developing and using support systems, persistence and resilience, compassion, and courage, but there are many more. While life hands us hardship, and it will, we decide how to respond and move forward.

## References

Coutu, D. (May, 2002). How resilience works. *Harvard Business Review*. https://hbr.org/2002/05/how-resilience-works#

DeSteno, D. (October 18, 2015). The funny thing about adversity. *New York Times, Editorial*, p 11. http://dictionary.reference.com/browse/compassion

McCall, M. W. Jr., Lombardo, M. M., & Morrison, A. M. (1988). *The lessons of experience: How successful executives develop on the job*. New York: The Free Press.

Manning, J. C., Hemingway, P., & Redsell, S. A. (2013). Long-term psychosocial impact reported by childhood critical illness survivors: A systematic review. *Nursing in Critical Care 19*, 145–156.

Moxley, R. S. & Pulley, M. L. (2003). Tough going: Learning from experience the hard way. *Leadership in Action 23*(2), 14–18.

Stoner, C. R. & Gilligan, J. F. (2002). Leader rebound: How successful managers bounce back from tests of adversity. *Business Horizons* (November/December), 17–24.

Youssef, C. M. & Luthans, F. (2007). Positive organizational behavior in the workplace: The impact of hope, optimism, and resilience. *Journal of Management 33*, 774–800.

# 10

# MAKING THE MOST OF YOUR KEY EXPERIENCES

As the findings from the students in my research demonstrated in Chapters 6, 7, 8, and 9, developing your leadership boils down to what you do with your challenges, opportunities, and even hardships. In your leadership development journey there are two things that stand out: (1) You need to seek challenging experiences rich in opportunities for leadership learning, development, and growth; and (2) You need to figure out the learnings from those experiences. The purpose of this chapter is help you do this in three ways. In the first part of the chapter, you will analyze your past key events to determine the messages you have learned about leadership, who you are as a leader (right now), and what skills and knowledge you have learned up to this point. In the second part of the chapter, you will analyze the challenging experiences, people, and coursework in your current situation for learning opportunities, and if necessary, consider ways to enrich your current experiences. Finally, in the last part of the chapter, you will be encouraged to take personal control of your ongoing leadership learning by setting goals and initiating plans for your own leadership development during college or in the next few years.

As you proceed through this chapter, remember that you are on your own leadership learning trajectory. Your learning and development path to leadership is yours. What is right for you is different from what is right for other people. There is no right starting point, no single path to your leadership development, no right amount, and no end point. There is no level of IQ, no traits that you are born with. There is no big-name school to attend, no "right" experience that you must do, no set list of competencies to master, no magic, no guarantees. There will be hard work, special interests, and talents that guide you in certain directions, along with unexpected opportunities and challenges, a little luck (good and bad), and the need for courage. The closest thing to a secret recipe for leadership development is: "Go for it, and make the most of it."

## Determine Your Past Key Events, and Lessons Learned from Them

Even if you are not aware of it, you already have ideas about leadership and who you are as a leader (or not) that guide your actions. These ideas have been developed gradually over time from observations and experiences. Most people are not aware of the degree to which these ideas influence their thoughts about leadership, their readiness to learn leadership, their motivation to lead, their leadership identity, and their own leadership behaviors. It is helpful to begin this part of your leadership learning trajectory (no matter where you are on it) with a look at the past to determine key events that have had an impact on you and what you learned about leadership from them.

In this exercise, you will discuss (and write about) the key events you have already encountered that have changed or affirmed your ideas on what leadership is, your own motivation to lead, your leadership identity, and the way you actually lead, and the lessons that you have learned from each of those experiences.

Go back in your life as far as you can remember. Come up with as many key events as you can. Think of events that happened in your family, school, community, religion, camp, jobs, or even with your friends. These events could have been something you experienced or something you observed. List each experience separately, describe what happened, who was or were the leader(s), and why it stands out in your mind. Was it a challenging event such as joining and participating, a first leadership role, an increase in scope and scale, an organizational switch, leading task force, a start-up, a turn-around, or something else? Was it a specific person or persons such as receiving powerful feedback, a boss, teacher, parent or family member, clergy member, community member, mentor, or coach, a peer, someone that you mentor, or someone else? Was it a class or a program? Was it a hardship? Was it a positive experience or a negative one? Compare your events to the ones on the charts. Are they similar or different?

For each event, list all the lessons you learned from it. Did the event change (or reaffirm) your ideas about leadership? Did you learn something about yourself in general or something about you as a leader? Did you learn something new, a skill, or a new way of doing things, a new way of seeing things, or even a new idea or theory about leadership? Did you learn how not to do something? Compare and contrast your lessons to the lessons on the charts. Analyze each lesson: Was this a useful lesson to learn as you move forward or do you think you might want to continue to tweak and modify it or change it completely?

Once you have listed all the lessons for each event, consider all your lessons together. Are they clustered in a few areas or have you learned a variety of lessons? What have you learned about what leadership is, about your own motivation to lead and readiness to learn leadership, about your leadership identity, or about your own leadership behavior up to this point?

If you are discussing this with a partner or in a group, compare your experiences with each other. Do you have similar experiences (e.g., RA), but discovered they were interpreted in different ways? Compare your lessons learned. Did you learn similar or different lessons for similar experiences?

If you discussed this with others, also capture these events in your leadership learning journal. Write a paragraph on each event and the lessons you learned from that event. Put the events in chronological order.

At the end of the events, write a paragraph for each of the following topics: (1) what you have learned about leadership and your general thoughts about leadership; (2) what you have learned about your motivation to lead (or not) and where this comes from; (3) what you have learned about yourself as a leader; (4) what your strengths are and what you need to develop or work on; and (5) how your understanding of leadership has changed over time. As a note, you will probably recall additional events and additional lessons over time that you had forgotten before this. Make sure to capture them as well and include them in your journal. You will use the events and the paragraphs later in this chapter, then again in the next chapter.

This set of events and the lessons learned represent where you currently are in your leadership learning trajectory. This is your starting point as of right now. And I assure you, wherever you are right now on this journey is the right place for you to be.

## Determine How Developmental Your Current Situation Is

In this section, you will take a look at your current position or positions to determine how developmental they are for you in terms of your leadership learning and development. In terms of positions, think broadly. Consider jobs (both on campus and off campus), roles in clubs, fraternities, or sororities, work you are doing with professors, work you are doing with your church, volunteer work, family responsibilities, and any other positions that you might be engaged in.

Within each position, you are encountering different experiences. While experiences are necessary for you to learn leadership, not all experiences are learning experiences. To be a learning experience, they must trigger your learning processes. As I stated in Chapter 2, learning processes are triggered by pressures, demands, challenges, and opportunities that affect you in such a way that you cannot continue what you are doing in the same way and be successful. When you are unfamiliar with a task or situation, or if you are exposed to a circumstance that is difficult or either extremely intense or highly meaningful, your activation level increases and starts your learning processes. Research identifies five task-related characteristics that make experiences developmentally challenging for the development of leadership: unfamiliar responsibilities, high levels of responsibility, creating change, working across boundaries, and managing diversity (McCauley, Ruderman, Ohlott & Morrow, 1994).

Take the following survey (see Table 10.1). If you have more than one position, re-take the survey for each one.

**TABLE 10.1** Developmental Challenge Exercise[1]

Once you have thought about your current position, rate each of the following on a five-point scale. Add your scores for a total score for each position:

**Rating Scale**

0. Not at all descriptive of my current position.
1. Slightly descriptive of my current position.
2. Moderately descriptive of my current position.
3. Very descriptive of my current position.
4. Extremely descriptive of my current position.

| | |
|---|---|
| 1. This position involves doing something very different from what I've done in the past. | |
| 2. This position involves a tremendous intellectual/strategic/problem-solving challenge that is different from any I have encountered before. | |
| 3. This position requires building a club (or organization) from scratch or fixing/turning around a club (or organization) in trouble. | |
| 4. My success or failure are both possible and would be obvious to others and myself. I think I could fail or not perform well in this position. | |
| 5. There is high pressure for me in this position (deadlines, high stakes, long hours, my work viewed as critical). | |
| 6. This position requires me to take-charge. I need to show individual leadership. | |
| 7. This position requires building a team. | |
| 8. This position requires influencing people, activities, and factors over which I have no authority or control (I am working with supervisors other than my boss or I am working with partners or peers, or I am working with outside parties, political situations, or customers). | |
| 9. This position involves working with new people, a lot of people, or people with different skills. | |
| 10. I am closely watched and monitored by people whose opinion counts. | |
| 11. This position involves interacting with a boss (whether or not supportive) and their view is critical to success. | |
| 12. I am missing something important that would help me be successful (little management support, limited resources, missing key skills or technical knowledge, lack of credentials/credibility, etc.). | |
| **Total** | |

**TABLE 10.2** Interpreting Your Scores

Now that you have your score or scores, you need to understand what the scores mean. Here are some interpretative guidelines:

**Your Score**

| | |
|---|---|
| 40–48 | This position may be too challenging for you, making it difficult to develop yourself. Are you feeling overloaded and very uncertain about how to do many things? If you are feeling this way, rather than devoting your energy to problem solving, decision-making, and learning-related processes, you may be focused on worrying over possible performance failures and evaluation anxieties. |
| 30–39 | This position is suitably developmental. One-half or more of the challenges are present in a big way. |
| 20–29 | You may have been in this position for a while and it is no longer much of a challenge. Your performance might not be as good as it once was because you may be getting bored. You need to spice it up to make it developmental. |
| 0–20 | You've been in the position too long, it's old hat, it's no longer challenging. You need to spice it up to make it developmental. |

If you scored in the 40s for any of your positions, take a moment to consider your options. Will this position continue to be this challenging for a short time or for a longer time? Is there anything you can do or anyone you can speak to that can help reduce the challenges somewhat? You need to actually reduce the challenges a bit to make this an experience where you can work on leadership development. Skim the next section, but definitely don't add more challenges at this point in time.

If you scored in the 30s for any of your positions, you are being suitably challenged at the moment. You are in a situation that can help you develop your leadership. Read the following section for ideas to incorporate once you have mastered this situation and are ready to add new challenges.

If you scored below 30, you may be in some fun and interesting positions, but they are not challenging you to develop your leadership. Read the following section for ideas on how to add challenges to your current position or positions to ramp up the leadership development potential in what you are already involved in.

## Develop Your Leadership In Your Current Position[2]

It is not always necessary to change or add positions to what you are already doing to create opportunities for leadership development. Rather, you can add challenges to what you are doing now. Read over the following for ideas and pick ones that you have not done before (or have not done well) to add to whatever positions you are in. Again, you can add these to jobs, to roles in clubs, fraternities, or sororities, work you are doing with professors, work you are doing with your church, volunteer work, and any other positions that you might be engaged in.

1.  *Think about small challenges to add to your existing position.* For some, these might be challenge enough. For others, these can add up to something bigger. Here are some examples:

    - Organize a meeting and put together the agenda.
    - Run a team meeting or briefing session.
    - Develop and implement a training program to teach a skill.
    - Find a way to cut costs, implement it.
    - Streamline a process or operation to make it faster, or smoother, or easier.
    - Speak at a meeting.

2.  *Take on a challenging temporary "stretch" assignment.* Here are some examples:

    - Volunteer to fill in for your supervisor or manager when they are on vacation.
    - Volunteer to participate in or lead a small project from start to finish.
    - At work, take a temporary lateral move to another part of the organization.
    - Volunteer to help launch a new initiative or program.
    - Help turn around a struggling project.
    - Develop a new product or service.
    - Teach a process or course to your team or others.
    - Benchmark other teams that are known for high performance and create a plan to help your team meet or exceed expectations.
    - Solicit feedback from peers, direct reports, and key constituents regarding a project, program or process that is under-performing. Propose several improvements.
    - Attend a regional or national conference put on by your professional association, fraternity, or sorority.

3.  *Add a new responsibility to your current role.* Here are some examples:

    - Offer to manage project budgets to develop financial and budgeting competencies, or shadow the person doing this.
    - Represent your group at a cross-functional meeting on campus or serve as a liaison between groups on campus.

4.  *Add some direct leadership experience to your current role.* Here are some examples:

    - Run for a leadership position in a club, fraternity, sorority, or professional association on or off campus that you are already a member of.
    - Take on a leadership role in a social, community, or volunteer organization that you are already involved with.

- Serve as a mentor to other colleagues, supervisees, or staff members.
- Lead a division- or campus-wide project or task force that will have campus policy implications.

5. *Put yourself into situations where you interact with people who might become a mentor or role model.* Here are some examples:

   - Go to faculty office hours to discuss a topic of interest in the class or to ask questions.
   - Join a favorite professor's research laboratory.
   - Be a teaching assistant for a favorite professor.
   - Serve as the student representative on a university committee or task force.

6. *Put yourself into situations where you interact with people who you might be a role model and mentor to.* Here are some examples:

   - Put in place and run a session to onboard new members to your club, fraternity, sorority, or eboard.
   - Work with incoming freshmen or transfer students in some capacity.

7. *If you are working on research, ask you professor if you can present at a conference.*
8. *Seek feedback about your performance from your bosses, peers, and others.* Put in place a plan to improve. Implement the plan.

The above list suggests a few ideas for adding leadership development opportunities to your current position. The possibilities are endless once you know about and begin looking for challenges. But remember, learning doesn't automatically occur because you have added a challenge or two to your position. You could do these new tasks using the same techniques, methods, or behaviors that you have used in the past. To learn something new, not only do you need to challenge yourself, you also need to do something different within those situations.

Another way to add challenge is to decide ahead of time what you would like to challenge yourself on. Do you have a strength you would like to hone or take to the next level? A skill or competency that you have never addressed or that needs development? An area that you are curious about and want to learn about or how to do it more or better? You can pick a challenge or experience that will push you to learn more about or how to do something or how to do something differently. Here are some examples:

- *You have been content being a follower and doing whatever others suggest.* You might plan a weekend with and for your friends when you return home over the holidays. Figure out who is in, what time, and where everyone should meet; make reservations; if need be, collect money ahead of time, etc. Or plan a social gathering and figure out the venue, the decorations, the meal plan, etc.

- *You are not sure yet whether you really want to be a leader.* And are not terribly confident that you would be any good anyway. But you figure everyone should know how to plan and run a meeting. For a group project in a class, take this role on. Do some research on the web about how to develop an agenda and how to run a meeting. Develop an agenda before each meeting. Try to get students to stick to the agenda at the meeting (you might have to experiment with how to do this). Take notes during the meeting. Keep a record or minutes of what happened and who agreed to do what by when. Journal about what worked and what didn't work.

- *You are comfortable leading people you already know, but your communication skills go downhill with new people.* Your goal might be to attain a level of comfort and confidence in speaking with people you don't know. Attend a conference (maybe don't present at this first one) and make a goal to network at events and become more comfortable talking to people you don't know. Agree to represent your group at a cross-functional meeting on campus. Join (not necessarily lead yet) a campus-wide project or task force and plan to speak at every meeting.

- *You have been working as a server at the local ice cream store part-time since high school and you want to learn a little bit more about how to run a business.* Talk to your boss about adding more general management duties to your position. Let your boss know that you can "take over" for a few hours if need be (or regularly manage a shift), or volunteer to train the newcomers, or streamline the store workflow so that customers move through more smoothly. Ask if you can help with paperwork (ordering supplies, etc.).

- *You are the president of a club and think you are doing okay.* But you have never actually confirmed that or asked for feedback. Seek feedback about your performance from your advisor, peers, and others. Put in place a plan to improve. Implement the plan. Go back to the people you asked and determine if they notice a difference. Have you improved?

For this exercise, it would be great to have a one-on-one meeting or small group meeting with a boss, advisor, coach, mentor, teacher, or even a peer (you can do this for each other). In this meeting, plan to discuss the fact that you would like the opportunity to add more challenges to your position or role. You might go into the meeting with some ideas about what you would like to develop, learn, hone, or do differently. Or you might start the meeting brainstorming with the person on what you might like to learn or develop next. Choose one or two to target. Then brainstorm ideas for how to create opportunities and challenges for you to learn from. Use the lists above to begin your thinking, but be creative. Set up another meeting to debrief how you did before you leave this meeting. If the challenge will take some time to do, you might also want to set up some brief meetings to check in and discuss how the challenge is unfolding. Then implement your plan. Journal as you are implementing your plan regarding what is working and what is not working. Some questions you might consider include: Where are you improving your skills? Where are you struggling? Do you need something to help you (for example, more support from a coach)? Remember, it will probably not go smoothly as you are learning as you go. You should plan on tweaking and experimenting and changing. If your challenge is going smoothly, you might want to explore why—are you doing anything new? Once you have completed your challenge, debrief with the person you originally met with regarding what you did, what worked, what didn't work, and what you learned as a result. Discuss such things as what you learned, whether you reached your goals that you laid out before you started your challenge, and how you plan to use or apply this learning and development moving forward. Also include where you succeeded, where you struggled, and if you had the chance to do it over again, what you would do differently. Write a short description of your challenge and what you learned, and add this to the section of your journal that you started in the first exercise. Then repeat! This is a process you can use throughout your life to develop your leadership or many other things.

## Planning Your Leadership Development While in College

Just as you can purposefully choose challenges within your current position to give yourself learning opportunities, you can also be proactive in your leadership development plan in a larger way and purposefully develop or modify your own leadership identity, change the way you think about leadership, build or improve on leadership skills and competencies, and learn formal knowledge about leadership by setting goals, putting in place multi-year plans (and then semester by semester plans), implementing the plans (implementing back up plans if the original plans don't work), and getting feedback, and making changes to your goals and plans. In other words, you can plan your leadership development while in college (and beyond) rather than letting it happen to you.

This type of development is a self-paced process that works on the principle of progression. It is self-paced because you decide what and how much you want to take on. If you live on campus and don't have a job, you might be able to do a great deal of leadership development while in college. If you live off campus, have family responsibilities, and work full-time, you may have to be creative to find ways to focus on your leadership development. In terms of the principle of progression, you do similar things, but gradually build the scope of what you take on. Here in college you may be doing smaller or different versions of much larger leadership endeavors that you will take on later in life. Becoming comfortable communicating with larger and larger groups while in college may turn into a TEDx talk with thousands of viewers, post college. Starting a club in college may turn into starting your own business later.

In this next exercise you will be creating what I call a "living document" regarding your leadership development plan for the rest of your time in college (or in the near future if you are near the end of your college years). You will continually edit and update this plan. It will never be "quite right" and that's okay. No one's life unfolds exactly as planned.

## Leadership Development Goal Setting Exercise

1.  *Visualize yourself at the end of college (or the near future) in terms of yourself as a leader.* Consider this in terms of your career goals and your other interests. What are your long-term goals? Write this down in your journal and title it "My future self as a leader." Just allowing yourself to visualize something, you will begin to think about it and how to make it happen. And if you think about being a leader and how to develop yourself as a leader, you will begin to see opportunities and take steps to make that happen. Walt Disney said, "If you can dream it, you can do it. Always remember that this whole thing was started by a mouse." By envisioning yourself as a leader, you allow yourself to think of yourself as a leader, and the more you act as though you are a leader. Your leader identity starts emerging.

2.  *Having a vision is a great starting point.* As I stated above, you will almost unconsciously begin moving in the direction of that vision. But an actual plan will help get you there. In these next few steps, you will put your leadership development plan in place.

    a.  *First, to remind you, in Chapter 3, I listed four areas to learn about leadership.* These were: (1) learning about yourself in general and yourself as a leader; (2) learning about ways of thinking about leaders and leadership; (3) learning leader skills and competencies; and (4) learning formal knowledge about leadership. To the extent possible, you want to try to grow in all four areas while in college. Try to include all of these in your plan.

    b.  *Gather your materials regarding where you are today.* If you have a resume, include that. Include the scenarios from the first exercise in this chapter. Go back to the exercises in the assessment chapter. In this step, identify gaps between where you are now and where you hope to be at the end of college (your goal from Step 1, above). What are your strengths? What and where do you need to develop? Do you need to work on your leader identity? Your motivation to lead? Your formal knowledge about leadership? What skills and competencies will you need to reach your vision? Write all of this down in your journal. If you are able, it would be great to discuss this with someone you trust. They may affirm what you are seeing, or they may suggest other ways of seeing yourself. Write all of this in your journal. Title it: "My current self as a leader."

    c.  *Using that analysis, identify what you want to develop now and in the near future (during your time in college).* Pick a few strengths that you would like to hone, and a few areas that you would like to develop. You cannot and should not try to develop everything. Write this list down in your journal. You can always change, modify, or add to this list later.

d. *Find, research, and consider your options to develop your leadership.* As I discussed in Chapter 6, universities have numerous roles you can use to develop yourself as a leader. These include student governance organizations (student government associations, residence hall government, honor councils, and judiciary boards), intercollegiate and intramural athletics, academic and professional organizations, volunteer and service-related activities, multicultural activities and organizations, the arts, clubs, and fraternities and sororities. There are also on-campus jobs (for example, Residence Hall Assistants). You can volunteer to do research with professors, or volunteer to be a teaching assistant. If you are a commuter and it is difficult to get to campus on a regular basis, consider off-campus jobs, community associations, your house of religion. If you are caring for family members, you can think about that in terms of leadership development as well. Find out what leadership courses, certificates, minors, and majors are available at your college. List options that you are interested in; include roles, courses/certificates, and minors/majors that you are interested in pursuing as well as roles you are currently in (developing yourself within your current situation, as you addressed above can and should be part of this plan).

e. *Draft a four-year action plan (or however long you have left in college) as to how you will develop yourself.* Plan on doing something each semester. If your plan includes being selected for a position or being elected to a position, you should definitely put in place back-up plans (for example, if you would like to apply for an RA position, or run for vice president of a club, you should have a second plan in place in case you are not selected or elected). This plan should be viewed as flexible and changeable. For example, if you are planning on running for a position on your sorority board, but a teacher or advisor unexpectedly suggests that you join a campus-wide project planning team that looks really interesting, don't feel bound by your original plan! You may find that once you make up your mind to develop your leadership, you actually have more opportunities than you realized and that you will have to pick and choose.

f. *Consider progression in your plan.* Here are some examples: Join a fraternity or sorority. Then lead a special project in that fraternity or sorority, then run for a cabinet or eboard position, then run for a position on the Greek council. Work as a referee for intramurals, then work on getting promoted to the next level, and the next level. Become a Residence Hall Assistant, then work your way up to Residence Hall Assistant Coordinator.

g. *Write the plan down.* Title it: "My leadership development action plan."

3. *Begin to put your plan in place.* What was the first action that you decided to do? What do you need to do to make this first step in your plan a reality? Within your positions and roles, engineer the right kind of developmental

experiences using the exercise you conducted above. Take the initiative to look for ways that you can learn new skills through experiences that also help your supervisor/manager, team, unit, or department achieve its goals.

4. *Change plans as necessary.* Did you change your major? Did your vision change? How does this influence your plan? Make changes as necessary. Is your plan working? If you find that the plan is not working as expected, put your back-up plans in place. Or go back to step 2 and make some decisions on what to do differently. And capitalize on opportunities or challenges that arise unexpectedly. Your vision and plan will not unfold exactly as you wrote it. You will need to continually modify it.

5. *Get feedback.*

   a. *Set up meetings with your boss, advisor, teacher, mentor, or coach to discuss your proposed development experiences.* Discuss and confirm with them the learning and development that you are prioritizing. Ask them to help you track your progress.

   b. *Set up regular check-in meetings with your boss, advisor, teacher, mentor, or coach.* The time frame for these check-ins are flexible. What is right for you? Once a year? Once a semester? Once a month? This might change depending on what you are working on or where you are on your plan. Review your plan before the meeting so you are prepared. Send your boss, advisor, teacher, mentor, or coach any major changes before the meeting so they are aware of them. Leave meetings with notes on your progress and updated plans.

   c. *Remember to check in with your peers for feedback as well.* Are there others you should ask for feedback?

6. *Monitor your progress.* Keep a leadership journal for reflection. Having one experience after another is not sufficient for learning, development, and growth. Instead of plunging immediately into the next experience where you will probably repeat your mistakes, you need to reflect on what you learned. Constantly ask yourself: Am I meeting my goals? What am I learning, what do I need to do differently, what habits have gotten too comfortable, what do I need to do from a leadership perspective? Determine if your plan is working and adjust your plans if need be. Other questions to ask yourself periodically include What did I use to think leadership was and what do I think it is now? and How am I changing as a leader?

7. *Celebrate!* If you meet a goal, then take a moment to celebrate it.

8. *Plan ahead for the next step on your plan.* As your leadership development experience is progressing, update your plan to mark accomplishments and learning acquired. As you are completing one step, ensure that you are already planning on putting the next step into place.

9. *Realize that visioning, creating goals and plans, implementing plans, and getting feedback, and monitoring progress are all key leadership skills.* You are learning and developing your leadership by doing this exercise!

## Summary

A famous psychologist, Albert Bandura (2003), theorizes that people have the ability to exercise control over the nature and quality of their life, that they can intentionally make things happen by their own actions, and that this is the essence of what it means to be human. In Chapter 2, I discussed that in order to learn, you need triggers to learn and a readiness to learn. In this chapter, drawing on his work and my work, you have been encouraged to take control of your own leadership learning and development. In the first part of the chapter, you have reflected on your past experiences to glean previous triggers to learn leadership and your learnings. Then in the second and third parts of the chapter, you designed challenging experiences and long-term plans to trigger your learning— you have developed goals and visions, created action plans, and put in place ways to help you persist in accomplishing goals and reaching your vision, again reflecting along the way and making changes as needed. Finally, taking control in this manner helps you become more open and ready to learn.

I want to end this chapter with a note of caution and an odd statement to make in a book on leadership development. Somewhere, somehow, along your leadership learning trajectory, you will fail. You may fail epically. Your leadership learning journey is not a straight line up. Failing is part of your journey and if you don't fail, you haven't taken challenges and risks. I read a sign on Pinterest that said, "F.A.I.L.: First Attempt In Learning." When you fail (and you will), pick yourself up, reflect, talk to someone (which we will address in the next chapter), log your lessons, and if need be change your vision and change your plans.

## Notes

1 These items are drawn from: Lombardo, M. M. & Eichinger, R. W. (1989). *Eighty-eight assignments for development in place: Enhancing the developmental challenge of existing jobs.* Greensboro, NC: Center for Creative Leadership.
2 See http://hrweb.berkeley.edu/learning/career-development/skill-development/developmental-experiences

## References

Bandura, A. (2001). Social cognitive theory: An agentic perspective. *Annual Review of Psychology 52*, 1–26.
Lombardo, M. M. & Eichinger, R. W. (1989). *Eighty-eight assignments for development in place: Enhancing the developmental challenge of existing jobs.* Greensboro, NC: Center for Creative Leadership.
McCauley, C. D., Ruderman, M. N., Ohlott, P. J., & Morrow, J. E. (1994). Assessing the developmental components of managerial jobs. *Journal of Applied Psychology 79*, 544–560.

# 11

# YOUR SUPPORT NETWORK FOR LEADERSHIP DEVELOPMENT

*Something that I think was important in my leadership development was the support system here. My professor, the university staff, they are really good at supporting you, at bringing out the potential that they see in you. I think, with all the support of my boss and other staff members on campus that I've dealt with my whole four years, I don't think I would have done it. The support system here is good and it helps build and bring out leaders.*

*(College student leader in my research)*

Have you ever watched a child learn to jump into the deep end of a swimming pool . . . where the water is over their head? If a trusted adult were there to catch them, with a lot of encouragement, they could be convinced to jump. It is similar with leadership development. It would be difficult to choose to jump into risky and challenging positions where you could fail without a trusted person (or more) at your side to support you. And it would be hard to learn while you were in the midst of a challenge without that support—you would be more concerned with getting your proverbial head above water and breathing than learning and developing. And without that support, you might not be willing to try another challenging experience. During leadership development, "support helps people handle the struggle and pain of developing. It helps them bear the weight of the experience and maintain a positive view of themselves as capable, worthy, valuable people who can learn and thereby grow" (McCauley, VanVelsor, & Ruderman, 2010: 12).

The purpose of this chapter is to explain the final element needed for your leader development in the ReAChS model: support. This chapter explains how you will learn and develop as a leader if and when your feelings of insecurity and anxiety caused by participating in challenging leadership experiences are grappled with through assistance from people in your support network. The chapter also includes exercises to help you determine who is already in your leadership development support network and if need be, how to expand your support network.

## What Is Support and Why Is It Important for Leadership Development?

As you saw in Chapters 6, 7, 8, and 9, and the exercises in Chapter 10, leadership development can be difficult, failure is possible, and it might be downright scary and anxiety provoking. You need to step out of your comfort zone. You need to let go of what you know and do something different. You need to do this in front of other people who are watching and evaluating you. You are at risk of failure. When demands exceed capacities, people tend to get anxious (DeRue & Wellman, 2009). Your leadership development support network provides the support, assistance, and resources you need during these times.

You have a social network. This is all the people that you associate with and have relationships with; it is everyone you know, everywhere (take a moment and think about all the people you know). Your social network can include people in your family, your community, your social circle, school, and work. You might be close to some of these people or see them on a regular basis. Others you might see once in a while. Others might be "friends" on facebook, "connections" on LinkedIn, or followers on other social networking sites. Still others might be people you have only met once or a few times (for example, friends of your parents that you see once a year or less).

Your leadership development support network is a subset of this social network. It is a resource pool of people from your social network that you draw on selectively (that is you choose the appropriate individuals to be in this support network and keep those persons who are not particularly helpful in your leadership development from getting in the way) that gives you resources or assistance in developing and growing as a leader (Seahore, n.d.). This leadership development support network can include people from anywhere in your social network: people from school, work, community, family, and friends. Interestingly, supportive people may or may not be aware that they are part of your leadership development system network. Your relationship with them may be close and personal or distant and impersonal.

## Why Do You Need a Leadership Development Support System?

Your leadership development support systems can be used for different purposes during your leadership development process, depending on the situation or situations that you are dealing with. Here are five possibilities (Seahore, n.d.):

- *Gaining new leadership competencies*: One function of the people in your leadership development support system is to help you develop new skills and competencies. You need individuals to help you find challenges and encourage you to actually do them and try out new skills. People who serve in this function may also serve as teachers and models during your challenging experiences, and provide the emotional support when you may be feeling awkward or inept in dealing with new skills or situations, or are anxious, or scared.

- *Re-establishing competence*: As you are learning, you have to let go of old strengths and develop new skills. As you go against the grain, you feel stressed and uncomfortable. You will feel awkward at the new skill—it doesn't come naturally. You may find yourself with a performance decrement—you aren't doing as well as you did before. You may find yourself functioning at a very low level of competence. You need individuals to help you cope with the stress and return to your previous level of functioning (while using the new skills and competencies gained along the way instead of reverting back to the old way).

- *Achieving specific objectives*: Many of the objectives you strive for as you participate in leadership cannot be met by yourself. You need to collaborate with others and you need contributions from others. You need to include individuals who have skills and resources that you don't have to work with you and be a part of your leadership development support system.

- *Maintaining high performance*: It is important to include people in your leadership development support network even when you are doing well, in order for you to continue working at a high level. However, when things are going well, it is tempting to neglect your support system! Unfortunately, this leads to two problems. First, these individuals can continue to help you during the good times. Second, it is difficult to go back and ask them for help when you need it again.

- *Emotional support*: Finally, all along your leadership development trajectory, you will need people who are there for you through thick and thin, who help you handle the struggle and pain of developing, and help you maintain a positive view of yourself.

## What Are the Different Roles that People in Your Leadership Development Support Network Play?

A well-developed leadership development support system includes a variety of people. These people will play a variety of different roles and provide different types of support. Some will be with you for a long time. Some might just be in your life for that particular leadership development experience. Here are some of the roles needed in your leadership development support network:

- *Mentors*: These are people who are experienced and knowledgeable practicing leaders who help guide and advise you along your leadership development trajectory, usually for a sustained period of time. You do not have to officially ask someone to be your mentor. Often the relationship will build over time as you find yourself reaching out to them for advice and guidance. Or they approach you.
- *Teachers*: These are people who are willing to teach you a particular skill, how to do something, or impart practical wisdom. They are not necessarily the faculty within a university; they can be anyone including peers or even people younger than you.
- *Role Models*: These are people that you respect and emulate in terms of their behavior, or ways of doing and being, or the choices that they make. You may have a role model that you want to be like in many ways. Or you may watch someone in one instance and decide to try something that they did. Interestingly, you might learn what not to do. You may be close to this role model. Or your interaction with them may even be non-existent beyond your observations.
- *Referral agents and sponsors*: These are people who can connect you with resources through their own networks of people and organizations, as well as their knowledge of opportunities. They can refer you to those places where you can obtain needed assistance or funding. They find and provide opportunities for development, important assignments, exposure, visibility, and are willing to sponsor you or advocate on your behalf (in terms of introducing you or writing letters, etc.).
- *Protectors*: During your leadership development process, you will make mistakes. Some will feel like epic disasters. Protectors are people who will help you deal with your mistakes, advise you on how to fix them, help you show your face in public, speak on your behalf, and if need be even shield you. And then help you turn what happened into an opportunity for leadership learning and development.
- *Challengers*: These are people who can help motivate you or even demand that you try new ways of doing things, develop new skills, and work on your leadership development. They may not be people who you count on as personal friends, but they are demanding of you.
- *Confidence boosters and cheerleaders*: Just as you need people who will push you to the next level, you also need people who make you feel worthwhile right where you are now. These are people who respect the skills you have already developed and who value the contributions that you are already making in a given situation. They are particularly helpful during times of transition when you may be feeling unsure of yourself in developing new skills.
- *Helpers*: These are people who can be depended upon to provide assistance when needed. They are often experts in solving particular kinds of problems. They provide technical assistance, advice, expertise, resources,

and even the elbow grease when work is needed. They are great people to have in your acquaintance, on your side, or on your team. However, they do not need to be the type with whom you would choose to have a close personal relationship.

- *Common interests*: These are people who share common interests, concerns, or passions and can be especially important in keeping you motivated in not only your leadership development but also your leadership practice. These are the people who will join teams with you and work with you on common causes. Some people with common interests may be your friends. Others may not be, but you know that they are willing, dependable, and will help you move a project forward (as you would for them).
- *Close friends*: And yes, some of your close friends should be part of your leadership development support network. These people care for you, have some of the same interests as you do, and keep you from becoming down in hard times. These are the people you turn to for your emotional well-being and psychosocial support.

## Developing Your Leadership Development Support Network Exercises

In the remainder of this chapter, you will do three exercises in your leadership development journal. First you will evaluate who is in your current leadership development support network. However, as your leadership learning trajectory unfolds over time and you change over time, your leadership development support network must also evolve and develop over time. In the second exercise, using your leadership development action plan that you developed in Chapter 10, you will strategically enhance and extend that support network to fit your action plan needs. Third, just as you are developing yourself as a leader and are in need of a leadership development support network, others around you are also developing as leaders and need a support network. In this exercise you will analyze the roles you play as part of someone else's support network.

### Exercise 1: Who Is in Your Current Leadership Development Support Network?

- Think about the all the people who currently (in the last year) have taken an active interest and action to help you advance in your leadership learning and development in some fashion. The words leadership, learning, and development may not have occurred to you before this in your interactions with them). So think broadly: these may be people from school, work, your family, community, or social circle.

- Copy Table 11.1 so you can store it in your leadership development journal. List the names of all the people in your leadership development support in the first column on the table (if you have more in your network, feel free to add more lines). Look this over again; who are you forgetting? Add them to the list. Fill out the table.
- Analyze your current leadership development support network (see Yip & Kram, in press, 2017). Look closely at the table and write your answers to the following questions in your leadership development journal.

    1. *Is your network the right size?* Do you have all the roles filled (multiple roles may be filled by one person and some roles may be filled multiple times)? What roles are missing? What roles are over represented? While you need many people in your network to fill these roles, when you have too many people, it is difficult to find the time to deepen the quality of all these relationships. There is a balance to achieve between quality and quantity.
    2. *What is the strength of your ties to the people in your network (consider closeness and amount you communicate)?* You should have a balance of strong ties and weak ties. Are there some weak ties that really can or should be strong ties?

**TABLE 11.1** Your Current Leadership Development Support Network

| Name | How many years have you known this person? | What is your relationship with this person?* | How often do you communicate with this person?* | How close do you feel to this person?* | What role does this person play?* | Describe their interests and actions |
|------|------|------|------|------|------|------|
|  |  |  |  |  |  |  |

*What is your relationship with this person?* This can include such people as family member, community member, friend, boss, work colleague, teacher, school administrator, student, etc. Use labels that are meaningful to you.

*How often do you communicate with this person?* Less than once a month, Once or twice a month, 3–5 times per month, a few times a week, daily? Again, use labels that work for you.

*How close do you feel to this person?* Very close, close, less than close, distant.

*What role(s) does this person play?* Mentor, teacher, referral agent/sponsor, protector, challenger, confidence booster/cheerleader, helper, common interests, close friend, other.

3. *What is the range of your network?* Are the people you listed all from the same place (for example, all at your college) or from the same background? Are you including people different from you in terms of background, or race, or gender? Having a diversified network will help give you different perspectives.

4. *How dense is your network?* Do these people know each other? It is helpful if some people know each other: they can coordinate. On the other hand, it is also helpful to have people who do not know each other. Again, a balance is good.

5. *How influential or powerful are the people on your network?* Look over everyone on your list. Put a star next to those individuals who you think have significant power or influence. It is useful to have at least a few influential and powerful people in your network for a number of different roles.

- Look over your answers to these questions. You may discover through answering these questions that there are people you forgot to add. Go back and add them to your list. What are your network strengths? What do you need to develop in your network? Use the answers to these two questions (strengths and development areas) to help you think through Exercise 2.

## Exercise 2: Strategically Enhance/Extend Your Leadership Development Support Network for the Next Step in Your Leadership Development

You can also be strategic about who is in your leadership development support network rather than letting it develop organically. You can learn to ask the right people for the right support at the right time. As a student in my research said:

> I learned to ask other people for help and assistance when I need it. . . . The biggest thing I can say is that you need to learn how to ask other people and that was probably the biggest thing and the greatest part of what I learned being a leader is being able to ask for help.

- For this exercise (see Kram & Higgins, 2013), you need your leadership development action plan that you created in Chapter 10.
- Look at the first action you decided to do (you will do this for one action now but remember to do this exercise again as you move forward in or change that plan).
- Answer the following questions:

1. Looking at the next action that you are planning to take in your plan, how will your current leadership development support network help you achieve this? (be specific here, name individuals from the list in the first exercise and exactly what they can do to support you).

2. Look over this list. What support role is missing from this list that you need? (look at the first exercise above to remind yourself of the different support roles you may need).
3. How can you leverage your current network to meet people who can help you? (Who might know whom?)
4. Plan to reach out to at least one (but preferably all) of the new people you need to add to your leadership development support network for this next step. In this step, you need to plan your communication strategy and then actually do it. See Table 11.2 for an example of what you might do.

• Write in your journal and capture everything that you did.

**TABLE 11.2** Strategically Expanding Your Leadership Development Support Network Meeting

| | |
|---|---|
| Step 1 | *Let people in your current network know what you are planning on doing next in your leadership development.* Let them know what support role you are looking for (I think I'm going to need someone to help me do X) and ask them if they have names of people who might be good to talk to. Ask if you may contact that person and if you may use their name when you contact that person. Thank them. |
| Step 2 | *Practice talking with people that you have never met before.* When you are at a meeting, make it a habit to introduce yourself and to try to find common interests with those you are meeting. If this is very difficult for you, watch someone you know who is comfortable with meeting people they don't know and establishing a connection, listen to what they say, and then try it with people who agree to help you (by the way, this is using someone as a role model). |
| Step 3 | *Plan a specific brief few sentences (that only take about 60 seconds), which express your interests and commitments.* Outline what kind of help you are looking for. Practice this short speech until you can say it naturally and conversationally. Practice in front of a mirror or video yourself. |
| Step 4 | *Arrange to talk to the person you want to add to your network.* In today's world, a good way to do this is to send an email introducing yourself, why you want to meet them, and what you will be asking for (basically a written version of step 3 above). If someone referred you, mention their name. Ask if they would be available for a 15-minute phone chat or face-to-face meeting. |
| Step 5 | *Plan and practice the meeting.* Again, practice your introductory statement that you created in Step 3. Let the person know why you are contacting them. Then write a list of questions you would like to ask this person, then choose one or two. Finally, ask if they would be willing to help you with your next step. |
| Step 6 | *Meet.* If this is face-to-face, dress appropriately. Keep the meeting to the time allotted. At the end of the meeting, thank them. |
| Step 7 | *Send a thank you email as soon after the meeting as you can.* Outline any next steps that came from the meeting. |
| Step 8 | *Follow up* as necessary and appropriate. |

## Exercise 3: Who Are You Currently Supporting in their Leadership Development Support Network?

Leadership development support networks are not one way. Are you reading this book in a class? If yes, look around you—everyone else in the class also needs to develop a leadership development support network. They can play a role in your network and you can play a role in theirs. In addition, there are people above you and below you who are also developing as leaders. Playing a supporting role in someone else's leadership development will help expand your own leadership development support network. For easy examples, playing the role of helper, someone with common interests, or close friend for someone else will probably lead them to reciprocate those roles in your own leadership development support network.

Here is a quote from a student in my research concerning being a part of someone else's leadership development support network: "I have always been the mentee and I am a big believer in mentors. Now being on the other side as an upperclassman, it was interesting to see how other people grow and evolve."

- *Think about all the people whom you have supported, taken an interest in, or taken some sort of action in their leadership development in the past year.* Think broadly, these may be people from school, work, your family, community, or social circle. If you graduated from high school in the past year, think about all the students in your high school you may have made an impact on. If you worked with children (for example, as a camp counselor), include that. And if you have younger siblings or other family members that you interact with on a regular basis, include that. If you were a contributing member of a team led by someone else, include that.
- *Copy Table 11.3 so you can store it in your leadership development journal.* List the names of all the people you have supported in their leadership development in the first column on the table (if you have more in your network, feel free to add more lines). If there are groups of people (for example, the campers in unit 12), put in the whole group as a unit. Look this over again: who are you forgetting? Add them to the list.
- Similar to Exercise 1, analyze the roles you are playing in other people's leadership development support networks. Look closely at the table and write your answers to the following questions in your leadership development journal.

  1. *What roles are you filling in other people's leadership development support network?* Include your interests and actions as well. Are you playing multiple roles or do you specialize in a certain type of role? Are you supporting many others or a few others? Again, there is a balance to achieve. Supporting too many others may lead to spreading yourself too thin. Supporting few others and you may find it difficult to expand your own network when needed.

**TABLE 11.3** People You Are Currently Supporting in their Leadership Development Support Network

| Name | How many years have you known this person? | What is your relationship with this person?* | How often do you communicate with this person?* | How close do you feel to this person?* | What role do you play in this person's leadership development support network?* | Describe your interests and actions |
|---|---|---|---|---|---|---|
| | | | | | | |
| | | | | | | |
| | | | | | | |
| | | | | | | |
| | | | | | | |

*What is your relationship with this person? This can include such people as family member, community member, friend, boss, work colleague, teacher, school administrator, student, etc. Use labels that are meaningful to you.

How often do you communicate with this person? Less than once a month, once or twice a month, 3–5 times per month, a few times a week, daily. Use a term that is meaningful to you.

How close do you feel to this person? Very close, close, less than close, distant.

What role(s) did you play in this person's leadership development support network? Mentor, teacher, referral agent/sponsor, protector, challenger, confidence booster/cheerleader, helper, common interests, close friend, other.

2. *What is the strength of your ties to the people you are supporting (consider closeness and the amount you communicate)?* You should have a balance of strong ties and weak ties. Are there some weak ties that might be beneficial to strengthen? You may also find that you had temporary ties (for example, if you graduated high school, you may not continue those relationships.)

3. *What is the range of your support?* Are you supporting others just like you? Or are you supporting people from different backgrounds, races, and genders? Just as you need a diversified leadership development support network, so do others.

- Look over your answers to these questions. Where are you strong in your support of others' leadership development? Is there anything missing or that you could be doing better? How might you improve the support that you give to others (without spreading yourself too thin).

## Summary

- Leadership is not something you develop all by yourself. To develop in your leadership, you need the support of many others.
- Support is assistance and resources given to you by others that is designed to help you handle the struggle and pain of developing as a leader.

- Your leadership development support network is a subset of your social network. It is a resource pool of people from your social network that you draw on selectively and that gives you the resources and assistance you need in your development.
- Your leadership development support network can help you gain new leadership competencies, re-establish competence when you let go of an old way of doing things and begin a new way of doing things, achieve specific objectives, maintain high performance, and provide emotional support.
- The people in your leadership development support network take on many roles. These include mentors, teachers, role models, referral agents and sponsors, protectors, challengers, confidence boosters and cheerleaders, helpers, people with common interests, and close friends.
- Your leadership development support network may happen organically. As you move along your leadership learning and development trajectory, you will meet people along the way. Some may stay with you over a long period of time; some may be part of your development for only short amount of time or for one project.
- You can also strategically develop your leadership development support network and ask people to help you by fulfilling roles.
- A leadership development support network is a two-way street. As you are learning and developing your leadership, others around you are also developing—your peers, people senior to you, and people junior to you. Supporting others in their leadership development is important. It will also help you create and strengthen your own leadership development support network—when you are there in supporting roles for others and providing assistance and resources, others will be more willing to help you.

## References

De Rue, D. S. & Wellman, N. (2009). Developing leaders via experience: The role of developmental challenge, learning orientation, and feedback availability. *Journal of Applied Psychology 94*, 859–875.

Kram, K. & Higgins, M.C. (2013). Developmental network map. www.rochester. edu/diversity/wp-content/uploads/2014/11/Developmental_Network-Assessment KramandHiggins.pdf.

McCauley, C. D., VanVelsor, E., & Ruderman, M. N. (2010). Introduction: Our view of leadership development. In E. Van Velsor, C. D. McCauley, & M. N. Ruderman (Eds.) *Handbook of Leadership Development* (3rd ed.) (pp. 1–28). San Francisco, CA: John Wiley & Sons.

Seashore, C. N. (n.d.). Developing and using personal support systems. (http://socialwork. ou.edu/Websites/socialwork/images/MSW/resources/Developing_and_Using_ Personal_Support_Systems.pdf).

Yip, J. & Kram, K. E. (in press, 2017). Developmental networks: Enhancing the science and practice of mentoring. In D. A., Clutterbuck, F. K. Kochan, L. G. Lunsford, N. Dominguez, & J. Haddock-Millar (Eds.) *The Sage Handbook of Mentoring*. Thousand Oaks, CA: Sage.

# PART III

# Capturing and Telling Your Leadership Development Story

# 12

## BRINGING IT ALL TOGETHER

### Telling Your Leadership Development Story

Early in my career, I had a really impressive student in the leadership development minor I was directing. He did everything right. He was first in line to sign up for the new leadership development minor that my school was putting in place. Through the minor, he had an internship working with military veterans. He started up and led a club. He was president of his fraternity, then moved to vice president so that he could lead the university-wide Greek council. And grade-wise, he was holding his own. He also had a job working in the residence halls, checking people in. Not an impressive job, but it paid his expenses and allowed him the time he needed for all his leadership development. When he graduated, I knew that his career would be off to a great start, I knew he would have his choice of positions. But he struggled to find a job. Why?

Too late, I asked to see his resume. There, under job experience was his residence hall job. His low-level paid position. His leadership positions were briefly mentioned in a word or two, buried deep under his education. There was no mention of his start-up club or his internship. The lesson I learned that day is that students not only need to develop themselves to participate in leadership, but they also need to understand what they have learned and developed for themselves, and they need to learn how to communicate what they have learned and developed to others. Jacob, I know you eventually landed on your feet. This chapter was inspired by you. And hopefully many students will capitalize on my learning moving forward.

The purpose of this chapter is to ensure that you don't make the same mistake that my student did. It doesn't matter what the next step is in your career after college—hiring managers, graduate schools, the judges on Shark Tank—they are all looking for candidates with leadership skills. Even if you have not been the person in charge, by this point in this book, hopefully you are aware that you participate in leadership and in fact have some leadership skills to offer a variety of situations. As you have hopefully learned or realized, your leadership skills that you bring to the situation make you a good follower or a good team player as well as a good leader. Participating in leadership from any role (standard terminology would be "leader," "follower," or "team player") requires many of the same leadership skills and competencies.

In this chapter, you will be starting or completing a leadership development portfolio. If you are early in your college career, you will be starting the portfolio. It is easier to build a little at a time as you proceed through your college years. If you are reading this book closer to graduation, you will be making the entire portfolio. Either way, this portfolio should be considered as a "living document" that is continually edited and updated. I recommend creating the document in two forms at the same time. You should have an electronic version and a hard copy. For the hard copy portfolio, it should be in a three-ring binder with dividers for the different sections to make it professional and organized. For the electronic portfolio, if your school already has a leadership or co-curricular e-portfolio, plan to use that one. If not, you should create the document in Microsoft Word (or similar word processing software). Your portfolio should include separate sections. Each section should be clearly labeled, either with a title page or with a distinct header. Page breaks should be used to clearly mark the beginning and end of each section. Be creative, but in the end, the portfolio should look professional as well. While the portfolio in its entirety is for your eyes only, if you create it to look professional, you will be able to copy the pieces you need or want to show to others. Finally, you might also consider a LinkedIn (or similar) profile. You can also place different parts of this leadership portfolio on line in a searchable format.

## Leadership Learning and Development Portfolio

A learning portfolio is a systematic and organized collection of evidence that you use to monitor, understand, and communicate your change and growth in your knowledge, skills, and attitudes. Using leadership learning and development from all the experiences you have had during college (and perhaps some from high school), leadership development programs you have participated in, and leadership courses you have taken, you will develop a leadership learning and development portfolio. The purpose of the portfolio is for you to better understand and take control of your own learning and development as a leader. In it you will identify, analyze, evaluate, and communicate your experiences and the learning that came from them.

There are seven sections to your portfolio. I describe these below. Then in the remainder of the chapter, you will be guided in developing each section in its entirety.

1. *Personal statement on leadership.* Writing a personal statement on a topic is a process that can help you develop a stronger sense of what the topic means to you. In this case, defining and describing what leadership is and what it means to you will help to develop an understanding of why you participate in leadership. Your statement should include: your definition of leadership (you can use the definition from this book or if you have one you like better, use that one); why you think leadership is important; and why you have spent your valuable time developing yourself as a leader. This should be in your own words. It may be short and succinct or longer and more detailed (but not longer than one page).

2. *Essay on your leadership learning trajectory during college.* In this section, include an essay on your leadership learning trajectory during college. How has your definition and understanding of leadership changed over time? What is your leadership style and how has your leadership style developed and changed? How have your skills and competencies developed and changed? The difference between this section and the first section is that in the first section, you are stating where you are now. In this section, you are analyzing your leadership learning trajectory to determine how you got to where you are now in your leadership beliefs, identity, and style.

3. *Resume ready statements of jobs, positions, and experiences that you have had.* In this section, you will create a chronological list of all your leadership development experiences from college (with dates) that are ready to be used in a resume. This will include the important outcomes of the experience. If you have a number of these experiences, you will be able to pick and choose the most relevant ones depending on your needs. This way you will be able to customize your resume and application forms. In addition, if you are comfortable doing so, you can also put all of these on your LinkedIn profile.

4. *A summary of your accomplishments, competencies, and skills.* In this section, you will list your accomplishments, competencies, and skills in such a way that you are prepared to articulate them in a conversation.

5. *Your accomplishment stories.* In this section, you will learn and use a technique for developing all your accomplishment stories to be used in showcasing your leadership skills and competencies.

6. *Artifact/documentation collection.* This section is a storage area for all things leadership learning and development related that you have collected during your time in college. This artifact collection serves three purposes. First, it serves as a repository for all things leadership learning and development. Everything is now in one place. Second, it is a memory prompt for what you did and when. And third, you can use it to learn and demonstrate your own leadership change, development, learning, etc.

7. *Additional sections as necessary.* If you find that you need an additional section, add it. Put it in the order that makes the most sense to you.

## Building Your Leadership Learning and Development Portfolio

It is easier to build the portfolio from the back forwards, starting with your artifact and document collection and moving through to your essay and statement. In this portion of the chapter, you will be asked to create your leadership learning portfolio beginning with the last section and working your way forwards.

### Putting Together Your Artifact and Document Collection

This section is a storage area for everything leadership learning and development that you have accumulated during your time in college. When you get a certificate in class for your service learning work, pop it in. When you get an email with feedback from someone, pop it in. This section could include assessments (such as those you filled out in Chapter 5), your leadership development plan (that you developed in Chapter 10), work samples (for example, if you created a training program for your club or Greek organization, put this in here), papers, letters, sketches/drawings/paintings, snapshots, projects, videos, presentations, collaborative work, certificates, your leadership learning and development journal(s), feedback you received, etc.

Plan to be inclusive in this section. The information that you collect here will help you flesh out the rest of your portfolio. Even if you are not sure whether an item is relevant, include the information. It is easier to weed out items you don't want later than wish you had captured something because you need it to help you craft other portions of the leadership learning and development portfolio. While it may be tempting to just use this section to dump items in, at some point, it pays to organize it in a form that is useable. Organize in a way that makes sense to you, although including a chronological order will help you in crafting the remainder of your leadership learning and development portfolio. For example, all the assessments should be put together (perhaps even into their own subsection) in chronological order. That way you can see how you have changed in your assessments over time.

### Writing Your Accomplishment Stories

In this section, you will be writing out, in detail, all of your accomplishment stories using the SOAR technique.

The first step is to identify your accomplishments. Accomplishments are indicators of one or more skills and competencies "in action." Look over your artifact/document collection. What are some accomplishments of yours from that? Write these down. As you have worked your way through this book, you have identified "key events" that impacted who you are as a leader. Look them over. Some of these may be added to your list of your accomplishments. Add these to your list. In addition, think back over your time during college (and perhaps high school). What are you most proud of during that time? Add these to your list. What things that you did excited you the most? Add these to your list. See Table 12.1 to prompt you for other accomplishments. Once you begin thinking about accomplishments, others will arise, often when you are doing something else. Plan to capture these and add to your list.

The second step is to flesh out the "story" of each accomplishment you listed and determine what skills and competencies you used to accomplish it. When you are successful or accomplish something, you have used some sort of skill or competency to do it. An analysis of your accomplishments and the skills/competencies you used can help you identify your particular and unique skill set.

**TABLE 12.1** Accomplishment Prompts

Use the prompts listed below to help you identify your accomplishments while in college. Look at each item. Have you done this? If yes, briefly note where you did this.

| Accomplishment | Where you did it | When you did it |
| --- | --- | --- |
| Elected to office | | |
| Hired or selected into a leadership position | | |
| Led a team or committee | | |
| Served as a student representative on a university committee | | |
| Managed a budget. How much? | | |
| Saved your club/organization money. How much? | | |
| Identified a problem and solved it | | |
| Participated in decision-making or planning | | |
| Developed a new product or service | | |
| Introduced a new system or procedure | | |
| Effectively managed a project | | |
| Effectively managed people | | |
| Wrote a major report, program, publication, newsletter, etc. | | |
| Started up a club/organization | | |
| Took a club/organization to the next level (e.g., grew the organization in terms of membership or level) | | |
| Served as a liaison between clubs/organizations | | |
| Served as a mentor | | |
| Created and implemented a training program | | |
| Did a research project from beginning to end | | |
| Spoke at a conference | | |
| Published a paper | | |
| Won an award | | |
| Received particularly strong positive feedback about something you did | | |
| Struggled to do something, but overcame it successfully | | |
| Other accomplishment | | |

In this next exercise, you will write your accomplishment stories using the SOAR technique. If you have a number of accomplishments listed, you will probably not be able to write all your stories at once. Plan to write these by continuously adding them over time. Also, once you know this technique, you can add accomplishments stories as you do them and the details are fresh in your memory. There is no magic number of accomplishments, but the more you can pull from, the better you can understand and communicate your skills.

For now, start with a recent accomplishment, or one that you are most proud of, and do the following:

1. Describe the (**S**)ituation. Capture as much detail here as you can recall. You never know what might arise as an important detail.
2. Describe the (**O**)bstacles that you faced.
3. List the (**A**)ctions that you took.
4. Describe the (**R**)esults that you obtained or helped obtain and the benefits of these results (to the club, organization, team, etc.).
5. Finally, what skills or competencies did you use in this accomplishment? In some cases, your skills and competencies are apparent. If you are not sure what skills/competencies you used, look over your assessments from Chapter 5 (or any others you have done) for key words. Also see Chapters 4, 5, 6, 7, and 8 for lessons learned. Finally, Corey Seemiller (2013) has a book that lists 60 student leadership competencies. Your challenge here is to use formal leadership terminology to describe your skills and competencies in a way that others will recognize.

Continue to write up all your accomplishments this way. The more of these stories you have, the more you have to draw from for the next parts of your leadership learning and development portfolio, the more examples of your accomplishments you can use in conversations, and the more information you have for your resume and for filling out applications.

Finally, put these accomplishment stories in order. For example, group them by club, or organization, or position, etc., then into chronological order. This will help in crafting the remainder of your leadership learning and development portfolio.

## A Summary of Your Accomplishments, Competencies, and Skills

The first step in this section is to identify the skills and competencies you have used, learned, and developed by analyzing your accomplishment stories.

1. *Start by creating a master list of all the skills and competencies you listed in all your accomplishment stories.* If you used certain skills and competencies more than once, note how many times these have arisen in your accomplishment stories. Note which skills and competencies you like to use.

2.  *Categorize all the listed skills and competencies into related topics.* Topics may include: self-awareness, learning and reasoning, interpersonal interactions, group dynamics, managing others, managing projects, civic responsibility, communication, and getting the job done. You may find that you want to use a different organizing scheme: use one that makes sense to you. Are your skills clumped into a few categories or are your skills and competencies spread across a number of areas?
3.  *Go over your lists.* Pick 3–5 skills and competencies that represent your most commonly mentioned, or your strongest, or your most preferred skills.

In the remainder of this section, I will pose questions. These are the kinds of questions you might get asked in an interview. In some cases, you might be asked for examples of these in applications (for example, a graduate school application or essay). People who are writing you letters of recommendation might ask you for this sort of information. You never know where you might have the opportunity to talk about these.

Write the answers to the questions down by drawing from your skills and your accomplishment stories. There should be little or no new information in this section. You should be drawing directly from your accomplishment story collection. If you are finding you are using new information here, go back and incorporate the changes in the accomplishment story.

## Question 1: Tell Me About Yourself

This question presents you with a great opportunity to succinctly and positively position yourself to someone else. The key here is to create a short statement that you can naturally say in a conversation, with a smile. You will probably need to write a number of these and show them to people before you get it right. You may find that you actually have more than one answer depending on who you are speaking with. There are four parts to this statement.

1.  *What is your identity?* People already established in their career might use their professional identity (e.g., marketing executive, organizational development professional, etc.); most students do not yet have this sort of identity. You can try using your major ("I am a college student majoring in psychology" or "I am a recent college graduate with a major in physics"). You might also use something like the following: "I am an emerging leader." Are there other ways that you define yourself? Here you can choose to be narrow (for example, if you are talking to someone about a particular position), or broader (more general conversation).
2.  *What is your expertise?* Here you will talk about your three strongest or most preferred skills from the previous section. You would tack this on to the above statement. I am a . . . with strengths in X, Y, and Z. Or I am a . . . and I have strengths in X, Y, Z.

3. *Summarize the organizations and environments that you have worked in* (this one is optional). For example, if you did an internship at a Fortune 500 firm, or a public agency, include that. If you were on a club eboard, include that. This statement might be something like, "My experience spans from being a member of a college club eboard to a Fortune 500 firm."

4. *What differentiates you from other similar people?* What makes you unique? Here you can list a few skills that are different from the ones you listed above. Or you can list personal attributes. Are you easy going, have a sense of humor, collaborative, resourceful, etc.? Did you manage the budget of your club? Look over your assessment for help. Or ask your friends to describe you and see what they say.

5. Here is an example of a more broadly written answer: I am a recent college graduate with a major in political science and a minor in leadership development. My strengths include identifying problems, managing projects, and making decisions. My experience spans from the legislature of the college student government association to an internship in a medium-sized not for profit organization. My organization skills have been a great asset to help teams I have worked with stay on track and be successful.

6. Write and edit your statement on Table 12.2 until you can say it with ease and with a smile on your face. Again, you might have several of these or variants depending on the situation.

7. If you have a LinkedIn profile, post this statement here.

**TABLE 12.2** Positioning Statement

Include identity, expertise, organizational experience (if any), and what makes you unique)

## Question 2: Give Me Three Words or Phrases that Describe You (This May or May Not Have the Additional Phrase, "As a Leader")

You are already prepared to answer this one! To answer this question, use your top three skills (your strongest or most preferred) from your categorization above. "I would describe myself as a problem solver, project manager, and decision maker." If you have the opportunity, continue with this question in more depth: "Here is an example of me as a problem solver . . . " Recount your problem-solving accomplishment, using the SOAR ((S)ituation, (O)bstacle, (A)ction, (R)esults) method, from the previous section. Or "Here is an example of me as a project manager . . . " Recount your project manager accomplishment, using the SOAR method. "And here is an example of me as a decision maker . . . " Recount your decision-making accomplishment, using the SOAR method. Practice answering this question out loud until you can say it naturally. Begin recording your answers in Table 12.3.

## Question 3: Name a Personal Strength

Here, use your most relevant skill for the situation for the strength. If you are not sure what the most relevant skill is, pick a favorite one from the list below. "One of my strengths is managing an organization's yearly budget." Recount your budget management accomplishment, using the SOAR method. You may be able to pull a strength from Table 12.3. Just in case you have been asked a question similar to Question 2, be prepared with another strength to speak about here.

## Question 4: Name a Personal Weakness

You have a number of options in answering this one. First, you can look over your skills and compare them to lists of skills and competencies. Is there something

**TABLE 12.3** Three Words or Phrases that Describe Me

| Word or phrase | Accomplishment story (from previous section) |
| --- | --- |
| 1. | Situation<br>Obstacle<br>Actions<br>Results |
| 2. | Situation<br>Obstacle<br>Actions<br>Results |
| 3. | Situation<br>Obstacle<br>Actions<br>Results |

you are missing that you would love to add to your skills? If that is the case, you might say, "A skill I am interested in developing, but haven't found the opportunity to do so is X." Second, is there something you have done in one situation but would be interested in trying in another situation? For example, "I was the treasurer for our SGA where I managed a budget of $X. I am looking forward to honing my budget management skills in a large corporate setting." Third, is there something that you have learned but have not had a chance to try out? For example, "In my entrepreneurial class, I learned how to build a business plan. Even though we developed one in class, I am looking forward to working at a start-up and working with someone to do this for a real organization." Finally, note that I did not include as an option listing something negative about yourself, or something that might raise a red flag indicating there is something wrong with you. You have plenty of experiences you have not yet had the opportunity to engage in. Concentrate on those and looking forward in a positive manner.

### Question 5: Tell Me about a Time When . . . (You Delegated, You Managed a Team, etc., the Variations Are Endless)

This is another reason why your accomplishment stories are so important. It is difficult to prepare for every variation ahead of time. The more accomplishment stories you are able to write down ahead of time, the less likely you are to struggle with answering these sorts of questions. The last thing you want is to be asked this question and you don't have a situation at ready to describe. When you tell your story, tell it using the SOAR technique. There may be a question that you do not have experience with yet. Say that. Assuming that you are able to articulate a truthful answer about demonstrating other skills, having one or a few that you have not experienced is okay. You might say, "I have not had the opportunity to do that yet and it is one of the skills I am hoping to develop in the near future. " You might even be able to add, "while I have not done that exactly, I have done something similar . . . (SOAR)."

### Resume Ready Statements of Jobs, Positions, Experiences You Have Had

The purpose of this section is to take your accomplishments and turn them into resume ready statements. In today's world, resumes are used for many purposes. And you will modify your resume for each and every situation. For example, you would want to use a different resume in a graduate school application than you would in a job search or when networking. You will probably slightly modify your resume for every job that you apply for. The key in this section is to have a number of resume ready statements that you can pick and choose from depending on the situation and the message you want to send about yourself.

In your resume, you can also include relevant paid jobs. These may be different from the ones that you are writing in this section. For example, if you are a server at a restaurant, or work in a clothing store, or de-tasseled corn in the summer, you can include these as well. This will demonstrate that you are multi-talented! I will not be covering these in this section. But you can set up these positions the same way you do your leadership positions.

First, look through your accomplishment stories. If any were part of internships, note those. If any were part of a paid or volunteer job, note those. If any are part of an elected position, note those. If any are part of a class project in which you created and communicated an outcome of some sort, note those. If any are service projects from a course, note those. If any include laboratory work or teaching assistance, note those. If any include committee work (in which you were either a member or you led), note those. Are any accomplishment stories within the same position? You will want to make sure you represent both of those in the same statement. Look through the remainder: are there other options that might be included that I have not mentioned?

Second, write up the statements. These should be ready to cut and paste straight into your resume, so I will leave the formatting up to you. Your school probably has resume writing classes and resume templates. And there is a plethora of information on the web. Find a format that works for you and write the next section in that format.

Each statement should have:

- The name of the organization (if it is part of your university/college, make sure to include both the name of the college and the name of the club/organization/class, etc.).
- The city and state of the organization.
- The position you held. If you had an official position title, use that (e.g., president). If not, give a short descriptor (team leader or member, committee chair, co-chair, or member, project team leader or member, etc.).
- The period that you were in this position.
- A brief description of your duties. Use your skill words.
- One or two bullet points that use the skills that you demonstrated and the results. Go back to your accomplishment stories.

Here is an example:

Montclair State University

Psychology Club

Vice President                                             September 2016–Present

Conducted meetings using Robert's Rules of Order. Formulated and coordinated ad hoc committees as needed to accomplish the goals of the club. Organized club trips. Served as de-facto president of the club in the absence of the president.

- Grew the club from 35 active members to 50 active members
- Negotiated with the university to increase budget from $2,500 to $3,500.

Montclair State University

Emerging Leaders Learning Community

Tutor at Orange Community Middle School     September–December 2015

Worked individually and in a group setting with seventh-grade students to improve study habits and reading and math skills.

- Worked 2 hours weekly for 10 weeks as part of course requirements.
- Helped students increase their reading test scores and math test skills by 10 percent.

Try writing these on your own. In addition, utilize your resume writing services at your university to hone these into concise statements that communicate your use of leadership skills.

Third, list these in your leadership learning portfolio in chronological order. Again, chronological order will be helpful for the essay in the next section.

Fourth, if you are comfortable, put this on your LinkedIn account. You may put all or a few favorite select ones on here.

### Essay on Your Leadership Learning Trajectory During College

In this section, you will write a short essay on your leadership learning trajectory during college. The purpose of this section is for you to understand how you have grown and changed in your leadership during college. Read carefully over your artifact collection and your accomplishment stories to help you think this through. If you have already written essays on this topic, certainly re-read those as well (if they are not in your artifact collect, definitely put them in there now!). Address these topics in your essay:

1. *How has my definition and understanding of leadership changed over time?* What did you think leadership was when you entered college and how is it different from your definition and understanding now? For example, did reading this book and doing the exercises in this book change your definition and understanding of leadership? Did other experiences cause you to change your mind? As I stated in Chapter 3, leadership is not something that exists in the real world like a tree. In fact, when you speak to people, you will find that there is little agreement on what leadership is. And your own understanding of leadership will change as you think about it and as you practice it. To help you think this through, I am re-including Wilfred Drath's principles of leadership (2001):

    a. *Personal dominance*: leadership comes directly from the formal leader. Leadership is what the leader does and is a personal characteristic of the leader. Most college students understand leadership from this principle.

An individual in the formal role of leader who understands leadership from this perspective sees themselves as the "authority." Followers or observers who understand leadership from this perspective think that if the leader's actions don't make sense, or if someone doubts or challenges the leader, then leadership is ineffective or is not happening.

b. *Interpersonal influence*: leadership is an influence process and a leader emerges from a process of negotiation with the rest of the group where the individual(s) of greater influence emerge as the leader(s). Leadership is occupied by the most influential person and can change over time. An individual in the formal role of leader who understands leadership from this perspective would see their job as listening to and being influenced by followers but having greater influence on their followers through reason and negotiation, and by virtue of their formal title as leader.

c. *Relational dialogue*: leadership is when people participate in collaborative forms of thought and action to complete tasks and accomplish change. If there is a person who has the label of "leader," the role this person takes is only one aspect of participation in the larger process of leadership. An individual in the formal role of leader who understands leadership from this perspective might see their job as to "act with" the other members of the group and to use his or her talents and skill sets as needed to reach goals and effect change. For example, their contributions to leadership might involve facilitating the group in creating a direction together, and in submitting the actual report of progress or goals reached.

2. *What is my leader identity and style, and how has it developed and changed since I started college?* What was your leader identity and style when you started college? What is it now? As I stated in Chapter 3, developing a leader identity is one of the most important leadership learnings. After reading this book, what is your leader identity? At the very least, I'm hoping you now realize that you participate in leadership regularly. I'm hoping some of you have tried out a leader position. And others who started with an already established leader identity—how are you now different? To help you think this through, I am re-including the leader identity stages suggested by Susan Komives and her colleagues (2005, 2006):

a. *Leaders exist out there somewhere.* Parents are leaders, the president of the United States is a leader, girl/boy scout leaders are leaders. You don't identify as a leader.

b. *You join groups and taking on responsibilities, but typically don't take on positional leadership roles.* In addition, even if you are in a leader role (e.g., the president of the speech club), you still do not see yourself as a leader.

c. *You believe that leadership is a position, and therefore, the person in that position is the leader.* The typical college student is at this stage.

    d. *You tend to see leadership as what an individual does as a positional leader, but also have noticed leadership being exhibited by non-positional group members, including, perhaps, yourself.* A group member could be "a leader without a title."

    e. *People work together regardless of their official role or title.* They express a passion for their commitments and care for the welfare of others, including the sustainability of their own groups in which they are working. Really everyone is participating in setting direction, aligning, committing, and managing complex challenges.

    f. *You realize that you do not need to hold positional leader roles to engage in leadership.* Leadership is something you do when it needs to be done.

3. *How have your skills and competencies developed and changed?* What were your skills and competencies coming into college? Have you deepened these skills? And how? Have you added new skills? As listed in Chapter 3 (Dreyfus and Drefys 1986), which of the following were/are you:

    a. *Novice:* focus on accomplishing immediate tasks, typically require clear rules that they follow closely.

    b. *Advanced beginner:* use rules as guidelines, applying them in new situations, but not able to handle exceptions or unforeseen problems.

    c. *Competent performer:* form conceptual models of what they are doing; can handle more complex situations based on their experience; typically rely on heuristics or surface features.

    d. *Proficient performer:* have experienced a wide variety of situations and challenges; see the big picture, monitor their own performance, and interpret underlying principles to adjust their behaviors based on the context; can handle relatively novel or complex situations.

    e. *Expert:* able to identify and solve problems intuitively, with little explicit analysis or planning; see underlying patterns effortlessly and adapt principles to generate and apply appropriate solutions, even to complex and unique situations, in such a way that they generate consistently superior performance. The "expert" level does not signify that development stops, as expert practitioners need to evaluate their practice and keep up-to-date with new evidence.

## Personal Statement on Leadership

The purpose of this short, concise statement (no longer than one page) is for you to put a stake in the ground, right here, right now, and clearly record what leadership is to you and what it means to you. It is different from the last section, which was an analysis of your leadership learning trajectory in college, because in this section you clearly describe where you are right now.

Start your essay with the following words (or something like this), "As a result of reflecting on my leadership learning trajectory and my accomplishments during college, my definition of leadership is . . . . " Then answer the stems, "Leadership is important because . . . " and "I have spent my valuable time developing myself as a leader because . . . "

## Summary

The purpose of this chapter was to push you one step further. Throughout this book, I have argued that it is important for you to develop yourself to participate in leadership in a number of different ways. But developing yourself is not enough. You also need to be clear on what you are developing, how you are developing, and why you are developing so that you understand it yourself and so that you can communicate it to others. This chapter outlines a leadership learning and development portfolio, and then gives ideas on how to create your own. But always remember, as with all other chapters in this book, this chapter gives you ideas and suggestions but you need to make it your own. Do create your own leadership learning and development portfolio but if something doesn't work for you, or your school suggests something different, or you have an innovative idea on something to include that I did not mention, modify to make it work for you. In addition, remember that this is a "living document." It can be changed and modified as you yourself change.

## And Moving Forward

At this point in the book, you need to take a moment to pat yourself on the head, hug yourself, celebrate in some form or another. You have moved along your leadership learning and development trajectory. Some things that you may have learned, or changed your ideas on in this book including what leadership is and the idea of participating in leadership (rather than being a leader), that learning and developing your leadership is like learning and developing in general, the ReAChS (Reflection, Assessment, Challenge, Support) model of leadership development and how to use it, and the importance of and how to create your own leadership learning and development portfolio. This is important learning. Monumental learning. And worthy of at least a moment of your time, celebrating at least a little, to honor this portion of your journey. But don't stop here: go forth and lead!

## References

Drath, W. (2001). *The deep blue sea: Rethinking the source of leadership*. San Francisco, CA: Jossey-Bass.

Dreyfus, H. L. and Dreyfus, S. E. (1986). *Mind over machine: The power of human intuition and expertise in the age of the computer*. Oxford: Basil Blackwell.

Komives, S. R., Longerbeam, S. D., Owen, J. E., Mainella, F. C., & Osteen, L. (2006). A leadership identity development model: Applications from a grounded theory. *Journal of College Student Development 47*, 401–420.

Komives, S. R., Owen, J. E., Longerbeam, S. D., Mainella, F. C., & Osteen, L. (2005). Developing a leadership identity: A grounded theory. *Journal of College Student Development 46*, 593–611.

Seemiller, C. (2013). *The student leadership competencies guidebook: Designing intentional leadership learning and development.* San Francisco, CA: Jossey-Bass.

# INDEX

abilities 62, 63
academic experiences 18–19
academic organizations 92
accomplishment stories 193, 194–196, 199, 200, 201, 202
accountability 36; challenging experiences 117; first leadership role 95, 96–97; increase in scope and scale of role 100, 101, 103
ACS (Assessment, Challenge, Support) model xi
action 52, 59
adaptability 36; being a mentor to others 137, 138, 140; challenging experiences 117; learning though others 141; organizational switches 105, 106–107, 108–109; peer interactions 131, 133, 136; start-up clubs 115, 116; task forces, project teams and committees 110, 111, 113
adaptive learning 13, 17, 24, 26, 29
After Action Reviews (AARs) 54–56, 57
After Event Reviews (AERs) 54, 55, 57
agendas 35, 172
agreeableness 67–68
alignment xii, 2–4, 6
ambassadors 134
andragogy 14
anxiety 52, 178–179
artifact collection 193, 194, 202
arts organizations 93, 175
assessment 39, 42, 43, 61–86; assessment centers 65; character strengths 69–74;

continuous 62; definition of 61–62; feedback 64; individual psychological 65; leadership competencies 79–84; leadership courses and development programs 153; leadership learning and development portfolio 194; personality 66–69; questions for reflection 44; readiness to learn 75–79; self-assessment 39, 42, 63–64, 66–86; simulations 64–65; what can be assessed 62–63
assignments 40, 170
Association of Leadership Educators 145
athletic teams 24, 92, 109, 150, 175
authentic leadership 153
authority 33, 203

balancing roles 36, 105, 106, 109, 117
Bandura, Albert 14, 177
Barber, James 19
beauty and excellence, appreciation of 74
before action reviews (BARs) 55–56
behavior, assessment of 62, 63
Big Five personality traits 66–69
Blue Hen Leadership Development Program 145
Bonners 148, 150
boundaries, working across 40, 41, 88, 167
brain processes 12, 25, 38
bravery 72
Buccino Center for Leadership Development 143

 Taylor & Francis eBooks

## Helping you to choose the right eBooks for your Library

Add Routledge titles to your library's digital collection today. Taylor and Francis ebooks contains over 50,000 titles in the Humanities, Social Sciences, Behavioural Sciences, Built Environment and Law.

**Choose from a range of subject packages or create your own!**

**Benefits for you**

» Free MARC records
» COUNTER-compliant usage statistics
» Flexible purchase and pricing options
» All titles DRM-free.

**Benefits for your user**

» Off-site, anytime access via Athens or referring URL
» Print or copy pages or chapters
» Full content search
» Bookmark, highlight and annotate text
» Access to thousands of pages of quality research at the click of a button.

REQUEST YOUR **FREE** INSTITUTIONAL TRIAL TODAY

**Free Trials Available**
We offer free trials to qualifying academic, corporate and government customers.

## eCollections – Choose from over 30 subject eCollections, including:

| | |
|---|---|
| Archaeology | Language Learning |
| Architecture | Law |
| Asian Studies | Literature |
| Business & Management | Media & Communication |
| Classical Studies | Middle East Studies |
| Construction | Music |
| Creative & Media Arts | Philosophy |
| Criminology & Criminal Justice | Planning |
| Economics | Politics |
| Education | Psychology & Mental Health |
| Energy | Religion |
| Engineering | Security |
| English Language & Linguistics | Social Work |
| Environment & Sustainability | Sociology |
| Geography | Sport |
| Health Studies | Theatre & Performance |
| History | Tourism, Hospitality & Events |

For more information, pricing enquiries or to order a free trial, please contact your local sales team: www.tandfebooks.com/page/sales

 Routledge
Taylor & Francis Group

The home of Routledge books

www.tandfebooks.com